EDWARDIAN MURDERS

ROY·HARLEY·LEWIS

DAVID & CHARLES
Newton Abbot London North Pomfret (Vt)

British Library Cataloguing in Publication Data

Edwardian murders.
1.Murder, 1875–1935
I. Title
364.1'523'09034

ISBN 0-7153-9157-7

Typeset by Typesetters (Birmingham) Ltd
Smethwick, West Midlands
and printed in Great Britain
by **Billing & Sons Ltd, Worcester**
for David & Charles Publishers plc
Brunel House Newton Abbot Devon

Published in the United States of America
by David & Charles Inc
North Pomfret Vermont 05053 USA

CONTENTS

	Introduction	7
1	Brides in the Bath	11
2	Other Ladykillers	31
3	The Worm That Turned	46
4	Miscarriages of Justice	59
5	The Role of the Defence	87
6	Science and the Murderer	114
7	Unsolvable Puzzles	129
8	It Helps to be Rich	145
	Selected Bibliography	155
	Index	157

INTRODUCTION

We tend, for the sake of convenience, to relate memorable periods in history to a monarch or outstanding statesman who stamped his or her personality on the age. In a reign spanning sixty years, the diminutive Queen Victoria rose in stature to become larger than life, and continued to over-shadow her son, Edward VII, even after death. Indeed, as the king inherited many of her ministers and advisers, it could be argued that the Victorian age extended far beyond, thus blurring the parameters of the much shorter Edwardian reign.

Chronologically, the new age began in 1901 when Edward, already sixty, came to the throne – ending in 1910 when he was succeeded by his son, George V. However, historians generally accept that a more practical demarcation was 1914, with the outbreak of the Great War. The outcome of that horrific conflict was not only to change the map of Europe – forging a breakthrough to the modern world – but imperceptibly end the English feudal system through an 'explosion' of the middle classes coinciding with a contraction of the so-called ruling classes. And in view of its short span, the Edwardian age was a period of considerable change – a fascinating transition, or buffer zone, between nineteenth and twentieth centuries.

The most visible impact was in the form of scientific and engineering advances – many spectacular, such as the development of the aeroplane. In the space age we take the aeroplane for granted, but even after the Wrights' first powered flight in 1903 there was still a strong body of opinion insisting that 'If God had intended us to fly, we would have been given wings', an attitude which persisted until 1909 when Bleriot flew the Channel. There was also a marked change in other forms of travel. By 1903, electric trains were beginning to replace steam. A year later, London saw its first motorised taxi, to be followed by buses and in 1906 the first tube train. The bicycle became increasingly popular. Meanwhile, the first transatlantic wireless transmission was made in 1901, although no-one took the facility very seriously until 1910 when it was used to ensure the apprehension of Dr Crippen, fleeing from a murder charge to Canada. In the home there were more mundane inventions which, nevertheless, helped improve the quality of life, eg the incandescent gas mantle which replaced the Victorian gas jet.

Although many thousands still struggled to survive in abject poverty, the wealth of the nation (the accumulated benefits of the industrial revolution and vast colonial exploitation) finally manifested itself in improved living standards. After the unplanned greyness of Victorian urban development, the Edwardians established Britain's first Garden City development at Letchworth (Herts), and introduced reforms such as the Old Age Pension Act, and the Coal Miners Act, which cut the number of hours men were allowed to work underground. It is with these slow but significant advances that the reader of this book should be most concerned because of the effect on public attitudes; in turn the treatment of crime, and murder in particular. While we must be wary of blaming Society for all violent crime (after all, people do not change, and most murderers would have behaved in the same way whatever the age), there are undoubtedly social pressures unique to certain periods.

When Victoria was on the throne, the number of women charged with murder in Britain and France rose considerably, and it is impossible to dissociate these figures from the ignorant demands made by a male-dominated society, which expected women to conform to its own unreal image of female saintliness. Among the growing middle classes, respectability had been everyone's prime consideration, which meant that women had to be above reproach; virgins *incapable* of sin – and often acquitted, despite overwhelming prosecution evidence. For different reasons, married women were no less 'pure' and automatically given the benefit of the doubt – provided they had the astuteness to maintain the desired image. Juries would even accept a defence premise that the unfortunate victim committed suicide, rather than believe a respectable woman was capable of murder.

Long before the end of the nineteenth century, women had asserted their right to be treated as ordinary human beings – in other words, that they were entitled to the same social privileges as men – and insisted on climbing down from the pedestal on which they and been placed by the Victorians. For a time a significant number of women used this new found 'equality' to get even with husbands and lovers who had abused them, and they were often treated sympathetically by the courts. But despite the militancy of the suffragette movement, it was not until the Great War when women in all walks of life were needed for the war effort that emancipation became a reality. Meanwhile, in the run-up to that inevitable change, there was a marked change in attitude. Women were allowed to compete in male-dominated sports, such as cricket and rowing – and even at work. No longer having to resort to violence (ie poison or firearms) to make whatever point it was that had once led to death, there was a marked drop in the number of women committing murder (as distinct from infanticide). Hitherto, murder had invariably been motivated by emotional issues but in the Edwardian period, when the number of women charged with the capital offence had shrunk to a mere trickle, significantly there was even one suspected of intruding on a hitherto male preserve – murder for material gain, although even she was found 'not guilty'.

Other murders linked in one way or another to the Edwardian Age involved the products of other scientific advances. In the same way that Victorian doctors had 'discovered' new poisons, imagining that they were unusual enough to remain undetected, so their successors in the first decade of the twentieth century realised the killing potential of something even more novel – bacteria. In fact, forensic medicine was an area in which progress was rapid, turning laboratory technicians into detectives.

1

THE BRIDES IN THE BATH

George Joseph Smith

It took two thousand years for ordinary people to accept bathing (in the context of cleanliness) as normal behaviour, yet only a decade for someone with a warped mind to recognise the potential of the bath as a murder weapon. The 'Brides in the Bath' case could not have happened in the nineteenth century, when the private bath was the prerogative of the rich; the Edwardians, enjoying higher living standards, came to expect bathrooms built into new middle-class property, while even a few working-class cottages had model bathrooms, or various types of portable bath housed in the scullery, for whatever use a tenant wanted to make of it. Boarding houses, as well as grander hotels, were now able to offer this optional extra.

To the many thousands as unfamiliar with the risks of submerging themselves in hot water, as they were the dangers of the 'high speed' automobile, it would not have been unduly surprising to learn of a person accidently drowned after fainting or falling asleep in the tub. Even coroners were aware of such mishaps and would not necessarily bother with an inquest when there were no suspicious circumstances. The bigamist, George Joseph Smith, would therefore have got away with drowning one of his wives, having first persuaded an unwary doctor that she was subject to fits; nor, in another part of the country, under a different name, was it surprising that he was not suspected when the same thing happened to another wife – but *three* times was pushing his luck, and when those circumstances made newspaper headlines (he had only been married for a day, and even in those days certain sections of the press had a fascination with honeymoons!), at least two newspaper readers had good cause to recognise a pattern, and contact the police. The irony is that Smith had no interest in personal hygiene, and there is evidence to suggest that he took a bath himself on only one occasion – his excuse being that he could not bring himself to sit in a bath already used by someone else . . .

So novel was the case that Smith was one of only two murderers featured briefly in *The Investigation of Murder* (Michael Joseph, 1966), in a chapter entitled 'Original Murders', in which the eminent pathologist, Dr Francis Camps pointed out that the importance of the case – from the medico-legal aspect – lay in the method which, owing to the lack of signs of violence and the negative findings at the post mortem, could disguise the fact that murder had been committed. Reminding us that the truth only came to light because of the way the method and preparation was repeated, Dr Camps speculated on the advantages of a central registry, with causes of unexpected death classified under relevant headings – which would bring many such coincidences in different parts of the country to the attention of the authorities. Sophisticated computers have since made these dreams a reality.

Although a murderer does not necessarily have to be an unsympathetic character, Smith was contemptible – not only because of the heartless way he treated his victims, but for his unbelievable meanness. He was not, after all, an indiscriminate killer helpless in the face of overwhelming impulses; he was content most of the time to simply rob his wives, and the other women he did not bother to marry. But the three he murdered brought him unfamiliar wealth, and were each buried in a pauper's grave because he refused to pay for a decent coffin, let alone a headstone. Not only did he plead poverty, but he regarded it as a matter of *principle*, maintaining that 'when they're dead, they're done with'.

In fact, Smith did not have one redeeming feature, and must be included among the half-dozen most evil murderers of all time. A study of murder trials shows that when the defence prospects are hopeless, counsel has at least been able to fall back on pleas of mitigation, enabling them to speak movingly of the accused's 'finer qualities' – the love of an ailing mother, devoted wife, dependent child, and even faithful pets. At

Smith's trial he was represented by possibly the most eloquent lawyer of the age – Edward Marshall Hall, who would have had the jury in tears, if there had been *anything* to say in his client's favour. Indeed, Marshall Hall had accepted the brief partly because the obvious hopelessness had represented an irresistible challenge, but after an initial argument on a point of law (whether evidence relating to two other murders could be admitted when he was facing one specific charge) was lost, he was left with virtually no ammunition. All he could hope was that, since Smith could not be 'tied' to the scene of the crime at the relevant times, the prosecution could not actually prove Smith had drowned his victim(s). The Crown evidence in all other respects was overwhelming, but Marshall Hall remained convinced that the women had not died in the manner alleged – although he was obliged to remain silent on his client's character, having to concede later that Smith was a complete rogue.

Statistics indicate that most murders are committed by normally law-abiding people, but Smith was one of the exceptions – a petty crook who resorted to murder when the profit motive was strong enough. Despite an early apprenticeship (he was only eight when he was sentenced to eight years in a reformatory), he would never have made the grade as a professional criminal. He was lacking in every respect, except for an instinctive talent for captivating and exploiting women. Born in January 1872 in London's East End where most of his contemporaries remained for life, Smith travelled the country as constantly as a gipsy, never settling for long, as though frightened to put down roots. His own were fairly stunted, barely knowing his father, an insurance salesman, who was also seldom at home.

It is pointless to speculate now on why Smith was in trouble with the law so young, although it seems reasonable to suggest that he may have been striving to obtain his mother's attention. Equally, there can be no doubt that such a savage and totally unwarranted custodial sentence (the reformatory was a particularly harsh regime) on an impressionable child would have had a highly detrimental effect. Although he was to return to a relatively affectionate mother, it was not long before he was in trouble again. In his early teens he was given seven days for petty crime, and shortly afterwards six months for stealing a bicycle*.

He gained a temporary reprieve from life in the underworld by taking the only escape route available in those days – the army. In fact, there is no available proof that he was ever in the army and the police were later sceptical, dismissing the claim as yet another of Smith's many lies. However, he was not in prison, and he told his first wife that he had been three years in the Northamptonshire Regiment, which may well have been true, because he managed to glean a rudimentary education during that period – or, at least, to discover what else life had to offer – and a degree of confidence. Another reason is that he changed physically, developing an upright bearing, which he never lost, offsetting an otherwise shifty appearance. In fact, Smith was not a bad-looking man – above average height, fair and with a ginger moustache; he had clean-cut aquiline features, and piercing eyes (hypnotic in the view of some, unnerving to others). Nevertheless, this new assertiveness, manifesting itself in easy conversation when he tried to impress, was not enough to encourage him to go straight. In consequence of his childhood environment he was now probably incapable of behaving honestly.

In circulation again and calling himself George Baker he made his first known 'conquest', quickly persuading an innocent young woman infatuated with him that the only way they could afford to set up home together was if she could earn the necessary funds quickly enough – by stealing. Unfortunately, he was no more successful as a teacher and 'mastermind' than he had been as a thief. The girl was soon caught, and Smith was sentenced to twelve months' prison; the only lesson he had learned was not to use his real name, otherwise the sentence would have been heavier.

Undaunted, on his release in 1898, he moved to Leicester. Now, posing as George Oliver Love, he met and soon proposed

* Bicycles were just becoming fashionable

marriage to an inexperienced eighteen-year-old, Caroline Beatrice Thornhill. Even though he did his best to impress her family, they were not taken in, and when she insisted on getting married they stayed away. Apart from giving a false name on the marriage certificate, he also described his father's occupation as 'detective'. From his subsequent behaviour, it would seem that he regarded Beatrice as someone rather special (she *was*, in the sense that she remained his only legal wife), and for a brief spell he tried to run a baker's shop. However, he had no head for business, and his concern for his young wife did not prevent him from setting her up as a thief, despite his previous misfortune. The plan this time was to keep on the move, trying his luck not only in London but on the south coast, particularly in Brighton and Hastings. Providing impressive references (forged), he found Beatrice potentially lucrative employment as a maid, and when she had stolen whatever he considered worthwhile, they would move on to the next job. The problem was that although his young wife was impressionable enough to do as she was told , she was basically too honest, and it was only a matter of time before she was apprehended at a seaside pawnbrokers, trying to sell some silver spoons.

When Beatrice went to gaol for a year, Smith disappeared; in need of money – he proposed marriage to a boarding house keeper from London, affluent enough to keep him in relative comfort. He came and went as he chose, using her as a bank offering free loans, yet she put up with the humiliation, even when he beat her, revealing – in common with so many of his victims – a masochistic streak, matched by a sadistic one in Smith, fortunately not demonstrated too often. Meanwhile, Beatrice had come to her senses, realising that she had been used, and on her release she tracked down her husband and identified him as the person behind the thefts. Charged with receiving stolen property he was sent down for two years – benefitting from the fact that George Love was apparently a first-time offender!

Smith's sense of morality was outraged by such disloyalty, and on his release he even threatened to kill her, but the threat was nipped in the bud by Beatrice's two brothers who gave him an overdue good hiding. Ashamed of her experience, and to prevent any further trouble, Beatrice emigrated to Canada – remaining Mrs Love until after his execution twelve years later, when she remarried.

On his release from prison in 1903, Smith made a conscious decision to forget conventional crime in which he now realised his limitations, and to play to his strengths – indeed, his only strength – his power over women. From now on, he earned his living from loving and leaving a succession of women. He got back on his feet initially by returning to his first bigamous wife, the boarding house keeper, where he could at least eat and laze about at no cost. (The reason why women were prepared to take him back after the initial humiliation is that – apart from the sexual attraction – he invariably established the ground rules from the outset, which was that a man's business was his own, and that a woman should remember her place and be grateful for small mercies! This would imply that the women he exploited were a bunch of desperate spinsters, plain and lonely, but the opposite was true. His conquests included many attractive women, albeit vulnerable in some way. The factor common to all was the humiliation that prevented them from speaking out.) From his point of view, anyone who had *any* money, was fair game, and he moved about the country in search of conquests – regularly changing his name although in the early years, perhaps to avoid confusion, he stuck to his own Christian name.

As his resources accumulated he began to dabble in antiques and eventually took a small shop in Bristol. He was never any good at business (over the years his income from gullible women was considerable, but he invariably lost money on business and property transactions), yet it seems he had an instinctive 'feel' for certain antiques, such as *objets d'art*, and especially Chinese porcelain. Nevertheless, antiques were seldom more than a supplementary income, his bread and butter coming from women prepared to draw out their life savings on his instructions. No doubt it was his meanness that ensured he did not have to waste money on a marriage licence unless it was absolutely necessary.

Mrs Florence Wilson, a widow whom he met in London in June 1908, was only his second bigamous bride. He had calculated that she was too shrewd to draw out her post office savings of £30 until married and confident of security of another kind, and he had found how simple a matter the marriage service could be. How a mature woman can innocently hand over her life savings to a brand-new husband she has known only briefly (in this case, it was all of three weeks) defies explanation – but it is another indication of Smith's powers (some say hypnotic) of persuasion. Smith was not the first, or last confidence trickster to exploit women – but certainly the meanest. Money and jewellery is one thing, but Smith took everything and anything that was not too heavy to carry off. The pattern was usually the same. Straight from the post office, he took Florence to a public exhibition (invariably a venue that was free) and, clutching her £30, he went off to buy a newspaper. While she waited naïvely, he returned to their lodgings and made off with all her belongings, leaving her with just the clothes she was wearing at the time. It is surprising he never hit on the idea of taking his victims to a Turkish bath, when he might also have grabbed those clothes too.

Smith returned to Bristol and within a month he was married again, but this time he may have miscalculated because his fourth bride, Edith Mabel Pegler was not discarded in the usual fashion. It is possible that was never his intention. At twenty-eight, only eight years younger than him, Edith was an attractive woman who had advertised for a job as housekeeper in a household which had a servant to do the heavier work. Smith answered the advert, despite the fact that he had no servant. We do not know his reason, but for Edith it was infatuation on sight. He would not have expected her to have much money of her own, and it would not have been practical for him to disappear from his home, in the vicinity of his own antiques business. More likely he decided it would be cheaper to marry her than pay a housekeeper's wages, because Smith was not the sort of husband who believed he had any marital obligations. If he was living at home he was prepared to find the money for their food, but when away – which was most of the time – Edith had to fend for herself. The difference this time was that he announced his departures – describing them as buying or business trips – and his intention of returning in due course, so that when she was desperate, Edith could go to stay with her mother. His treatment of Edith was quite uncharacteristic – almost considerate, by his standards. It might even be speculated that, in his way, Smith 'loved' her – actually sending her money occasionally (not much, but a £1 note once in a while), although when she complained of his neglect too strongly he was not above putting her in her place with a thrashing. Edith obviously came to terms with his gipsy way of life and, when invited, joined him on his travels through the south of England.

However, he was on his own a year later in Southampton when, posing as George Rose, of independent means, he wooed and married Sarah Freeman, after establishing that she had sufficient funds to make it worth his while. Sarah was a cut above him socially but although he retained a cockney accent, he dressed well (befitting his 'occupation') and had sufficient personality to persuade people he possessed the ability to rise above his humble origins. His knowledge of antiques and the people in all walks of life he met in the course of that business, undoubtedly added to his ease of manner and conversational ability. For a man of no formal education he could read and write (after a fashion) and had an aptitude for music, somehow learning to play the piano and harmonium with a degree of competence. Wherever possible, he would disorientate his victims, uprooting them from familiar surroundings – in the case of Miss Freeman finding new lodgings at Clapham in south London. Then, telling his latest wife that the business was a little short of funds for new stock, he took everything she had – a 'profit' on the marriage of £50 in cash, £260 drawn from the bank and £30 in Government bonds. He used an outing to the National Gallery as the opportunity to disappear, asking the unsuspecting Sarah to wait while he went to the toilet;

instead, he returned to their lodgings, where he collected her clothes to sell.

Smith returned to the faithful Edith in Bristol, but whether to cover his tracks or whether he had ants in his pants, he immediately took her to Southend where he invested part of his latest income in a cottage with a small second-hand furniture business. But once again there seems to have been no thought to the investment potential. At no stage had Smith ever made proper use of the money he stole from his women; he seemed to regard it merely as a means of eliminating the need to work for a living. Beatrice Thornhill, his only legal wife, maintained that in their short time together she never saw him do a proper day's work, looking to her to provide their income – and he never changed. Edith Pegler earned her keep by working the shop while he did nothing, or dabbled (if the mood took him) in antiques, gradually moving 'upmarket', so he could eventually justify calling himself an art dealer.

Southend was another dead-end, and he sold the property at a loss in order to return to Bristol, apparently regarded as a permanent base, and where he bought another property, this time on a mortgage – which meant another injection of capital from somewhere. It could be argued that trying to find an 'available' woman of substance, starting from scratch, is like looking for a needle in a haystack and therefore might qualify as work of a kind. There can be no doubt that Smith was industrious in this direction and his persistence paid off. Woman-hunting in nearby Clifton in August 1910, he was attracted by a striking, smartly dressed woman with whom he managed to strike up an acquaintance. She turned out to be Beatrice ('Bessie') Mundy, 33, who did not need to work, living on an inheritance. It says much for his attraction to women that Miss Mundy, whose background was highly respectable, allowed herself to be picked up by a stranger – and to accompany him to Weymouth where they were married three days later. She was a well educated young woman, as tall as Smith and very good looking, which does not make her seem like a lonely spinster; in fact, it is more likely that many men would have found her somewhat intimidating. But she was putty in the hands of Smith, posing as Henry Williams, a picture restorer. Once he had learned about her inheritance, there was no stopping him.

Bessie had inherited £2,500 (a considerable sum in those days), on the death of her bank manager father, six years earlier. The money, controlled by a trust supervised by her uncle, had been well invested and brought in an annuity of almost £100, more than enough to live on, although she had little cash to spare. However, Smith realised that interest would have accrued on her investments, and on their wedding night penned a terse note to her uncle: 'Bessie hopes you will forward as much money as possible at your earliest by registered letter'.

Bessie's uncle, always concerned that she had no head for money matters, was suspicious of the mysterious Henry Williams and sought legal advice over withholding the £138 due to her; but he had no option and eventually (five months later) Smith got his hands on it – and promptly walked out. This time, instead of simply disappearing, he left an unpleasant letter – presumably in retaliation for the inconvenience of having to wait so long for 'his' money. He wrote:

> Dearest, I fear you have blighted all my bright hopes of a happy future. I have caught from you a disease which is called the bad disorder. For you to be in such a state proves you could not have kept yourself morally clean . . . For the sake of my health and humour, and yours too, I must go to London . . . to get properly cured of this disease. It will cost me a great deal of money, because it might take years . . . Tell the landlady and everyone else that I have gone to France. But tell your uncle the truth . . . If he happens to ask you about money, tell him that you kept all the money which was sent to you in a leather bag, and two days after I had gone you happened to go on the beach and fall asleep and when you woke the bag of money was gone . . . Whatever you do, stick to everything you say. Never alter it or else you will get mixed up and make a fool of yourself . . . Mark what I say. Now tear this letter up at once and throw the pieces in the road.

His totally false allegation of VD was based on her naïve confession of an earlier love affair, so he was really rubbing salt into the wound. By the time the news had sunk in, Smith was back in Bristol with Edith Pegler, proudly showing off the financial return on some of his lucrative fictitious business deals. For no discernible reason they returned to Southend, and on to London before going back to Bristol, once again. It was not long before funds were again at a low ebb, but this time he did not have to search for his next meal ticket – she found him. He was in Weston-super-Mare, wistfully gazing out to sea, when he was spotted by the wife he had deserted, Bessie Mundy, who was now staying with an old school friend at a seaside boarding house.

Incredibly, Bessie was overjoyed and Smith managed to convince her that the meeting was no accident; that he had been searching for her for the past year. Her friend took an instant dislike to him, supporting the theory that people were seldom indifferent to Smith; they either loved or hated him, which might be described as some form of magnetic attraction or repulsion. However, despite the warnings, Bessie had totally forgiven her 'husband'. If she needed any further proof of his genuine intentions, Smith volunteered to repay the £138 he had 'borrowed'. It did not occur to her that he could afford to be magnanimous, with a far greater sum at stake – her inheritance.

Smith immediately explored every possibility of getting his hands on the £2,500, but soon came to the conclusion that the only way would be as the sole beneficiary of a will. Realising that on hearing of the reconciliation, her uncle might take steps to change the conditions relating to her estate, he knew he had to act quickly. His first step was to get Bessie away from other possible influences and, unquestioning, she accompanied him back to the east coast, this time to Herne Bay where he rented a house for their second honeymoon. To reassure her, he demonstrated his change of heart by making a will – leaving everything to Bessie. Since Henry Williams did not exist and had nothing to bequeath, he was giving nothing away, but Bessie felt honour-bound to reciprocate – making her own will in his favour.

How blind my friends and relations are, Bessie must have thought, especially when her considerate husband realised that in his haste to obtain a pleasant place for their reconciliation he had overlooked the fact that it had no bathroom. He was determined to rectify that omission at once by getting a portable bath which would at least do until they found a proper home, and 'Henry' proved as good as his word, returning with a metal bath, the type which has to be filled (and subsequently emptied) by bucket. She may not have been so starry-eyed had she heard him haggling with the ironmonger, eventually getting the price reduced from £2.00 to £1.17s 6d (£1.75p).

Next, Smith prepared the ground by consulting a local doctor about his wife's health, telling him that she suffered from fits. When the doctor called he found 'Mrs Williams' in bed, somewhat drowsy but apparently well, apart from a slight temperature. She denied any history of fits, but admitted suffering from headaches. Yet the same night Bessie wrote to her uncle, announcing that she had suffered *two* fits.

> Last Tuesday night I had a bad fit, and one again on Thursday night. It has left me weak and suffering from nerves and headache, and has evidently shaken my whole system. My husband has been extremely kind and done all he could for me. He has provided me with the attention of the best medical man here, who is constantly giving me medical treatment, and visiting me day and night.
>
> I do not like to worry you with this, but my husband has strictly advised me to let all my relatives know and tell them of my breakdown. I have made out my will and have left all I have to my husband. That is only natural, as I love my husband.

The tone of the letter contained strange inaccuracies, such as the reference to two fits, which she had not mentioned to the doctor . . . the 'best medical man' visiting day and night: the young GP had in fact been qualified for less than two years, and had seen her only twice when he had prescribed a mild sedative . . . this and the references to a 'breakdown', have all the hallmarks of being dictated. Besotted as she was, Bessie could have conveyed the same message far more naturally – unless the hypnosis theory is valid.

The letter was Bessie's death warrant. The very next day she took an early morning bath, after which a note was despatched to the same GP, asking him to call at once. He found the bride, her head still under the water, dead; in one hand was clutched a bar of soap. From what he thought he already knew about Mrs Williams, and because the scene was so peaceful, he assumed she had died from natural causes, drowned after being taken ill. A more experienced doctor might have been more aware of the odds (at least 12 to 1) against any person having a first epileptic fit at the age of thirty-five, and also puzzled by the fact that a fit while in the water had not caused more of a mess. Thus Smith felt justified in writing to Bessie's uncle the same day, claiming that the doctor said she had suffered a fit in the bath (in fact, he had not). In view of their suspicions, Bessie's brother wrote both to 'Williams' and the coroner asking for a post mortem, but the coroner, knowing the deceased's medical 'history', and the letter testifying to the husband's attentiveness, decided it was not necessary. The family also tried to fight the recently filed will, but were unable to stop the money going to the apparently grieving Henry Williams.

Meanwhile, Smith was on the move again, this time to Margate, stopping only to return the tin bath to the ironmonger, reclaiming his money and refusing even to pay for its hire. On the Kent coast he was joined by Edith Pegler, but with the legacy in his hands they were off again on their travels. After a short spell in Tunbridge Wells, they were back in Bristol where he 'invested' in several more properties. It is an indication of Smith's poor record in handling money that in one short period he purchased a number of houses for a total (cash) investment of £2,187.10s, and sold them for £1,455 – a loss of over £600 (a significant sum) in just a few months.

A year later, in the summer of 1913, Edith was informed that funds were low, and that her tireless husband had to go off on one of his business trips again – alone. At Southsea

(Hampshire), in October he found his next victim, plump but attractive Alice Burnham, a twenty-five year old private nurse. Daughter of a successful fruit grower, she must have seemed a lucrative catch, and he may have been disappointed to discover she had little money of her own, apart from a small bank account (less than £30), and her savings of £100, which her father was holding for her together with interest accrued. That was not enough to justify murder, and Smith would probably have followed a former pattern and simply disappeared with the cash, but Bessie's money had made him greedy, and the day before they were married (less than a fortnight after the first meeting), he insured Alice's life for £500, and persuaded her to make a will in his favour.

Mr Burnham had taken an instant dislike to Smith, describing him as a man of 'evil appearance' – so much so that he could not sleep while Smith was in the house, fearing 'something serious' would happen. Cautiously, he got a solicitor to enquire into the suitor's background, but Smith was confident enough to treat and dismiss this interference with contempt. Within a few days of the marriage he wrote a terse note demanding the money 'owed' to Alice. She too was so much under her new husband's influence she even instructed a solicitor to write to her sister, demanding the immediate return of a £10 'debt'.

Funds replenished, Smith (he actually used his own name on this occasion) took Alice on their honeymoon, a short stay at the seaside. Bearing in mind that the English seaside is hardly at its most attractive in winter, and the fact that they were already in a holiday resort on the relatively warm south coast, one wonders why he chose Blackpool, in the much colder north west. It was just a couple of weeks before Christmas, a particularly bleak time of year.

The boarding house he chose was not as cheap as he would have liked, but the attraction was use of the bathroom. Blackpool was already a popular resort, and despite the time of year, had its fair share of attractions, but Smith was not interested in the surroundings; on arrival his first visit was to a local GP, to complain about his wife's headaches – and that he was concerned about her health. The doctor made a careful note of the symptoms listed by the so-considerate husband, promising to examine her in due course. There was not time.

Forty-eight hours later, the landlady Mrs Crossley noticed the young bride entering the bathroom, and soon became puzzled when she and her family realised that water was beginning to seep through the kitchen ceiling from the bathroom above. Before they could do anything, Smith stuck his head round the door, producing a bag of eggs he had just bought for the following day's breakfast. When his attention had been drawn to the water, he went to investigate – calling down from the top of the stairs to fetch a doctor 'in a hurry'. When next seen he was holding up his wife's naked body. It did not occur to anyone until later the significance of the fact that Alice's head was towards the taps. In fact, the doctor's initial reaction had been one of surprise that Smith had not attempted to lift his wife out of the water. In response, Smith simply retorted that he could not. When asked why did he not pull the plug out, his lame reply was that it had not occurred to him!

Considering that the couple had been married so recently, Mrs Crossley was stunned by Smith's obvious indifference, and affronted when he refused to spend any extra on a deal coffin, maintaining 'once they're dead, they're done with'. As he left, Mrs Crossley helplessly called out 'Crippen!' She would have been even more vehement had she realised that he was on his way back to her lodgings in Southsea so that he could collect and sell the rest of his wife's belongings. While he was there, he refused to pay a small food bill Alice had run up. Meanwhile, there had been an inquest, but accidental death was the only verdict which could have been brought in the circumstances.

Edith welcomed him back, and they were on their travels again until he felt the need to be left alone – travelling to London just after the outbreak of the war – to marry Alice Reavil, a pretty young domestic servant. Charles Oliver James, as she knew her husband, persuaded her to sell her piano for which she obtained £14. Next was her life savings of £70 in the post office, and confident that there was nothing else to detain him, he took her out, then made the usual excuse so as to double-back to collect her clothes and jewellery. It could be argued that she was lucky to escape with her life, but at the time I'm not sure that Miss Reavil would have agreed; apart from the humiliation, the prospect of starting life again without a penny in the world, in the days long before the welfare state, must have been daunting.

With his money 'tied up' in property, Smith's latest windfall did not go very far, and although he returned to Edith in Bristol, he disappeared again almost immediately to marry for the *ninth* time, on this occasion to a thirty-eight year old spinster, Margaret Lofty, who was on the rebound from an unhappy love affair with a suitor who turned out to be married! Despite her obvious vulnerability, it speaks volumes for Smith's charisma that this clergyman's daughter went out to tea with him on 15 December, and did not bother to return home. Two days later they were married in Bath, the bridegroom giving his name as John Lloyd, an estate agent.

In the interim, he had taken out an insurance policy on her life for £700. All Miss Lofty had in her savings account was £19, and this was withdrawn to pay for train fares to London where he had already reserved accommodation at a boarding house in Highgate. However, when he had called originally the manageress had taken a dislike to him. Possibly she was unduly suspicious, having recently been robbed by some lodgers, but she later told police that she did not like the way he had questioned her about the bath. It was as though 'he was measuring it with his eyes'. His subsequent appearance with a wife merely confirmed her unfavourable impression, and she arranged for someone to tell him the rooms were not yet ready, and to come back. Meanwhile, she asked a policeman friend to call in. Although the witness had no real grounds for suspicion, he was not happy with Smith's manner and his answers, and asked him to leave on the pretext that he had no references. What Miss Lofty thought of this unexpected complication is not known, but Smith managed to find another boarding house with a bath.

At that stage, his bride must have been exhausted, but

Smith insisted on dragging her to the nearest doctor where he announced that she was troubled by violent headaches. Presumably Margaret had experienced a stressful few months so she would not have protested, and the eventful day had left her with a slight temperature, so the doctor prescribed a sedative. Next morning they visited a solicitor so that she could make a will in her beloved husband's favour - an act of love because on returning to their lodgings she wrote to her mother, announcing her good fortune in marrying such a 'thorough Christian man'. That evening she took a bath, while Smith was downstairs playing 'Nearer my God to Thee' on the piano. A few minutes later the landlady, Miss Blatch, heard the front door shut but did not pay any further attention until she answered the door-bell ring to find the man she knew as John Lloyd, apologising for having forgotten his key. He was carrying a bag of tomatoes he had brought for his wife's supper. He asked if she was down yet. When she did not respond to his call, he went upstairs.

If Smith had been a little more cautious, and waited a few months, the inquest might have gone unreported, but the story of a bride found naked in the bath at the start of her honeymoon was a 'natural', and one of the more lurid reports caught the eye of Alice Burnham's father, and the Blackpool landlady's husband, Joseph; both of whom recognised the similarity with their own unpleasant experiences. As a result, Detective Inspector Arthur Neil of Scotland Yard was assigned to the investigation, an exhaustive enquiry in which he visited forty different towns, examined twenty-one different bank accounts, and interrogated 150 witnesses, of which 112 were to be called at the trial. His thoroughness (he was later commended for it by the judge) was rewarded, and he soon had sufficient reason to instruct the solicitors dealing with 'Mrs Lloyd's' will to delay the legal formalities as much as possible. When Smith eventually called to collect his £700, he was arrested by Inspector Neil – at that stage merely with 'causing a false entry to be made in the marriage register with Miss Lofty'.

But the pattern was now clear, and on 23 March he

was charged with three murders. On 22 June, the Crown proceeded with the charge in reference to Bessie Mundy. It was to be the longest murder trial since that of the evil Dr William Palmer sixty years before, ending on 1 July. There was drama even before the start over the appointment of counsel for the defence. In view of his incredible meanness, one wonders whether Smith – with his own life at stake – would have been prepared to invest in a good barrister. We shall never know because the dilemma never arose, because in an early example of cheque-book journalism, a daily newspaper offered to pay for the best counsel of the day in exchange for Smith's side of the story, after the trial. His solicitor jumped at the opportunity to brief Edward Marshall Hall, but only three days before the trial the Home Office ruled that the arrangement was not in the public interest. Fortunately for the accused, Marshall Hall and his 'junior', Montague Shearman, considered it a matter of honour to stand by their client, and completed the brief for little more than token fees.

Marshall Hall knew that the mass of circumstantial evidence mustered by the prosecution made his case virtually hopeless, and banked on winning a legal point – persuading Mr Justice Scrutton that it was wrong to prejudice a jury hearing one charge with allegations of other offences, even if the accused had not been convicted of them (which is why a defendant's previous convictions have to remain secret until he or she has been convicted of a new charge). The only exceptions to the rule protecting the character of an accused, is if the defence attacks the character of a Crown witness, or if the defence case is based on death through accident or ignorance. In other words, if a defendant is believed to have caused someone's death on one occasion, he or she may claim it was an accident, or that he or she did not realise that the incident would result in death. But if the same thing happens three times, people will automatically *assume* guilt. The technical name for this is evidence of 'system'. Marshall Hall believed the Crown could not prove the murder of Bessie Mundy, but in proving the case to be part of a pattern, the system would itself prejudice the jury. He was overruled by the judge who warned the jury they must not infer anything from such evidence – but that was an impossible request. On the other hand, it would have been a travesty of justice if Smith had got off solely because the jury was not satisfied beyond doubt that he had been with Bessie at the time of her death.

The only area in which the defence could put up a fight was in that of the actual drowning. Marshall Hall maintained there was no evidence that Smith had drowned Miss Mundy; no evidence of a struggle when even a kitten being drowned would scratch. But the police had done their homework, experimenting with volunteer women in baths, with – and even without – water. Now they were able to demonstrate to the jury how easy it was to crook one arm under the victim's knees and lift, while using the other hand to hold down her head. This was supported by the Home Office pathologist, Dr Bernard Spilsbury who explained that the sudden immersion of the head (when the legs had been lifted) would throw water onto the back of the throat – drowning from posture or immobility. He also discounted the possibility of drowning caused by epilepsy or fainting – in the case of the former, the limbs would have been in a different position. While the soap found clutched in Miss Mundy's hand was typical of a case of drowning, in a faint or during a fit the hand would have relaxed, releasing the soap. The rigidity of the fingers would only have occurred if the drowning was almost instantaneous; or if the water entering the mouth, ears and nose had caused her to die of cardiac arrest (or shock) before drowning.

After the summing up from both sides, the Judge invited the jury to inspect three baths in an ante-room, and even proffered a theory of his own of how the accused might have drowned his victim. When Marshall Hall protested it was not open to the jury to consider any theory that had not been put forward by the Crown, Mr Justice Scrutton told them: 'If, on looking at the baths another theory occurs to you better than those which have been suggested, in my view you are quite entitled to consider it'.

The jury took only twenty-two minutes to find Smith guilty, and there can be no doubt the verdict was correct, although

Marshall Hall in a letter to the Bishop of Croydon shortly after the execution, speculated on the possibility Smith had maintained his plea of innocence because he had not physically carried out the act of drowning. He was convinced of Smith's hypnotic powers, having had a strange experience in Brixton Prison when he and Montague Shearman were interviewing their client. At one stage he became so aware of Smith's staring eyes that he broke off the consultation, believing their client was trying to hypnotise them. Mr Shearman shared his sensation. In the letter he says: '. . . I have most reluctantly come to the conclusion that Smith was responsible for the deaths of all three women, directly or indirectly. That he did not drown them in any of the ways suggested by the evidence . . . I am convinced; but I am equally convinced it was brought about by hypnotic suggestion . . . Once one accepts this theory, and the whole thing, including the unbolted doors, is to my mind satisfactorily explained; it also accounts for his very firm assertion of innocence of murder, he having satisfied his conscience that the act was induced by his will, and became to all intents a voluntary act on the part of the woman.'

An interesting hypothesis, but I think it far more likely that Smith maintained his innocence because lying had become second nature, and he no longer recognised the truth. As I said at the outset, George Joseph Smith had no redeeming features. His own mother had given him up as a lost cause many years before, and one would have thought that his passing would not have been regretted by anyone. Yet one person – Edith Pegler – wept at the verdict, unable to believe he was capable of such villainy. To her, he had merely been an occasional bully who threatened her from time to time, but never actually did her any harm . . . left her alone for months on end but never deserted her . . . indeed, he had even occasionally *given* her nice clothes, even if he hadn't admitted they were the property of other women . . . he wasn't perfect, perhaps, but he was all she had . . .

2

OTHER LADYKILLERS

Dougal, Hoch and Chapman

Forever victims of sexual abuse, it is relatively unusual for women to be killed for financial gain alone – which is what makes the odious George Joseph Smith such a fascinating study. Sex was a business instrument with which he manipulated women as clinically as a more educated man handled commodities on the stock market; seduction was a job pure and simple, and there is no evidence that he got any thrill from the act of murder, undertaken only when it made commercial sense. As it happens, Smith cornered a shrinking market because, with the approach of emancipation and the parallel growth in female self-confidence, marriage was no longer the number one priority in life – so women were correspondingly less vulnerable to exploitation.

The murderer who had most in common with Smith was Samuel Dougal, although their characters could not have been more different. Smith had the limited perspective of a computer – a woman's dulcet tones to his ears would have had no more sex appeal than a cash register. Dougal, no less unpleasant, was at least human; he enjoyed mixing business with pleasure. In fact, it is a reasonable bet that Dougal fathered more children than any murderer in history. My confidence for that bold assertion is based on the near impossible research entailed in trying to arrive at the exact number – well into double figures!

The problem with hindsight is that, knowing someone has killed at least once, we tend to place sinister connotations on the death of anyone ever associated with that murderer. There is reason to believe that Dougal did murder more than once, but we shall never know for certain. Born of a middle-class London family in 1846, Samuel appears to have grown up into a fairly ordinary, if headstrong young man with more than a passing interest in alcohol and girls. After the relative dullness of an apprenticeship in engineering, he endeavoured to satisfy a sense of adventure by joining the army, which gave him the opportunity to travel – and meet women. After spells with the Royal Engineers in Ireland and Wales, he was based in Nova Scotia, Canada, where he spent ten of his twenty-one years in the army, before leaving with the rank of quartermaster sergeant. Like Smith, he was fortunate that women were drawn to him. Striking more than handsome, his growing reputation as a sexual athlete undoubtedly added to his attraction and his seduction rate was impressive, although success made him increasingly ruthless, and it was not long before he added violence to his sexual bag of tricks. He lived a Jekyl and Hyde existence; in other respects leading an exemplary life, and becoming known as a model soldier, a solid and reliable administrator. The women he encountered may have learned how to relate to men on equal footing, but not how to protect themselves against unwanted pregnancy, and Dougal was certainly no gentleman when it came to doing the 'right thing'.

Having played fast and loose, at the age of twenty-three he made a major error of judgement in marrying, and – in the real sense of the expression – settling down. As a regular soldier, he could not simply walk out, and while he was tied to the army, a wife in whom he had quickly lost interest was like a millstone. Sixteen quarrelsome years and four children (his first legitimate offspring) later, Dougal finally obtained his freedom when his wife conveniently died. There had been no history of illness, and despite the fact it happened so quickly – less than twelve hours from first symptoms to death – and the pain during that spell excruciating, Dougal's superiors did not bother with an inquest. An army wife was at the time still merely an appendage, kept very much under sufferance; anyone who had the temerity to rock the boat by dying while under their jurisdiction was virtually swept under the carpet. Admittedly, there was no apparent reason to delay. Members of Her Majesty's forces – especially those who had earned promotion – were far too well disciplined to do anything that might bring dishonour on the regiment. On reflection, the reaction of the military authorities was to be expected; after all, how many unexpected deaths turn out to have been murders?

But when something similar happened only a few months later, one would have expected even a token enquiry. In August 1885, Dougal returned from compassionate leave in England with a new wife. It was a surprising decision. Dougal had been happy playing the field and at the age of forty he was still not ready for domesticity. As he had discovered years before, a marriage certificate seemed to bring out the worst in some women, and although there is no record of the relationship between Dougal and his second wife, it seems reasonable to speculate that it was a disappointment. All we know as fact is that after less than two months of wedded bliss, the new Mrs Dougal died – just as suddenly and in similar circumstances, following a violent stomach upset, indicating an irritant of some sort. Nevertheless, the army doctors chose to ignore the unusual symptoms, and since the civilian authorities had no jurisdiction (or interest) in what passed for military affairs, no enquiry was ever held. Like the first Mrs Dougal, the new bride was buried within twenty-four hours. As I said, all very suspicious, but only with the benefit of hindsight. There was no evidence at the time that Dougal had anything to gain from the death of either wife – certainly not financially, apart from the fact that it was undoubtedly cheaper not having to support anyone.

However, even if Dougal had nothing to do with their deaths, he did little to conceal his indifference, and by the time he returned to England eighteen months later he was accompanied by another young woman, posing as his wife. She had given birth to Dougal's first British offspring before she realised – somewhat belatedly, already battered and bruised – that a future with the self-centred Englishman offered little but grief, and she fled back to her family in Nova Scotia, just as Dougal was about to embark on a civilian life. Ironically, although his grasp of morality had always been sketchy, the army seemed to have kept a rein on his more criminal inclinations. Without that disciplined regime, Dougal began to look for easier ways of making money.

A good army record enabled him to get most of the administrative jobs for which he applied, but he could not settle down and changed jobs as often as he changed his women. By now he had become almost as callous as Smith, although he did not need to do the disappearing act – his behaviour was so violent that his victims were relieved to escape of their own accord; one was a widow who bore him two more children. It could be argued that, unlike Smith, he did not stoop to stealing the clothes off their backs, but that was because he was cold-hearted more than petty – it never worried him, for example, that he was saddling some of these women with the additional burden of a child (remember, there was no welfare state). Indeed, he was becoming more materialistic all the time, and for once even put sex on one side to exploit an older woman with money. Using funds to take over a public house in Hertfordshire, he insured this property and the adjoining house in which they lived – feigning surprise when they were both destroyed by fire. But Dougal's smooth talk did not impress the insurance company, and the only reward for his efforts was to be arrested.

He was fortunate, being acquitted through lack of evidence. But by now Dougal was on the slippery slope. A couple of years later, avoiding suspicious insurance companies to concentrate on individuals incapable of retaliation, he contrived to meet and seduce Emily Booty, a gullible spinster, persuading her to lease a home for them in Oxfordshire. As soon as they were installed, he brought in another woman to share their love nest. Miss Booty put up with the humiliation initially, but when his manner became increasingly threatening, she went to the police. A search of Dougal's luggage revealed several inconsequential items belonging to his benefactor, and he was charged with theft. Again, he was found not guilty. However, arrested yet again on a charge of forging a cheque, he was sent to prison for twelve months, emerging in December 1896.

The woman he had introduced into Miss Booty's house

was Sarah White, whom he had married in Dublin two years earlier, and with whom he had had two more legitimate offspring. She had been deserted when he returned to England, and whether he sent for her as a matter of belated conscience, or whether he preferred her company in bed to that of the unfortunate Miss Booty, is not clear – but from then on they had a chequered relationship with Dougal sending for her when it suited his purpose, and Sarah walking out when she could no longer stand his behaviour; like Smith he had the ability to merely snap his fingers, and make discarded women return to further humiliation.

An army pension had meant that he could more or less please himself about work, but the criminal conviction resulted in this being cut off and now, over fifty, it was no longer easy to find decent employment. His brother came to the rescue for a while but by now Dougal had lost the last vestiges of self-discipline and was eventually sacked. There was little prospect of a job, but he was still a striking person, and now he used his sexual magnetism to captivate a lonely spinster, Camille Holland, two or three years his senior. Attractive in her youth, Camille had wasted the early years of adulthood, mourning over the death of her fiancé in an accident, and by the time she had come to terms with what life still had to offer, she was well and truly on the shelf. Her social accomplishments (apart from her education, she was both artistic and musical) and good looks, maintained in middle age with cosmetics and by dyeing her hair, might have rescued her in a less class-conscious society than the late Victorian period, but she was probably resigned to spinsterhood when Dougal swept her off her feet. Although he introduced himself as an officer and supported the story with appropriate lies, there is no doubt that it was his sexuality that fascinated her; he possessed an aura of animal-like virility that a woman of her gentility had never encountered. Most of Dougal's exhaustive experience had been with gullible servant girls; now he found the highly respectable and educated Camille every bit as responsive – even prepared to live in 'sin' (in addition to the conditioning of class, she was a Catholic).

Poor Miss Holland was out of her depth. When Dougal pressed too hard, trying to persuade her to withdraw her savings (she had been left about £7,000 by an aunt) and invest them in his name, she realised her folly – but like other, more experienced women, she was drawn back to him, and put up with the suspicion that she was being used. She may have felt it was a reasonable compromise to lease a house in Sussex in her own name, in which Dougal could stay rent free, and she then left her home in London to join him –telling her friends that she was getting married. But Dougal was not satisfied with being a 'kept' lover; he wanted to control his own destiny. Persuading the infatuated woman that they would be happier in a place of their own, a 'love nest' tucked away in splendid isolation, away from mundane distractions, he found a remote farm at Clavering, in Essex. When Miss Holland saw the property and conceded that it was ideal, she would have been surprised to discover that her lover had already agreed a contract with the estate agents, and signed – in his name!

However, Miss Holland dug in her heels, refusing to accept the contract – although only a matter of days later, in January 1899, the farmhouse became hers. The transaction cost her more than £1,500, although they were able to furnish it well from her existing possessions. The area was remote and the property itself was cut off from the surrounding countryside by a wide perimeter moat, reached only by a single bridge. Different people see different qualities in isolation; Camille's images were romantic, and she renamed the place Moat Farm. Very much alone initially, it must have seemed like a dream come true, but they could not manage without a servant – the mistress because she was accustomed to being looked after, while the master needed the company of young women.

For once Dougal miscalculated: the first objected to his advances, and left after a week, while the second was totally innocent and terrified enough to run to her mistress for protection. It was one thing knowing that Dougal was obsessed with money, Camille still having the consolation that he probably loved her in his way – much more humiliating to realise he even preferred the favours of servant girls. She must have realised she either had to put up with his behaviour, or risk losing him – and it would have been almost impossible to go back to her old life style. Nevertheless, she was courageous enough to confront him, and it suited Dougal's purpose to promise it would not happen again. Even as he apologised, he must have been planning to end the pretence by getting rid of her in a way that would enable him to retain her money.

On the pretext of taking his wife shopping, once out of sight of the agitated maid, Dougal shot Miss Holland in the head and buried her body on the farm. Returning much later from the 'shopping trip', Dougal explained that his wife had decided to go to London, but would be back later. When she did not return that day, or the next, he informed her maid that Mrs Dougal would be staying away for a little longer. Meanwhile the maid's mother arrived to collect the girl, and was given the same explanation. Finally, all pretence was dropped and to subsequent enquiries he merely implied that his wife was 'away'. Since no-one knew them or their background, it did not occur to anyone to ask why Mrs Dougal had left all her clothes behind; nor why only a week or so later, Dougal's widowed daughter was suddenly installed at Moat Farm. You might be excused for wondering why I have never mentioned an adult daughter. The reason is that he did not have one; the woman in question was his wife, Sarah, who had earlier been happy to move in to the home of another exploited mistress (Miss Booty), and no doubt now blithely accepted his story that Miss Holland was 'away'.

Phase two of the operation was the systematic withdrawal of Miss Holland's money by forging her signature on bank cheques. By 1901 he had syphoned off over £3,000, although a significant proportion was frittered away on developing his image so far as impressing the local women was concerned, eg the purchase of an unusual locomobile, an expensive but primitive motor car, eye-catching enough to set tongues wagging about the rich eccentric in their midst, and even a couple of bicycles, which enabled him to teach some of the teenage girls to ride (it was rumoured in the nude, although I suspect his deeds were exaggerated by the legend that had begun to be associated with Moat Farm). His expansive nature and calculated generosity in matters of charity made him a popular local celebrity, and the image was assisted by his disregard of convention. Even his attitude to farming was eccentric. Apart from keeping a few cows and chickens he did not attempt to develop the land, and his only regular crop was hay, which required little or no effort. The indifferent villagers regarded him as inefficient, crazy or simply as an example of the 'idle rich'. The truth was that his only interest was an easy life.

All this was happening in the presence of the long-suffering Sarah, although by 1902 she had acquired an admirer of her own, and finally walked out on Dougal. Such was Dougal's reputation at this time that the women who became his mistresses seemed content to share him, as though acknowledging the fact that they could not expect to have him to themselves. At one stage, his 'harem' included three sisters and their mother, and there seems to have been no ill-will towards him as his activities began to boost the local population.

As the rest of Miss Holland's money found its way into Dougal's own account, followed by the transfer of the ownership of Moat Farm, he must have thought he was living in paradise – but the bubble burst when one of his concubines, the second of the attractive Cranwell sisters, stepped out of line, and Dougal was faced with a paternity suit. Ironically, Dougal could have well afforded the small financial commitment involved, but presumably it became a matter of principle to stand on his dignity. After all, he had never had any problems before; who did she think she was? It was bad diplomacy because by contesting the case, he attracted still further attention and gossip about the missing 'wife' who had never returned from her sudden visit to London. Eventually the local police constable formally drew the attention of his superiors to these rumours, and an investigation was opened – initially low key, because Dougal managed to reassure the officer sent to interview him, but once Miss Holland's family had been involved it was only a matter of time before the bank discovered that her signature in various transactions over the past three years, had been forged.

Probably realising that time was running out, Dougal withdrew several hundred pounds and took his current mistress – Georgina, the fourth Cranwell sister, also now pregnant – on what may have been intended as one last fling in London and Bournemouth. When the girl had returned to Moat Farm, Dougal walked into the Bank of England to change a quantity of £10 notes into smaller currency, and the cashier recognised the serial numbers as those in a series which had been stopped. When a police officer attempted to detain him, Dougal made a break for it and was chased through the city streets – into a cul-de-sac. Having acquired his athletic honours in one discipline only – sex – Dougal was in no condition to fight off two younger, fitter pursuers, and was subsequently arrested and charged with the forgery of one cheque.

With Dougal in custody, the police proceeded to search the house at Moat Farm, and then the grounds. It took them seven weeks during which the moat was drained, but their persistence was finally rewarded by the discovery of Miss Holland's body in a drainage pit, leading from the farmyard to a pond. It was identified by her distinctive clothing, and Dougal was charged with murder. At the trial in June 1903, he pleaded not guilty – the circumstantial evidence including the fact that the bullet found in the victim's head had been fired from his revolver! – and the only surprise was that it took the jury as long as seventy-five minutes to reach their verdict. It was only after an appeal had been dismissed that Dougal wrote to the Home Secretary, admitting that he had shot her, but claiming it had been a terrible accident. He offered no explanation for his decision to conceal her death and for his subsequent behaviour.

He was hanged at Chelmsford Prison a couple of weeks later, remaining self-centred to the last.

It is doubtful that Dougal ever experienced a moment's remorse, and he occupied his last hours in writing bantering letters to various girl friends, and even the wife who had turned the tables on him. He enjoyed his notoriety which extended beyond the newspapers. The broadsheets dramatising famous events, particularly crimes, had largely disappeared outside the provinces, in much the same way as music hall has been superseded by TV, but there was still scope for ballad melodrama, as Dougal had learned. As a result he wrote to one of his girl friends: 'I see there were at the show at Bishops Stortford two men, one playing a banjo and singing a ballad on the Moat House, etc, and the other was dispensing of the copies of the song at 1d each, and doing a good business. I saw one verse of the song in a local paper, and no doubt you may see a copy of it in your neighbourhood. If you do, see if there is the printer's name at the bottom of the page, and if so, make a note of it for me, please.'

If Dougal was a candidate for being the murderer who fathered most children, then Johann Hoch outstripped him and even George Smith as a bigamist. In the United States, between the years 1892 and 1905, he married twenty-four times – on average two or three times a year – and half of these women died suddenly in suspicious circumstances, the others surviving when Hoch decided it was less bother to simply disappear. Like Smith, although not quite as mean (*nobody* was that mean!), Hoch regarded women merely as a means of making money. Explaining his philosophy, he said: 'Marriage is purely a business proposition to me. When I found they had money I went after them'.

The most surprising feature of Hoch's bigamous and murderous career is that it took so long for him to be caught, and much of the blame must rest with the poor quality of doctors in the United States and Britain in the late nineteenth and early twentieth centuries, often failing to recognise the symptoms of poison unless the victim happened to be clutching a bottle clearly labelled 'poison'. Many of his 'brides' came from Chicago, where he was employed in a packing house, and the surrounding area, yet because most of the victims were alone in the world, or were too humiliated to report their missing husband to the police, his exploits were never publicised. Cases that were reported were never linked, and remained buried in the files.

But like so many criminals on to a good racket, he did not know when to stop, and eventually murdered once too often.

In December 1904 he advertised in the personal column of a Chicago newspaper for the acquaintance of a widow, with the object of matrimony. One of his replies was from Julia Walker, who owned a confectioner's shop. At forty six-and fearing she had been left on the shelf, Julia was desperate enough to leap at marriage with a stranger – and Hoch was no oil painting, being quite plain, and not possessed of any special charm or any attractive features. They were man and wife within a week when Hoch explained that despite his healthy investments, and a substantial inheritance, he was temporarily embarrassed by a shortage of cash needed for an immediate business transaction. Could she come to his rescue? Trustingly, Julia withdrew her savings and handed them over. Almost overnight she was taken ill, and within a month she was dead. Apparently broken-hearted, Hoch turned to Julia's sister Amelia for consolation. Such was her generosity of spirit that Amelia made him feel he had not so much lost a wife, as gained a sister-in-law, and four days after the funeral they were quietly married. Unaware that Julia had handed over her life savings, Amelia was sympathetic when her new, wealthy, husband mentioned his temporary problems and was only too pleased to hand over everything she had. She was fortunate that Hoch merely skipped town, and pocketing her pride she went to the police.

This time, the similarity of the pattern with earlier reported cases was noted, and a photograph of Hoch circulated to newspapers as far as New York. The blanket coverage ensured that a woman boarding-house keeper in New York recognised him as a new admirer who had just proposed marriage. Hoch was arrested, although at that stage there was only the possibility of a fraud charge at most. However, when he was searched detectives found a fountain pen with a false compartment. It contained a white powder he claimed to be tooth powder. The police were not satisfied, and he then conceded that it was arsenic, claiming it had been obtained in order for him to commit suicide. It was the arsenic which prompted the Chicago police to exhume the body of Julia; it contained substantial traces of arsenic.

The charge was changed to one of murder, and at Chicago in May 1905 he was found guilty; he was hanged in the following February.

George Chapman, hanged just three months before Dougal, poisoned three women in a series of murders that were remarkable if only to show the shortcomings of the doctors who treated them during their short painful illnesses – yet he is remembered more as one of the suspects in the Whitechapel Murders, with at least one detective believing he was Jack the Ripper. Unlike the other ladykillers, his actions were never motivated by money; in fact, there was no discernible reason for killing women he could simply have discarded – except the most probable theory that he was a sadist, who got his kicks from watching his victims suffer.

Dougal was a striking man, but Chapman (his real name was Severin Klosowski, having come to England from Poland in 1888) had no obvious appeal, although he undoubtedly possessed the same sexual magnetism that drew a succession of women to him. The son of a carpenter, Chapman (he picked up the name from an early girl friend Annie Chapman) claimed to have been apprenticed to a surgeon in his home country, although he never qualified. On his arrival in London he became a barber – a logical alternative in view of the historic tradition of barber surgeons. This skill with a razor and the alleged surgical training, coupled with an obsessive interest in women, was the main reason for his being suspected as the Ripper – plus the fact that he was a foreigner! In the rampant hysteria prevailing in the East End during 1888 foreigners were automatically suspect, and often had to be protected by the police – and prejudice was not confined to the lower orders. When Chapman was eventually sentenced to death for the murders he did commit, the judge, Mr Justice Grantham addressed him thus: 'Severin Klosowski, for I decline to call you by the English name you have assumed, the only satisfactory feature in the case we have just completed is that I am able to address you as a foreigner and not as an Englishman . . .' Such bias seems unbelievable by today's relatively enlightened standards, but it was not uncommon for courts to regard 'foreigners' as wicked seducers of innocent British women. The Ripper murders stopped just before Chapman married and went to America, so, by the same logic that M.J. Druitt who had conveniently drowned himself at the 'right' time must have been the killer, it was assumed that Chapman had taken a rest from using the knife, in favour of poison. When he was arrested, one of the detectives who had headed the Ripper enquiries, Chief Inspector Abberline, congratulated the arresting officer, telling him: 'You've got the Ripper at last!' Unfortunately, like so many officers on that case, Abberline was not as smart as he might have been.

Chapman not only possessed skill with a razor, but appears to have been a shrewd judge of male psychology, introducing his more attractive girl friends into the shop as assistants. They were not only decorative, but lathered the customers, and in one shop he installed a piano and they actually entertained with a tune as he worked. In 1890, he married Lucy Baderski, latest in a long line of girl friends; at least, the couple went through a registry office ceremony despite rumours that he already had a wife in Poland. The same month they 'emigrated' to the United States, settling in New Jersey, and although he tired of the place after a couple of years, for the rest of his life he chose to call himself an American, hanging the Stars and Stripes on the wall at all his future places of business.

To a womaniser like Chapman, being closeted with men all day in a barber's shop must have been a frustrating experience and although he continued to have relationships with a succession of women (in a number of cases the couple announced their intention of marrying, but there are no records of any further ceremonies in the three years after his return), he began to seek a change. Running a public house was more suited to his temperament, and the dream became a reality in 1895 when he met Mrs Isabella Spink, living apart from her husband. Isabella drank enough to make him appreciate the financial potential as well as the other attractions, and the small amount of capital she possessed may have been the incentive to poison her, although he had already become landlord of his first business in London's City Road long before her death at Christmas 1897. If money had been the sole motive he would not have waited two years to get rid of her; more likely he enjoyed watching her suffer over a period.

The extent of Chapman's knowledge of poisons is not known, but he obtained antimony from a customer who was a chemist, and was obliged to sign the poisons' register. However, he used it in controlled doses so that the illness appeared to be brought about by natural causes. Isabella suffered vomitting and severe stomach pains on-and-off over several months, gradually becoming weaker until the doctor signing the death certificate regarded it as a formality. Although Chapman claimed to be prostrate with grief, only a few months later he went through a form of marriage with Bessie Taylor, a young woman he employed in the pub. Almost at once she fell ill with the same symptoms, dying in February 1901. Again the doctors had no suspicion – one suggesting she was suffering from 'constipation' – and Bessie's certificate gave the cause as 'exhaustion' from vomiting and diarrhoea'.

Bessie's successor as barmaid, Maud Marsh, also fell under Chapman's spell and the couple were soon 'married', although her family were suspicious of his background and it was their concern which ultimately drew Chapman to the attention of the police. The honeymoon was barely over when Maud became ill. Chapman became the devoted husband, personally looking after her day and night, but she did not improve and eventually through the pressure of her parents, she was removed to Guy's Hospital where the doctors were no more perceptive than the GPs who had examined his previous 'wives'. Among a number of inspired diagnoses, were cancer, peritonitis, tuberculosis and even rheumatism – these in a young woman who was perfectly healthy when she met her 'husband'. However, the mere absence of poison in Maud's diet was enough to speed her recovery.

Back at home, Maud suffered a relapse and her suspicious parents sent their own doctor, Dr Francis Grapel to examine her. At the trial the judge complimented Dr Grapel as the first medical man to show 'some originality and some intelligence'; indeed, he was the first to realise that 'inflammation' of the internal organs had to have a cause, and that in Maud's case it was probably an irritant of some sort – arsenic, in his opinion. Acting on his fears he sent a telegram to Maud's current medical attendant (the man who certified Bessie Taylor's death), warning him of the possibility of poison. Unfortunately, Chapman had anticipated his reaction, and given Maud an extra amount of antimony, and she died almost immediately. The date was October 1902. This time her doctor, supported by his colleague's poison theory, refused a certificate, and a post mortem revealed the true cause of death.

After Chapman's arrest, the bodies of his other victims were exhumed, and traces of antimony found in both cases. Apparently oblivious of the enormity of the charge facing him (the trial only concerned the murder of Maud Marsh), Chapman sent an expensive wreath to the funeral of his latest 'wife', signing it 'from a devoted *friend*, G.C.'. The evidence against him was so overwhelming that the jury took only ten minutes to reach their verdict, and he was hanged in April 1903.

3

THE WORM THAT TURNED

(Hawley Harvey Crippen)

One assumes that murderers are necessarily evil, and few would have any quarrel with that label when applied to the men featured in the preceding chapters. But there are degrees of evil, of course, and history plays tricks with memories. Asked to name one black-hearted villain (identifiable, as opposed to a mere phantom like Jack the Ripper) to epitomise Murder, most people would single out Dr Crippen – for so many years the Chamber of Horror's star attraction. In fact, Crippen is the only murderer's name to pass into the language as an expletive. When George Joseph Smith left the boarding house where he had drowned one of his wives, the suspicious landlady screamed after him: 'Crippen!'

Crippen's notoriety is due to the fact that he killed his wife and dismembered her body, but the irony is that, despite his larger-than-life reputation, Dr Hawley Harvey Crippen was anything but evil. At his trial at the Old Bailey in 1910, the prosecution could not find one person to speak badly of him. In fact, everyone – including the detectives* investigating the case – liked and respected the little doctor, a henpecked husband who finally turned on the domineering woman who had provoked and abused him for years. Crippen was so insignificant an individual that his deeds might have been forgotten, but for his dramatic attempt to escape across the Atlantic with

*One, Cecil Bishop had met him socially in 1908 when they dined at the same Holborn restaurant. They became friends over a period in which Bishop had several teeth filled by the doctor, then acting as a dentist, and they played billiards together. The relationship had extended to an invitation to Crippen's home where he met Mrs Crippen whom he disliked on sight, describing her as 'vain and flamboyant'.

his mistress, Ethel le Neve, dressed as a boy (in itself quite outrageous in those days) – and their arrest through what was then a remarkable achievement in the use of wireless telegraphy, its first application in the detection of crime. The case – also the first murder trial involving the poison hyoscine – was therefore sensational, obscuring the moving love story of a man who committed murder, and ultimately sacrificed his own life for a young woman.

Crippen could not have been more different to the professional ladykillers who were able to dominate their victims, either by their sexuality, or sheer force of personality. He was a small (5ft 3in), mild-mannered man with a pleasant but weak face, kindly, protruding eyes half concealed by metal-framed spectacles, high forehead and a gingery moustache – the sort of 'mouse' ignored by most women, unless they were given the opportunity to know him and appreciate his many qualities. His marriage to the strikingly glamorous Cora was a cruel miss-match. Initially, she may have been attracted by his reticence and humble devotion, because she consistently manipulated him in accordance with her personal ambitions. But if they were an unsuitable match at the outset, the incongruity of the relationship was even more apparent with the years, as she put on weight and lost her youthful charm.

Born in Michigan in 1862, Hawley (usually known to his friends as Peter) graduated from university to medical training in the state of Ohio. In 1883 he visited England to study at various medical colleges, returning to New York where, two years later, he gained a diploma as an ear and eye specialist. In the next fourteen years he practised as a doctor in different parts of the United States. In 1887 he married Charlotte Bell, but after three years she died (from natural causes), leaving a son of the union, Otto Hawley Crippen, who was brought up by his maternal grand-parents, and about whom little is known other than the fact that at the time of his father's trial he was a young man living in Los Angeles.

Two years later, the quiet widower in his early thirties was working in New York, when he was introduced to a colleague's patient, a seventeen-year-old beauty known as Cora Turner.

For Crippen it was love at first sight, but it is difficult to ascertain what the girl, already being kept by an older man, saw in her new, unprepossessing admirer – unless it was a combination of potential respectability, and the instinctive recognition of a willing slave, unlikely to make any demands, and willing to indulge her fantasies. Cora may have pressured him into marriage by an ultimatum that her protector was intending to take her away, prompting the doctor to jump in to 'save' her. After the ceremony he took her to St Louis where he had secured employment as consultant physician to an optician.

There is little doubt that Crippen was infatuated by his small, plump wife's youthful beauty; it gave him special pleasure to show her off in public, and to this end he bought her expensive jewellery and fashionable clothes that showed her figure off to advantage. In her turn, Cora liked being the centre of attraction; indeed, her loud and extrovert personality may well have been a cloak for an inferiority complex. It was not until after they were married that she revealed her real name was not Cora Turner, but Kuningunde Mackamotzki, the result of Russian and German parentage; that she was not interested in a life of domesticity, and that she intended to be an opera singer.

Although Crippen knew nothing about the arts, it was obvious that she had a pretty voice, and he was impressed by the fact that her apparently knowledgeable friends were convinced she was destined to be a star – she told him so! The only reason she had not been taken up before, he was led to believe, was that her voice – while pure – was not sufficiently trained, and Crippen was only too happy to do the necessary, by paying for lessons. Cora found the most suitable teacher (and probably the most expensive) in New York, and her doting husband not only paid for lessons, but for her accommodation and living expenses, since his work prevented him from being on hand.

The ambitious Mrs Crippen was still taking voice lessons from her fashionable teacher in New York, when her husband came to England in 1900 to manage the London office of a patent medicine company. He took the job, unable to practise as a doctor in England because his American qualifications did not meet the required stringent standards, which is something of a joke in view of his considerable practical experience, and the appallingly low standards of so many British GPs.

But after about four months in London (they had already been obliged to live in different cities, during which it is difficult to imagine the headstrong young wife was short of male company), Cora decided there was no future in grand opera, and since England was the home of music hall, Crippen could be prevailed upon to provide the means of re-launching her career. This so-called 'career' only existed in her mind, since she was faced with an insurmountable problem – the total absence of talent. With the help of an expensive wardrobe of eye-catching dresses, Cora looked the part – until she got on stage and began to sing. Billed as Belle Elmore, and promoted by a variety of agents, the newcomer began as a star, aiming at the top – and gradually worked her way down, since no-one could be persuaded to actually book her. She did appear in a couple of depressingly bad bills, but the would-be career sank without trace. Despite what any other performer would have regarded as constant humiliation, the showbiz pretence was maintained in the Crippens' social life, and the little doctor was content to stand supportively in the background, as his wife dominated the only stage she knew – the party scene.

Belle enjoyed the attention, but gained little satisfaction from her husband's blind faith in her infallibility, regarding him more and more as a provider, taken for granted. It was inevitable that, surrounded by male admirers, she would find someone to whose 'affection' she could respond, and after two years in London, when Crippen had to return to the United States for business reasons, the seeds were sewn for her first discreet affair. In 1905, as her singing pretensions diminished, Crippen thought to console her by moving to a more attractive rented semi-detached house in a pleasant part of Camden Town. He refused to deprive Belle of anything in the way of material comfort, realising that a comfortable home, decorated in her own very personal style was important to her self- esteem. Throughout their marriage, and the gradual relationship that followed with Ethel le Neve, his own satisfaction was derived from the happiness of his partner. He was a most considerate man.

One of the most revealing accounts of the relationship was given at the trial by one of Belle's friends, a neighbour, Mrs Harrison, and repeated in Filson Young's *Notable British Trials* (William Hodge & Co 1920). After describing the way Mrs Crippen had been so extravagant in major outlays, yet so mean in matters of pence, such as searching for the cheapest food, and the way Dr Crippen had allowed himself to be converted by his wife to Catholicism, she mentioned the effect of the move to Camden Town. 'She appeared more contented and settled-down now she had a home to interest her, and look after. He was delighted with the air up at Camden Road, and he chuckled with delight when he told us his clothes were becoming too small for him, and that he was getting quite fat . . .'

Having described him as 'subservient to her wishes', Mrs Harrison continued: '. . . He was not a man's man. No man had ever known him to join in a convivial bout; he was always back to time, and never came home with a meaningless grin on his face at two o'clock in the morning attended by pals from a neighbouring club. He never paid compliments to women, or flirted even in a jocular spirit. His eccentric taste in the matter of neckties and dress generally may be attributed to the fact that it represented feminine taste. His wife purchased his ties, and decided on the pattern of his clothing. She would discuss the colour of his trousers with the tailor while he stood aside looking on, without venturing to give an opinion.'

Referring to the period in which the couple took in paying guests as Belle's 'little harmless whim', Mrs Harrison went on to discuss the domestic problems of four young Germans living with them. '. . . The doctor had to do his part. He had to rise at six o'clock in the morning to clean the boarders' rooms, shovel up the coal, lay the breakfast, and help generally. He was always at his office before eight. It was a trying time, and quite unnecessary exertion for both, as Crippen was earning well, and gave his wife an ample supply of money; in fact, she had the strings of the family purse . . . She annexed the extra money from the boarders for personal adornment, and he continued to pay the household bills.'

In fact, what Mrs Harrison may not have realised was that Crippen's business fortunes had suffered a series of setbacks, and it was not long before Belle's extravagance began to exceed his income. But the interest in paying guests was little more than a diversion until Mrs Crippen was able to resurrect what had passed for a career in show business – a career that had wasted away before it got off the ground. This time she was able to act the part without being put to the test. It was the formation of a charitable organisation, the Music Hall Ladies Guild, the aim of which was to help former artistes down on their luck. The expansive Mrs Crippen was a natural for any fund-raising committee, and then, as Belle Elmore – the 'star' nobody had ever seen in retirement – as Honorary Treasurer.*

Inevitably, the Crippens' social life took off again with Belle taking her responsibilities seriously, hosting parties and entertainments (usually at restaurants, which added to the cost) for a wide circle of show business associates, and potential big spenders for the cause. It was, of course, Dr Crippen who had to pick up her bills.

As Belle's extrovert personality went into overdrive, the mentally and physically exhausted little doctor discovered the only time he could relax was in the company of his firm's bookkeeper and typist, Ethel le Neve, a quiet pretty girl blessed with a temperament matching his own; a restful companion who made no demands on him. However, as over the years the mutual respect made way for love, the ever-considerate Crippen needed to demonstrate his affection in the tangible fashion he had with his wife – by gifts of jewellery and clothes.

*Ironically, the contacts made it possible for her to demonstrate her 'professional' talents, by making up a heavily depleted bill during an artistes' strike. This time Belle was booed and hissed off the stage, not so much for her shortcomings, but for being a strike-breaking 'scab'.

The problem was to find the funds. To complicate the issue, the consummation of their affaire would have been a traumatic experience in itself – having to resort to a hotel during office hours, bringing a sordid note to what they intended should be a 'spiritual' occasion. Afterwards they were obliged to stick to hotels; there was no-where else to go – which also added to the financial burden.

However, it cannot be said with any confidence that Crippen murdered his wife through financial pressures; in fact, no-one knows precisely when or why he decided to get rid of Cora. All that is known for certain is that she was not seen after a dinner-party at their home on 31 January 1910, and that two weeks earlier he had obtained five grains of hyoscine – a massive quantity – for which he was obliged to sign the poison book. The choice of poison – little known in 1910 – is fairly typical of this gentle man – it is no coincidence that he selected a poison that could not cause pain or suffering. Its known medical application was for decreasing sexual appetite, and the effect of the slightest overdose was to cause deep sleep.

On 2 and 9 February he pawned some of Cora's jewellery for £195, something he would never have dared to do had she been alive. On 1 February he had visited friends who had dined with him and his wife the previous night, and in response to a token question about her health, he replied that she was 'well'. But from then on, he told anyone who enquired that Cora had returned to the United States to conduct some urgent business on his behalf; that she was visiting a sick relative, and later that she had contracted pneumonia herself.

Had he been a more calculating man, Crippen would have kept Ethel at a distance, maintaining the pretence of an employer-employee relationship; but he was incapable of subterfuge, and she did not delay moving into the marital home, albeit initially posing as the housekeeper. Crippen justified the presence of his mistress by an advertisement in *The Era*, the journal of the entertainment industry, announcing his wife's tragic death in the United States after a short illness. To her friends, puzzled that such an inveterate letter-writer should not have kept in touch by even a short note, he sent more personal cards containing further details. When they asked where the service was being held so that they could send floral tributes, he explained that the cremation had been in Los Angeles, but that the ashes were being sent to London, at which time he would hold a small memorial service.

Those aware of the somewhat strained relationship would not have expected him to be totally distraught, but the presence of another woman in Belle's home, apparently enjoying her personal belongings, irritated some of her friends. The situation was exacerbated when Ethel appeared at a Guild charity dinner and dance at the end of February, wearing Mrs Crippen's most opulent jewellery and furs. When some close friends returned from the United States in June, they were unconvinced by Crippen's story (the biggest objection was to the fact that the glamorous Belle had gone anywhere, let alone America, without the fabulous wardrobe in which she took such a special pride), a visit was made to New Scotland Yard to acquaint the police with their suspicions.

On 8 July, Chief Detective Inspector Walter Dew, following up what was to him a routine enquiry, called at the house in Camden Town. He was received by Miss le Neve, who described herself as Dr Crippen's housekeeper. She conducted him to the doctor's office – he was at this time a partner in a dental practice – where the interview took place, between extractions and administrative duties, for the best part of the day. Crippen was frank, immediately admitting the story of his wife's death was untrue, that she had in fact left him for another man and that he had fabricated the account of her death to avoid a scandal. They broke in the middle of the day to have lunch at a nearby restaurant, but the statement Crippen gave in answer to Dew's questions satisfactorily dealt with all suspicions raised by Cora's friends. Dew and his assistant, Detective Sergeant Mitchell, then accompanied the doctor to his home where, with his full co-operation, they searched the place from attic to cellar. By the end of the long day, the officers had accepted Crippen's story, dismissing the reasons for their visit as groundless allegations, and apologetic that the doctor had been placed in such an invidious position.

Having emerged from the ordeal free of suspicion, Crippen might have relaxed in the knowledge that his wife would become just another statistic of the many thousands of people who simply disappear, mostly of their own free will. His decision to make a run for it is therefore one of the great unresolved mysteries. His coolness in the face of Inspector Dew's exhaustive enquiries indicates that he was not the sort of man to panic, especially as the immediate danger was over. And, in fact, there was nothing panic-stricken about their departure; his plans were laid with typical care, Crippen writing helpful notes to all his business associates to minimise any possible disruption caused by his absence. Nor, since he always claimed that Ethel le Neve knew nothing of Belle's death, does it seem likely that she lost her nerve and urged him to leave.

The escape plan hinged on them travelling as father and son, John Robinson, and John junior. Since Crippen was forty-eight at the time and Ethel only twenty-seven, and although a couple of inches taller, she was slightly built and the deception might have worked in the short term. The fact that it had to be maintained over a period of weeks, gave the plot all the ingredients of a suspense thriller. Stage one was to get to Rotterdam and then Antwerp where they would board the S.S. *Montrose*, bound for Quebec. They encountered no problems, but had to wait in Antwerp for a week before the ship sailed on the 20 July. Although they had no reason to imagine they were being pursued, each day must have seemed like a week.

Meanwhile the hunt had begun, albeit initially by mischance. Chief Inspector Dew, for no good reason other than he was efficient and needed to tie up a few loose ends, called at the doctor's office and learned that he had left, asking his partner to tie-up his affairs. The news inevitably caused Dew to reverse his earlier judgement, and he went straight to the Crippen home in Camden Town. That was the 11 July. This time his search extended to digging in the garden and testing floorboards and bricks in the cellar floor. He was still searching two days later when he discovered that bricks in the cellar floor were loose. Prized away, they left a patch of earth to explore. Only a couple of inches below the surface they found what must have seemed like animal offal, since there did not seem to be enough of it to be human remains. At that stage, he did not realise that Crippen had removed the head, the limbs and major bones, as well as the organs which indicated they belonged to a woman. The remains should have been destroyed, having been covered in lime, but not enough water had been added to assist the chemical reaction.

On the 16th, the police issued a warrant for the arrest of Dr Crippen and Miss le Neve, and the story of the murder, its gory aftermath and the dramatic flight, was taken up by the newspapers, with the *Daily Mail* offering a reward of £100 for information leading to the arrest of the couple, but copies of the London papers were read on the Continent, and Captain Kendall, master of the *Montrose* was forwarned even before the fugitives came on board. Crippen had shaved off his moustache, and removed his distinctive spectacles (still leaving the tell-tale marks high up on the bridge of the nose), but the feature which aroused his suspicion was the couple's affectionate behaviour. The older man seemed an unnaturally doting father, and the more he studied the lad, the more conscious he was of the ill-fitting suit, and the fact that the trousers were held up by two safety pins instead of the customary braces. In addition to an effeminate walk, the boy's table manners seemed almost lady-like, and on deck he tested his theory by calling out 'John!' and noticing that the youngster did not react. On the second day at sea he sent a wireless message, detailing the reasons for his suspicion.

On the 23 July Chief Inspector Dew, accompanied by Sergeant Mitchell, caught a faster liner from Liverpool, and were waiting for the fugitives on the other side of the Atlantic. Crippen and Miss le Neve had been kept in blissful ignorance by Captain Kendall, and it was not until the 'pilot' came on board at the mouth of the St Lawrence river, identifying himself as Chief Inspector Dew that Crippen realised that the whole elaborate exercise had been for nothing. His reaction was typically phlegmatic and when charged made no reply, although later he said: 'I am not sorry. The anxiety has been too much. It is only fair to say that Miss le Neve knows nothing about it. I never told her anything.' Ethel was in her cabin and missed the dramatic confrontation, surely as electric as that between the two explorers, Stanley and Livingstone. When Dew introduced himself, she screamed and fainted; the charge was the lesser one of being an accessory after the fact.

Chief Inspector Dew, who had already gained a favourable impression of Crippen now had further reason to confirm his earlier judgement. On arresting his quarry, he found a handwritten card which indicated that Crippen had contemplated taking his own life. Addressed to Ethel it read: 'I cannot stand the horror I go through every night any longer. As I cannot see anything bright ahead, and as our money has come to an end, I have made up my mind to jump overboard tonight. I know I have spoiled your life. I hope some day you will learn to forgive me. With last words of love.
Yours H'

It took three weeks for the extradition order to be processed, and Dew returned with the prisoners, incognito. The detective was moved to grant a request from Crippen to let him see (but not speak to) the woman who had been his constant companion for almost three years. They were brought to the doors of their cabins and faced each other across the corridor – a moment so poignantly intimate that Dew felt obliged to look away.

In the opinion of a number of lawyers, Crippen virtually committed suicide by offering a hopelessly weak defence, which gave his counsel little chance. Marshall Hall, who had declined the brief because of the defendant's obstinacy, maintained that if he had admitted administering the hyoscine (he was one who accepted the voracious sexual appetite theory) he could have secured an acquittal. How he could have persuaded the jury that a qualified doctor could have confused the suggested dosage – between a one hundredth and two hundredth part of a grain – for the half grain which is enough to kill, is another matter. Instead, Crippen insisted he knew nothing about his wife's disappearance, or of the remains; that there was no proof they were even human, let alone belonged to her; and that they could have been there for years, even before he took over the house.

His defence was destroyed piece by piece. Although there was little enough to go on, Sir William Willcox, Home Office analyst, conducting chemical tests on the internal organs, found traces of the very unusual poison hyoscine, and further concluded it had been administered by mouth – probably disguised in sweet tea or coffee – as opposed to being injected, which was the normal medical application. One of the few remaining portions of flesh – a piece of the abdominal wall – had a scar which a defence medical witness suggested was a crease in the skin and which was proved by the pathologist, Bernard Spilsbury(making his criminal case debut) to be an operation scar – one which could be linked to a mark seen by a couple of Cora's friends. The revolting remains had been buried wrapped in a man's pyjama jacket which the Crown was able to prove belonged to Crippen, having been bought for him the previous year by his wife. The prosecution case was overwhelming, and the jury took less than thirty minutes to reach their verdict. Ethel le Neve's case was dealt with the next day, and although she was defended by the great F.E. Smith, the Crown case was never really pushed, and an acquittal was more or less a foregone conclusion.

Since Crippen never offered his own account of what really happened (almost certainly in an effort to protect Miss le Neve) we shall never know for certain, but in his account of the trial (*Inquest* (Hutchinson 1941)) S. Ingleby Oddie, who assisted Richard Muir for the Crown, and later became coroner for central London, offered the theory that the murder, while deliberate, was the outcome of a plan that misfired. He suggested that Crippen intended to capitalise on Cora's fatness by claiming that she had a history of mild heart attacks, and to administer a fatal dose of hyoscine on 31 January. After death he would have summoned a doctor, and almost certainly been granted a death certificate. Because hyoscine is not detectable by the human eye, even a post mortem may not have shown anything other than a fatty heart, and by implication (with Crippen's background story) death from natural causes. Oddie supports the theory with the knowledge that Crippen had encouraged their guests for the evening to come, despite the fact Paul Martinetti had earlier been ill. In the event, the couple stayed until 1.30am, Crippen's intention being to demonstrate that he still had a pleasant relationship with his wife. Mr Oddie speculates that Crippen had not realised that a large, fatal dose of the poison would cause delirium and that Cora probably ran amok, shouting and screaming. This might account for Filson Young's account that Cora shouted and screamed at him for allowing Mr Martinetti to go upstairs to the lavatory unaccompanied. On the other hand I cannot accept the conclusion that in desperation, to stop the noise, Crippen produced a gun and shot her in the head. Since Cora's head was never found, we shall never know, but the assumption that Crippen ever had a gun (never mentioned by the police) is a wild one, as was Mr Oddie's justification that all Americans carried guns!

Three days before his execution, in a statement reiterating the innocence of the woman he loved, Crippen declared: 'This love was not of a debased or degraded character . . . Her mind was beautiful . . . Whatever sin there was – and we broke the law – it was my sin, not hers . . . As I face eternity, I say that Ethel le Neve has loved me as few women love men . . . Surely such love as hers for me will be rewarded.'

His last letter to her: 'When he (the prison governor) had gone I kissed your face in the photo . . . It was some consolation, although in spite of all my greatest efforts it was impossible to keep down a great sob and my heart's agonised cry.'

Crippen's remarkable stoicism concealed deep emotions and the public mask slipped only once. On the eve of his execution at Pentonville on 23 November, when the prison governor brought him Ethel's telegram of farewell, he broke down at last. His final request that her letters and photograph be buried with him, was granted.

4

MISCARRIAGES OF JUSTICE

Steinie Morrison and Oscar Slater

The death penalty has no place in civilised society although there are always exceptional cases capable of shaking one's convictions. However, if we dispense with the emotion which always influences public opinion, every argument – from the theological to that of the deterrent – collapses in the face of just one consideration: the risk of a miscarriage of justice. This happens more often than is realised by those who, through ignorance, retain a blind faith in the legal system.

There is, of course, the safety net of an appeals machinery to protect the innocent, but without new evidence (which is rare), an appeal usually depends on a re-evaluation of the same evidence. It is as well to remember what is meant by 'evidence'. Eye-witness reports from ostensibly impartial sources, for example, are almost impossible to discredit, and what happens when that witness has been mistaken, misled by the Crown or an irresponsible press, or is even prejudiced?

The two most glaring examples of such a breakdown in the system during the Edwardian period were Steinie Morrison, sentenced to death at the Old Bailey in 1911, and reprieved, but who died later in prison still protesting his innocence after a series of hunger strikes; and Oscar Slater, unjustly sentenced at Edinburgh in 1909, and also spared, but who still served nineteen years. Both were victims of questionable identification and conclusions by prejudiced witnesses, or by the police. It is no coincidence that both were foreign-born Jews, at a time when the scale of anti-semitism was comparable with the more obvious racism of the second half of the twentieth century.

Morrison's criminal background, made to seem even worse by the number of times he was caught out in obvious lies, undoubtedly had something to do with his conviction – still controversial inasmuch as the judge summed up in his favour. In their efforts to secure a guilty verdict, the police may well have cut corners, under pressure to restore the image of law and order in the East End after three policemen had been killed in Houndsditch and two more wounded, by Russian anarchists – the incident which led to the Sidney Street siege. The Glasgow police, with no such excuse in the Slater case, nevertheless manufactured a case, and contrived to obstruct the campaign for an enquiry into the handling of the prosecution by such formidable criminologists as Sir Arthur Conan Doyle, and William Roughead, who produced the first report of the trial. Slater's compensation for nineteen years of wrongful imprisonment was £6,000.

Today, most law enforcement agencies recognise the value of what they call 'psychological profiles' in the study of the criminal mind, which means that if Morrison was around now, it is unlikely he would have been charged. He had a long criminal career with a clearly defined pattern of behaviour, but absolutely no record of violence, and the circumstances surrounding the murder of Leon Beron on the morning of 1 January, 1911 were entirely alien to his character.

The trial in March was one of the most dramatic in legal history – for the wrong reasons. The atmosphere had the highly charged surrealism of a Marx brothers' farce, and was at times just as incomprehensible, since the majority of witnesses were foreigners, with little or no understanding of English. In some cases, interpreters were needed, but irrespective of their grasp of the language almost every witness responded to cross examination excitably and with varying degrees of defensiveness. Although Mr Justice Darling generally managed to keep control of events, there were moments of near chaos, such as when one of the Crown's highly-strung witnesses (the deceased's brother) completely lost his cool, attacked the hostile defence counsel, Mr Edward Abinger, and had to be removed (to a mental asylum).

More to the point, Mr Abinger seemed to have been affected by the general hysteria, which – giving him the benefit of the doubt – may have been the reason for his erratic performance, and for a major tactical blunder which played into the hands of the Crown prosecutors – and probably cost the acquittal many had expected on the questionable circumstantial evidence. The Criminal Evidence Act of 1898 is remembered for the legislation which allowed defendants to go into the witness box on their own behalf. What is often forgotten, is that the same Act ensured that a defendant's background, especially any criminal record, was not revealed to the jury for fear of placing undue influence on them. This was conditional, however, on the defence not attacking the integrity of Crown witnesses (ie evidence could obviously be contested, but only on points of fact – not on the alleged unreliability of the witness because he or she was a person of doubtful morals). Counsel who risked this line of questioning laid himself open to counter-attack, which was usually to his detriment, unless the client happened to possess the qualities of an angel. Despite warnings from the judge, Mr Abinger persisted, and reaped the consequences.

The characters in this drama were predominantly foreign, mostly Jews who had fled religious persecution in Russia and Poland at the turn of the century. Unlike the socially more privileged refugees from Germany in the 1930s they were largely uneducated, often illiterate, and restricted to their ghetto in London's East End, where the common language was Yiddish and where they struggled to survive – mostly as exploited tailors or furriers in countless sweat shops.

Morrison stood apart from the crowd – too proud to scratch a living with those he regarded as amiable serfs, and prepared to gamble on his brains and initiative to keep his head above water. This was not difficult. At 6ft 3in tall, strikingly handsome, and always well dressed, he looked the part, although in common with so many small-time crooks, he was alternately flush with money, or broke. Nor was he successful, spending much of his developing years in prison, and he was also known to the police and prison governors as Morris Stein, and occasionally Moses Tagger. However, Morrison was no fool, and it may be that he was handicapped by his very distinctive appearance; once seen, never forgotten

– unlike his Victorian counterpart, Charlie Peace, who could change his appearance at will.

He had come to England in his teens from Russia in 1898, via Germany and France, although he claimed to have been born in Australia and taken to Russia as a child – which seems unlikely, not only because of his record as a liar, but because for oppressed Jews in Czarist Russia the traffic was strictly one way: out. However, he had adapted well, and had a good command of English, albeit spoken with an accent, and knew the ropes well enough so that after one prison sentence he complained to the Home Secretary that he should be released because he was really a Russian citizen, Alexander Petropavloff.

The life style of the victim, Leon Beron, was also very different to his contemporaries in the Houndsditch ghetto, although they were linked by a common background and language. Almost twenty years older than Morrison, he had come to England after spending his formative years in Paris, and since his first language was French and he was surrounded by Yiddish-speaking expatriates, there was little incentive to learn English. Like Morrison, he scorned work, but received a modest income from the rents of nine small dwellings he owned in the neighbourhood – worth all of ten shillings a week. Since he spent 2s 9d on his own accommodation (one room above a greengrocer's), to which one of his brothers contributed the odd pence, and almost nine shillings for his food and drink at the Warsaw kosher restaurant where he spent most of the week, it will be seen that Beron could only just make ends meet. However, his appearance gave a very different impression; he was always immaculately dressed, a Van Dyke beard neatly trimmed and his moustache waxed at the ends. The impression of affluence was heightened by a large gold watch and chain, from which hung a five guinea coin. It is not known how he could afford to maintain this image, and the two most likely theories are that he was a discreet and occasional receiver of stolen property, or that he was a police informer, bearing in mind that in those days the police needed help in infiltrating such an alien environment.

The body of Beron, who had been seen in his favourite

restaurant on the evening of Saturday, 31 December, in the company of Morrison, was found at 7.30 the following morning under some bushes near a footpath across Clapham Common. He was lying on his back, feet crossed; death had been caused by one or more of eight heavy blows to the head, and while on the ground, he had been stabbed *after death* three times in the chest. There were also seven superficial cuts or scratches on the face. Two, one on each cheek, were S-shaped – described by a police surgeon at the trial as like the 'f' holes of a violin. A black silk handkerchief with red stripes partly concealed the face. It was obvious that Beron, who had died at about three o'clock, had been attacked elsewhere on the Common and dragged by his overcoat collar into the bushes for concealment. His gold watch and chain had disappeared, and there was no money on the body. He was, however, identified by his rent book.

The local CID contacted Chief Detective Inspector Frederick Wensley of 'H' Division, covering the East End who, it transpired, knew Beron and his circle at the Warsaw restaurant. Significantly, he also knew Steinie Morrison for other reasons, and when enquiries revealed the two men had been seen together at the restaurant on most days since the burglar's latest release from prison in September, he did not look any further for his suspect. Concentrating the investigation on Morrison, the police soon discovered that the two men had been seen together in the street in Whitechapel as late as 1.30am (apart from the fact that both were known to witnesses, they were very distinctive figures, with Beron about nine inches the shorter). Even more suspicious, in their view, Morrison had earlier deposited with a waiter at the restaurant a paper-wrapped package about two feet long, which he had said was a flute, but which the waiter suggested was too heavy, and felt more like an iron bar, such as a jemmy. Morrison had collected it before leaving the restaurant that night. In fact, the waiter was wrong because Morrison *had* bought a flute that morning for four shillings. In any case, it amounted to no more than speculation, because the murder weapon was never found.

They also discovered that on New Year's Day, Morrison had left another paper-wrapped parcel at a local railway station. It contained a revolver and forty-four bullets – another red herring, as it had not been fired. The hunt then switched to cab drivers in the hope of linking Beron and Morrison with Clapham Common, a distance of six miles – and, after a small reward was offered, three were at hand prepared to identify Morrison, although Mr Justice Darling was not impressed with the reliability of their evidence. However, the combination of circumstances was enough for the police. On Sunday morning, 8 January, Morrison was having breakfast at another Whitechapel restaurant when Wensley and several officers burst in and surrounded him. He was detained on the pretext of failing to notify the police (as a convict on parole) of a change of address. (He had lodged with an East End family since September, but at the end of the year told them he was going to Paris; instead, on New Year's day he moved in with a Lambeth prostitute.)

Chief Inspector Wensley later insisted that he refrained from telling Morrison the real reason for his arrest, and that the prisoner compromised himself by claiming that the police had made a blunder in accusing him of murder. Morrison was to deny that he volunteered anything, and this was to be supported by a PC Greaves, present at Leman Street police station at the time, although the row turned out to be a storm in a teacup because an investigation into Greaves' track record proved him to be unreliable. However, as much as he denied the police allegations, Morrison had no answer to the presence of a left luggage ticket found in the lining of his hat, which was for his revolver, left under a false name. The gun played no part in evidence, but its existence was enough to suggest that its owner was up to no good.

Throughout the trial, conflicting evidence made it difficult to establish the truth. At the preliminary court hearing, two witnesses made damaging statements which were later retracted. A young woman, Eva Flitterman, claimed to have seen Morrison on 1 January, wearing a five guinea piece on his watch chain, the implication being that it had been taken from Beron's body. Miss Flitterman later admitted her identification had been made on the basis of the coin's similarity to one worn by her father, ie a two guinea piece. Morrison may not have been a master criminal, but he was at least an experienced professional, and certain conclusions drawn by the police from initial evidence do not bear close scrutiny, eg it was ridiculous to suggest that having just murdered Beron, Morrison would openly wear the most easily identifiable piece of jewellery. Similarly, no self-respecting burglar would leave a jemmy wrapped in paper with a potential witness, particularly if he intended to use it the same night as a weapon.

At the trial in March, lasting nine days, the defence counsel's major headache was Morrison's inability to explain his movements without a string of lies, most of which would be shown to be patently false. His story was that he was not an intimate of the deceased, and had not been with him for long on the relevant evening when, in fact, he had gone to the Shoreditch Empire from nine until eleven, after which he went home, and was in bed by midnight. Unfortunately, the witnesses called to corroborate his evening alibi, teenage sisters Jane and Esther Brodski, were entirely discredited. Having claimed, independently, to have seen Morrison in the same row of the stalls, they could not remember any of the acts they had seen – despite the fact that the star-studded bill had included Harry Lauder and Harry Champion. Furthermore, statements that they had bought their seats the same evening for one shilling each, had to be incorrect because the management insisted that there were no stalls left, and that the prices for that one night had, in any case, gone up to one shilling and sixpence.

More credible were Morrison's middle-aged landlord and his wife who supported his claim to have retired early, by testifying the front door had such a noisy bolt that it could not be slipped again without waking them. Regarded by the judge as honest – unlike the infatuated young sisters – their evidence could not be so easily discounted, and when the Crown suggested that the accused could have left by the window in his room, it was established that the window frame was badly fitted, and would have been as noisy an escape route as the front door.

However, it was the evidence of the three cab drivers – two operating the traditional hansom cab, attracted by a reward offered by the police – which proved crucial, despite the judge's warning to the jury that the light at that time of the morning would have made it difficult to be confident of any clear identification. The first, Edward Hayman, who did not come forward until after Morrison was charged, claimed to have picked him up with another man in Sidney Street at two in the morning and to have taken them both to Lavender Gardens, by the Common, a journey of forty to forty-five minutes. By the time he identified the prisoner in a police line-up, he had already seen his picture in a newspaper, although he claimed to have remembered negotiating a fare of 5s with the taller of the two men.

The second witness, Andrew Stephens, was more suspect, having volunteered a statement only after he had seen Morrison's photograph in a newspaper, and not actually picking him out again until the 17 January. In his initial statement he was confident that he had picked up Morrison from a spot at Clapham Common – taking him to Kennington, south London – at 2.30am, confident of the time because it was an hour after the last tram went, at 1.30am. Someone must have drawn Stephens' attention to the difficulty of reconciling his statement with that of Hayman because at 2.30am Morrison and his companion would not yet have arrived at Clapham Common. For reasons he never explained, but possibly at the suggestion of a helpful policeman, he decided to check the times of the trams, and changed his story when he learned that on that date the last tram had left at two. He described his fare as being about 5ft 10in, and looking like an actor or professional man, a description fitting a man Morrison himself had previously seen with Beron.

The final witness, Alfred Castlin, who drove a modern motor-cab, actually came forward before the police appeal for witnesses; indeed he volunteered a statement on the 4 January, before Morrison was detained, although it was the 9th before he got round to identifying him – after a photograph had appeared in the press. He claimed to have picked up two men – one identified as Morrison – from near Kennington Church at 3.30am and taken them to Finsbury Park in north London, a fare he remembered because the price had been negotiated, and because the smaller man had spoken to Morrison in a 'foreign' language before pushing him into the cab.

However, there was a serious flaw in the murder time-table – one provided by another police witness, but unfortunately not fully exploited by the defence. Chief Inspector Wensley had first been alerted to the possible involvement of Morrison through interviewing local people who might have known Beron, and it was a Mrs Nellie Deitch, who stated she saw Beron (whom she knew well) in the company of a man fitting Morrison's description in Commercial Road, not far from the restaurant, at between 2 and 2.15 on New Year's morning. If her timing was accurate, the men could not have been in Hayman's cab at the time he remembered. Furthermore, like other Crown witnesses, she had changed her original statement, now claiming that she and her husband had been to a ham and salt beef shop, leaving just after two o'clock (they had earlier been to a New Year's party), when they saw Beron and his companion. Before the cab driver's evidence was taken, her times were all approximately half-an-hour later, which meant that they arrived home a few doors away at 2.45am. But even her 'revised' time cast doubt on Hayman's story, and if his memory was at fault, the rest of the 'timetable' would have been proportionally delayed – leaving *no* time for anyone to commit the murder.

Abinger's policy had been to attack the credibility of the Crown evidence, and at times sailed close to the wind when it came to touching on the reputation of the witnesses. At one stage he secured an admission from a waiter who had quarrelled with Morrison, that he had once attempted suicide – as though that might have had some bearing on his ability to tell the truth. But since suicide was a felony in those days, the judge warned him of the possible consequences of raising the issue.

The chances are that Sir Richard Muir, for the Crown, would have ignored the incident, treating it with the contempt it deserved, but when Abinger became enmeshed in a furious row with Mrs Deitch about her lifestyle, he over-stepped the mark. His decision to discredit her was also inconceivable in the light of her testimony, which contradicted other vital Crown evidence; indeed, it would have been sensible to treat her as a 'friendly' witness and exploit the loophole she had provided. Instead, he demonstrated his lack of flexibility by sticking to the planned strategy.

Counsel based his attack on the assumption that Mrs Deitch supplemented her husband's income as a gas-fitter by running a brothel from home. The allegations were probably correct; her style of dress, complete with expensive fur cape, belied the income she might have expected from her husband's job, but by making his case Abinger opened the way for the Crown to reveal the defendant's criminal record; up to that stage Morrison would have passed for some matinée idol – not the sort of man who could sink to murder. The cross examination of Mrs Deitch, since she denied the allegations, and the prostitutes called to substantiate the charges, made a mountain out of an irrelevant molehill, and had the effect of completely neutralising her earlier valuable contribution.

When Morrison took the stand, Muir's initial questioning was low-key, exposing him as a liar but not really shaking his composure. Muir had a tough reputation – in cricket terms, a hostile fast bowler – yet some of his deliveries might have appeared wide of the mark or even under-arm, none more so than an almost conversational reference to the fact that the weapon which had fractured Beron's skull was probably a heavy iron bar – nothing controversial about that . . . His next question was also innocent enough: 'Have you ever been found in possession of such an implement? Say a jemmy, Morrison, much used by burglars . . .'

One can imagine Morrison's visible indignation being shared by members of the jury, but it would have been short-lived as Muir set out to demonstrate that the defendant was no innocent caught up in circumstances beyond his control.

'When were you first convicted of felony?' Muir enquired, almost politely.

The question seemed to take Morrison by surprise, and for the first time he lost his composure, stammering his answer. 'I cannot say – 1900, or something like that.'

'Was it 17 December 1898?'

'That might have been it.'

Then came the grudging admissions, and blustering excuses as a stream of police witnesses testified to his long career in crime. There were so many of them that at one stage – to the fury of Muir – the judge called a halt, and only allowed him to continue after a short conference in his chambers with the Director of Public Prosecutions. By the time Muir finished, the jury were prepared to believe anything of the defendant, as though his earlier silence had been a deliberate attempt to mislead them.

Abinger maintained the element of drama throughout by basing his defence on the hypothesis that Beron had been a police spy, and that his death was a revenge killing by Russian anarchists active in London. Two days after the murder – on 3 January – the whole country was spellbound by the siege of Sidney Street at which the Home Secretary, Winston Churchill, accompanied armed police surrounding a group of anarchists responsible for the cold-blooded deaths of three policemen in Houndsditch on 10 December. He supported the theory with the suggestion that the letters 'S' scratched or cut on Beron's cheeks stood for 'spy', which is not as far-fetched as it sounds in the light of the larger-than-life events of the past few weeks – and more credible than the Crown allegations that the marks had been made by Morrison to mislead them.

In his summing up, Justice Darling dealt with the crucial importance of the times volunteered by the three cabbies, suggesting to the jury (who had been to the site of the murder, and retraced the likely footsteps of the deceased) that the time in which to commit the murder had been very short – no more than a few minutes. But he placed greater emphasis on the question of identity. 'With what certainty can you, do you think, swear to a man whom you saw on a night like that, by the kind of light that there was at these places which you have seen? Can you feel certain that a man would not be mistaken, and that he is not mistaken? You have heard the description that they gave. Suppose you had got that description, could you, from the description alone, if you had a dozen men, of whom the prisoner was one, before you, have picked him out? Do you think you could? You remember what they were. I do not mean the evidence given afterwards when they pointed him out, but the statements that they made as to his being 'tall' and 'medium complexion', and so on. What is a 'medium complexion'? That is the kind of evidence . . . I think, myself, it is a very difficult thing to describe a man. Suppose I look at a man in Court, and am asked to write down a description of him, do you feel certain, if I did write it down, that you could pick him out from other men in court I do not know? They gave a description. Let us assume they gave it to the best of their ability; let us assume they were honest. Even then, are you so certain that they really took notice enough, that they had opportunity enough, to be able some days afterwards to swear with certainty to the man they had driven?'

Despite a summing-up so favourable to the defendant that the Crown lawyers expected an acquittal, the jury took only thirty-five minutes to reach the opposite verdict. When asked if he had anything to say before sentence was passed, Morrison declared: 'I have got a great deal to say. For one matter, the evidence against me as to the funds which have been seen on me on 1st January being the proceeds of the murder. I can prove that in November I had a sum of £300, and out of this £300, I have still got £220. If I can prove that, will that in any way alter the jury's verdict?'

The question did not merit an answer, which was hardly surprising since there had been no reference to such a large sum during the defence arguments; and also because of his persistent lies – he had claimed, for example, to have won £28 playing faro, but could produce no evidence to substantiate it; also that he had received £20 from his mother in Russia, again taken with a pinch of salt, since he could not explain how she had obtained English banknotes, and nor would he supply her address. Justice Darling concluded his sentence of death with the traditional words: 'And may the Lord have mercy on your soul', and the solemnity of the moment was heightened by a sonorous 'Amen' from the court chaplain – and then dashed by a passionate outburst from Morrison. 'I decline such mercy,' he cried in a voice throbbing with emotion. 'I do not believe there is a God in Heaven either.'

In view of Morrison's record there was little to suggest there might have been a miscarriage of justice, and it was no surprise when his appeal failed, or when Abinger's plea to bring the case to the House of Lords was refused. Justice Darling said later he believed Morrison was guilty, but that it had been unsafe to convict on the evidence, particularly the question of identity. The defendant, was, however, surprisingly reprieved by the Home Secretary. In his biography, *Inquest*, S. Ingleby Oddie, who had assisted Richard Muir, wrote:

> For some reason, which I fail to understand, Morrison was, however, reprieved, and was sent to penal servitude for life. This interference with the decision of the jury, over-riding their verdict, especially after an appeal to the Court of Criminal Appeal which had failed, is an anomaly and seems entirely to nullify our system of trial by jury in such cases, substituting for it the opinion of a Government department.
>
> Muir was indignant that Morrison should thus have escaped the punishment prescribed by law for a brutal murder. He always thought that Morrison had had a confederate who actually struck the blow when Morrison had decoyed the victim to the lonely spot at that quiet hour, and this was the reason no blood in any quantity was found on Morrison's clothes.

Muir's theory, shared by the police, would counter my hypothesis that while Morrison was a professional criminal, he was no killer – and 'mugging' (even if he was merely an accomplice) would also have been a departure from his well known *modus operandi*, and the incentive would have had to be very great – a sum running into hundreds or even thousands of pounds, and Morrison knew Beron well enough to realise that he was far from rich. Furthermore, why would Morrison have risked taking any victim a distance of six miles, a forty-five minute journey involving three cabs – with the drivers of any one possibly able to recognise him – when he could have found a deserted spot, eg Hackney Marshes, only a fraction of the distance away? Relating Morrison directly with the murder, however, is even more unlikely; a man as powerful as he could have smashed Beron's skull with a single blow. And if he had remained, for no obvious reason, to stab the body *after* death, making it seem less like the work of a 'mugger', why had he not taken the trouble to remove the identifying rent book? Finally, why had he not attempted to disappear from London for a while?

However, that is all mere speculation – hardly grounds for the reprieve granted by the Home Secretary which so mystified Mr Ingleby Oddie. A probable explanation is offered by Julian Symons, in *A Reasonable Doubt* (Cresset Press, 1960), in developing Morrison's extraordinary statement just before sentence of death was passed – his explanation of having a large sum of money in his possession. Only after the verdict did Morrison admit to Abinger that in November he had forged a cheque for £200 on the South-Western Bank in Holloway. The proceeds had been taken to the travel agent Cooks, in Ludgate Hill, and changed into French francs – and then to another branch, where they were converted back to English currency. This was the money found on him after Beron's death, and for which he concocted other even more unlikely stories, confident that he would be acquitted, and not wishing to be further accused of forgery.

Morrison's solicitor, in checking the story, established not only that his client could be identified from photographs, but also that the police were in possession of the facts, yet had not raised the issue at the trial because it would not have helped the Crown case. Mr Symons points out that after the tragic events leading up to the Sidney Street siege, the police were under great pressure to clear up the Beron murder as quickly as possible, and believing Morrison to be involved, it was not in their interests to confuse the issue by introducing evidence which would have destroyed the motive for robbery. He also suggests that Beron *was* a police informer, which is why he was immediately known to Inspector Wensley, and this would support the defence theory of a revenge killing.

Stephens, the most suspect of the cab-drivers (he was even able to describe the *colour* of Morrison's overcoat – *after* such details had appeared in the press!) was originally quite vague, describing his fare as being about 5ft 10in tall, which makes interesting reading in the light of a statement made later by Morrison to the chaplain at Dartmoor prison.

'The man who killed Beron is no doubt a man who is exactly my double, but about four inches shorter. He met me in the East End of London one afternoon. He stopped me with a look of astonishment on his face and said, "Who the hell are you?" I said to him, jokingly, "It is singular that there should be two such good-looking men." He replied, "You may be damned sorry for it one day." He then told me that he was associated with some foreign secret society, and asked if I knew anything about them. I said, "No, and I don't want to."

In view of Morrison's long history of lies, one cannot give too much credence to that story, but what cannot be disputed is the vehemence with which he continued to protest his innocence. Prison was no new experience, and after his life had been saved, one would have expected him to accept the punishment as best he could. But he never came to terms with the conviction in eleven years at Dartmoor and Parkhurst, during which, in frustration, he appealed for the original sentence to be carried out on no less than four occasions. Eventually, ignored by the authorities, he resorted to a series of protest hunger strikes which resulted in his death in January, 1921. He was just forty-one years old.

In the confused and controversial evidence against Steinie Morrison, no-one could say with any certainty that he murdered Leon Beron. Equally, no-one could be sure that he did not. But the onus is on the prosecution to prove its case against any defendant beyond reasonable doubt. In the opinion of many authorities they failed in that respect. But at least there was no conspiracy to gain a conviction. The police in London may have 'juggled' with certain evidence, but they were convinced they had the right man. Their counterparts in Glasgow had no such excuse or 'justification' in pinning the murder of Marion Gilchrist, an eighty-three-year-old spinster, on Oscar Slater. It was not a question of reasonable doubt: he was clearly the wrong man.

From the time Slater first came under suspicion (and any unbiased detective would have given up when the initial lead proved to be a 'red herring') they ignored the wealth of evidence that pointed to his innocence, and ensured that witnesses came up with their preconceived version of events. They were aided and abetted at the trial by a prosecutor who skated over the suspect evidence of identification to attack the defendant's morals, which in any other trial would have earned a rebuke from the judge. No-one seemed to care very much that they were involved in an injustice in the making – Slater was, after all, only a foreign Jew. Scottish prejudice had changed little in the half century since the appealingly attractive Madeleine Smith was acquitted, against the evidence, of poisoning her lover, Pierre L'Angelier – shrugged off by the jury as yet another base foreign seducer of British women.

The circumstances of the murder are not in dispute. Miss Gilchrist had most of her wealth in jewellery, which she kept hidden among her dresses in a bedroom wardrobe. The flat was situated in a relatively affluent part of the city and, understandably wary of burglars, Miss Gilchrist kept the front door double-locked and double-bolted. She had already arranged with her neighbours in the flat below that she would knock three times on the floor if she was in need of assistance. However, she had no reason to fear she might be attacked in broad daylight, and in any case she employed a servant, which meant that she was seldom alone. Early in the evening of Monday, 21 December 1908, she sent the maid, Helen Lambie out to buy an evening newspaper. While she was out, the neighbour, Arthur Adams was sitting with his sisters when he heard a bump on the ceiling, followed by what he thought was the pre-arranged signal of three knocks. He went up to investigate, although his actions seem to have been somewhat half-hearted. After three rings at the bell, during which there was no response from Miss Gilchrist – merely the sound of what he described as 'someone chopping sticks' – he gave up. Why he did not call her, or bang on the door until he obtained a proper response, is not known, but his indecision must have played on his conscience because when he returned to his flat, and the noises continued ('the ceiling was likely to crack,' he said later), he climbed the stairs again. This time, he was on the point of ringing when Helen Lambie returned with the newspapers; she had been gone barely ten minutes.

When Mr Adams explained the reason for his presence the girl suggested that the noise had been caused by a pulley-operated clothes-line in the kitchen, crashing to the floor. Unconcerned, she opened the door and walked through the hallway to the kitchen. Mr Adams remained outside the door and was surprised a moment later to see a man emerge from the bedroom, composed enough to be a legitimate visitor, although as he brushed by on the landing, he broke into a run, and fairly tore down the stairs and into the street, slamming the front door behind him. The incident startled Adams and the maid, but did not yet have any sinister significance, and after a casual glance in the kitchen, Helen looked into the bedroom the stranger had just vacated before responding to Mr Adams's more pressing enquiry about her mistress.

The old lady was found in front of the fireplace in the dining room, her head savagely smashed in. Mr Adams hurried downstairs to find a policeman – although only a matter of seconds, the intruder had now disappeared – and came back with a constable who carried out a detailed examination at the scene of the murder. The motive for the attack was not immediately apparent, because the bulk of Miss Gilchrist's jewellery collection in the bedroom wardrobe remained undisturbed and a number of valuable rings, together with a gold watch and chain, and bracelet, still lay untouched on a dressing table; yet a box containing private papers had been broken open and the contents scattered on the floor. In other circumstances, one might have thought in terms of the killer searching for a blackmail note, but the initial assumption was that theft had been the motive, and that the old lady had opened the door to someone she knew and trusted.

With the killer practically caught in the act, the investigating officers might have been excused for an air of complacency, but their first disappointment was that Mr Adams, who had been face-to-face with the man, turned out to be short-sighted, and had left his glasses downstairs; the face he had seen for a split second had been little more than a blur. While there was nothing wrong with Helen Lambie's sight, she had had her back to the man when he emerged from the bedroom and had then, belatedly, caught only a fleeting glance. Hand on heart she admitted she would not be able to recognise him again, although there may be degrees of honesty when it came to relations with the police by certain members of the public, because later when Miss Lambie broke the dreadful news to her employer's niece, she had no doubt she recognised the assailant, and actually named him! Nevertheless, presumably by a process of elimination, the police managed to issue a description, which appeared in the following day's newspapers. It read '. . . between twenty-five and thirty years of age, 5ft 8in or 9in in height, slim build, dark hair, clean shaven, dressed in light grey overcoat, and dark cloth cap'.

Nevertheless, we have no reason to doubt that the police behaviour at that stage was beyond reproach. Two days later they were still carrying out what was ostensibly a correct investigation when they interviewed a third witness, Mary Borrowman, a fourteen-year-old messenger, who claimed she had seen a man running down the steps from Miss Gilchrist's home in Queen's Terrace, before colliding with her. He had then run off and disappeared round a corner. I use the word 'ostensibly' because there was later some question over her evidence; nor was she seen by Mr Adams who had followed the murderer into the street only a few seconds later. However, since Oscar Slater had not yet appeared on the scene, her testimony is interesting. Her recollection of another split-second incident on a dark and rainy night two days earlier provided the police with the following description:

'. . . about twenty-eight or thirty years of age, tall and thin, with his face shaved clear of all hair, while a distinctive feature is that his nose is slightly turned to one side. The witness thinks the twist is to the right side. He wore one of the popular round tweed hats known as Donegal hats, and a fawn-coloured overcoat, which might have been a waterproof, also dark trousers and brown boots.' The description was so detailed that the police concluded that they might be looking for two different men – but neither bore any resemblance to Slater who, apart from being ten years older, was powerfully built and impossible to mistake for 'slim' or 'thin' – had a perfectly straight nose, and far from being clean-shaven he had a dark moustache which could not be missed. Moreover, if he had any one distinctive feature that stood him apart from the average Glaswegian, it could be said that his face was clearly not Celtic or Anglo-Saxon – yet that obvious difference had escaped the attention of all three eye-witnesses.

Although there were no obvious signs of a robbery, Helen Lambie was convinced that one piece of jewellery was missing, a crescent-shaped diamond brooch, and when that description was circulated by the police it produced their first lead. On Christmas Day (not a holiday in Scotland), a bicycle dealer volunteered the information that a man he knew simply as Oscar, a German Jew, had been trying to sell a pawn ticket for a diamond brooch similar to the one being sought. He took detectives to Oscar's flat and although he knew nothing about the name 'Anderson' on the door, he was sure the man he knew was no dentist, as it stated. Already suspicious, the detectives were now prepared to arrest the mysterious Anderson, but when they called back later that night, their suspicions were confirmed – he had fled! What they could not know was that Slater and his French girl friend had been planning to go to America for some time, and left on that date only because a friend had managed to find two young women to take over the flat. In fact, when Slater arrived at their Liverpool hotel on the eve of catching the liner *Lusitania* across the Atlantic, he registered in his own name.

In fact, Slater had a number of aliases, his real surname being

Leschziner, although unlike Steinie Morrison there were no criminal reasons for the subterfuge. The initial change applied to many refugees with unpronounceable names from eastern Europe who, not speaking or understanding English, usually settled for some compromise conjured up by the immigration officer – this was particularly common in England and New York, where many thousands of emigrants to the New World were 'processed' through Ellis Island with little concern for accuracy. Later, Oscar used other names when travelling with his mistress, usually to conceal his real identity from the wife from whom he was separated.

So far, the police assumptions were not unreasonable, but the next day their case against Slater collapsed. The pawn ticket was for a diamond brooch which had been pledged a *month* before Miss Gilchrist's death. Refusing to accept the inevitable, they showed the brooch to Miss Lambie who was able to point out the marked differences between the two pieces of jewellery. However, when they discovered that Slater and his mistress were travelling under the false name, Sando, they sent a telegram to the New York police asking them to detain him, and to carry out a search for the pawn ticket, which they omitted to mention no longer had any bearing on the case.

Needless to add, when the apparently incriminating pawn ticket was found, the New York authorities had no reason to resist the application for extradition, but taking no chances, the Glasgow police sent their three 'eye-witnesses' to New York to identify their suspect. I use the phrase 'taking no chances' advisedly because this time they eliminated any question of doubt, by re-examining the witnesses with frequent references to Slater's photograph, so that by the time they had completed their primitive brainwashing there was no longer any doubt in the minds of the two women at least (Adams still resisted, maintaining that Slater only resembled the man). When Inspector Pyper waited with them outside the room where extradition proceedings were being heard, and Slater came out handcuffed to a New York detective, they excitedly exclaimed, 'That's the man!'; they had learned their lesson well.

However, the American lawyer representing Slater got a belligerent Helen Lambie (no doubt persuaded by the police of Slater's guilt) to admit that in her absence, Miss Gilchrist would not have allowed a stranger into the flat, and since her employer must have let him in (the door would have been locked and bolted) the implication was that she had known the person, and even the police did not suggest that Slater was known to her. In fact, Slater was advised that there was every chance the extradition order would be refused, and really only had himself to blame when he disregarded that advice, and decided to go back to clear his name. Having a clear conscience, he had no way of knowing the odds stacked against him. The principle of a police identification line-up, for example, is to 'bury' the suspect in a row of men of similar appearance so that the witnesses' identification counts for something. The Glasgow police in their search for fresh witnesses proceeded to break all rules by presenting a row of fair-haired, fair-skinned Glaswegian look-a-likes, offset by one distinctively swarthy odd-man-out, drawing the attention of the witnesses – who had all been shown photographs of Slater – to the odd one out.

When the trial opened on 3 May 1909, the evidence was so blatantly 'loaded' against Slater that, included in a crime novel, it would have been dismissed as 'far-fetched'. Restricted space means that I have to summarise from summaries, such as William Roughead's update on the case (*Classic Crimes*, Cassell 1951), which is appropriate since it was his report of the trial, published in 1910, which motivated Sir Arthur Conan Doyle to embark on his long crusade for justice.

From such modest beginnings – just two exceptionally vague eye-witnesses (one of whom even told her mistress's niece that she recognised the intruder – *not* Slater – and actually named him!) – the police came to court with no less than ninety-eight carefully rehearsed witnesses, some of whom had conveniently changed their original stories. They included some who identified the defendant as a man they had seen *watching* the Gilchrist house, and by implication acting suspiciously; and others whose testimony supported (false) allegations of Slater's suspicious behaviour in 'flight' – both after the murder, and en route for America. This veritable 'army' of witnesses was so comprehensive, they had to draw the line somewhere; except that the witnesses they declined to call would not have duplicated evidence, but contradicted it.

There was no excuse, for example, for failing to call the police surgeon, Dr John Adams, who examined the murder victim, and concluded she had been attacked with the heavy mahogany chair on which she had been sitting. He was convinced that the head wounds had been caused by blows from the chair legs, and while on the ground she had been stamped on, the action breaking several of her ribs. But this would have conflicted with prosecution evidence that Slater had inflicted the crushing blows with a tiny hammer which police had found in his luggage on board the *Lusitania* (among *seven* carefully packed trunks, which hardly suggests panic-stricken flight). As it was, even without Dr Adams' evidence, medical experts at the trial disagreed over the viability of the hammer as a weapon, free of any trace of blood; even the prosecution admitting that it might have taken 'not under' fifty-sixty blows which such a delicate weapon to cause the injuries sustained.

Nor did they call Mr Duncan MacBrayne, a local grocer whose testimony would have been embarrassing, having seen Slater standing at the door of his home at 8.15 on the evening of the murder. For a start, it would have cast doubt on the 'evidence' of a ticket clerk seated behind her small window at Kelvinbridge subway, some distance away, who insisted she saw a man 'flying' past her down the stairs, throwing her a penny, at 7.45pm. A fleeting glimpse was enough to convince her days later that the man had been Slater and that, by implication, he was fleeing from the scene of the crime. Even if she had been correct, it would have been impossible for the 'fugitive' to appear, totally relaxed, where MacBrayne said he was. It would also have made a dent in the relevant passage in eloquent summation by the Lord Advocate (Alexander Ure, KC), leading for the Crown, when in a voice heavy with irony, he said: 'We know nothing of the man's movements until a quarter to ten at night . . .'

George Joseph Smith, 'Brides in the Bath' murderer with one of his victims, Bessie Mundy (*The Mansell Collection*)

(*above*) Steinie Morrison in the dock (*Mary Evans Picture Library*); (*left*) Oscar Slater: a portrait taken in 1908 (*BBC Hulton Picture Library*) and (*below*) an unusual photograph taken at the trial (*BBC Hulton Picture Library*)

The brilliant defence lawyer, Sir Edward Marshall Hall (*BBC Hulton Picture Library*)

The Moat Farm murder: (*above left*) a portrait of the victim, Camille Holland; (*right*) the remains of Miss Holland, identified only by her clothing

(*left*) Samuel Douglas after his arrest (*All pictures on this page from Chelmsford & Essex Museum*)

(above) Crippen and Ethel le Neve at their trial *(The Mansell Collection)*; *(right)* Herbert Bennett, found guilty of the Yarmouth murder despite controversial evidence *(BBC Hulton Picture Library)*

Dr Arthur Warren Waite (*BBC Hulton Picture Library*)

Mr Ure's allegation (even if he did not know of MacBrayne's statement) conveniently ignored the defendant's alibi. Bearing in mind the murder took place just after seven o'clock, Slater *could* be 'tied' to other places for the previous hour: he was at the Central Station, sending a telegram in his own handwriting to London in respect of his watch which was being repaired; the time 6.12pm. From there he went to a billiards hall in Renfield Street where he was seen leaving at 6.30pm. He went straight home – much nearer than Queen's Terrace – and arrived at what his girl friend, Antoine, and the maid, described as his usual time, 7pm. If one wanted to discount the evidence of these two woman because they had an axe to grind, it is worth bearing in mind that when he left Renfield Street, he was seen to be wearing a waterproof and a bowler hat; whereas the prosecution placed great store upon the evidence of identification from one of its witnesses who claimed to have seen him staring up at the Gilchrist flat, before going up – she had no doubt the man was wearing a heavy brown tweed overcoat, and a brown tweed cap.

In fact, the Lord Advocate made no effort to cross-examine on Slater's alibi; he seemed less interested throughout in the facts, more on establishing that Slater was the *type* of man capable of committing such a crime. He used the opportunity of having Slater's maid in the witness box to question her about life in the Slater household. From his probing questions he secured at least two admissions, the significance of which the jury were asked to consider – the first was that Antoine 'received gentlemen' in the evenings; the other (by implication almost as sinful) that she frequented the music hall! It is doubtful that Slater actually lived on the immoral earnings of his girl friend. A 'wheeler-dealer', he had always been able to get by comfortably on his wits, originally as a bookmaker, and more recently by running 'social' (ie gambling) clubs. But even a hint was enough for Mr Ure who opened his speech to the jury with the solemn words: 'Up to yesterday afternoon I should have thought that there was one serious difficulty which confronted you – the difficulty of conceiving that there was in existence a human being capable of doing such a dastardly deed. Gentlemen, that difficulty, I think, was removed when we heard . . . that he had followed a life which descends to the very lowest depths of human degradation, for by the universal judgement of mankind, the man who lives upon the proceeds of prostitution has sunk to the lowest depths, and all moral sense has been destroyed and has ceased to exist. That difficulty removed, I say without hesitation that the man in the dock is capable of having committed this dastardly outrage.'

William Roughead draws attention to the fact that in a series of articles on the case, published in the *Daily News* in September 1927, Mr E.C. Palmer ('The Pilgrim') listed *twenty-five* inaccurate statements of fact or false inferences, eg the claim that on Christmas Eve, Slater had fled the country because he panicked when he saw his name and personal details in the newspapers on that day, when in fact his name was not mentioned until he was well on the way to New York. Before publication, Mr Palmer offered Lord Strathclyde (formerly Mr Ure) the opportunity to comment, but was met with a dignified silence. In fact, the Lord Advocate was a powerful and eloquent orator, and to be charitable it could be said that the plethora of errors was due to the fact that he spoke for two hours without a single note.

Unfortunately, it would be nearer the truth to suggest that Ure was less concerned with facts than with establishing a climate of such moral indignation that Slater's defence counsel decided it would be wiser not to put his client in the witness box, which may well have been the final straw to a jury which probably misconstrued his silence as a tacit admission of guilt. Nor were they helped by a judge who, if not positively prejudiced, was apparently moved by the Lord Advocate's persuasive powers, because in his summing-up he appeared to ignore many of the valid points made by the defence, and repeated Crown assumptions as though they were fact. In the circumstances, the most surprising feature of the trial is that the indoctrinated jury failed to bring in a unanimous verdict; indeed, after deliberating for one hour and ten minutes, the vote was as follows: nine 'guilty'; five 'not proven'; and one 'not guilty'.

When sentence of death was passed, the hitherto passive Slater sprang to his feet and shouted: 'I know nothing about this. You are convicting an innocent man!' – but he was ignored, and the date of the execution was fixed for 27 May. The farcical element of the verdict was highlighted by the way the £200 reward for the murderer's conviction was divided; one of the beneficiaries being the man who originally tipped off the police about Slater's link with the diamond brooch – the *wrong* one! However, public opinion, initially excited by graphic leads fed to the press by the Glasgow police, now underwent a significant change and not content with just reading between the lines of the evidence, 20,000 signatures were gathered demanding clemency while legal experts protested through more conventional channels. It was not until the 26th of the month, just one day before he was due to be hanged, that the reprieve came through, and another *five years* before there was any serious talk of an enquiry.

In 1914, pressure was mounting; it included the publication of a booklet by Sir Arthur Conan Doyle, in which he not only dealt with the inadequacies of the trial, but introduced some new theories of his own – such as the suggestion that the motive had not been a jewel robbery, but that the murderer who ransacked Miss Gilchrist's private papers had been searching for a document, such as a will. Another writer, David Cook, presented the Secretary for Scotland with a very clinical series of questions relating to Crown evidence, such as 'Did the witness to the identification on the night of the murder name a person other than Oscar Slater?'

But the terms of the enquiry, grudgingly conceded, made it impossible for a proper result; the authorities stipulated that it should be held in private, that it should deal only in *new* evidence (and therefore not relate to the conduct of the trial) and that it should be left to the discretion of the witnesses as to whether they attended. Slater was not represented, and the chairman of the enquiry was able to consult only the Procurator-Fiscal and the Chief Constable of Glasgow! Anticipating the inevitable outcome, Sir Arthur Conan Doyle wrote in the *Daily Mail* 'The police are as much on trial as Slater. If the methods of the police are not to be investigated the enquiry is futile.' It was.

While Sir Arthur's views of the conduct of the Glasgow police force were valid, there was one notable exception – the proverbial 'honest cop', John Trench, who in twenty-one years very distinguished service, had risen from the ranks to a position of seniority and respect in and out of the force. It was Trench who was sent to interview Miss Gilchrist's niece who recalled how Helen Lambie had broken the news of the murder, and the fact she had actually named the man. This genuine suspect was referred to only by the initials A.B., and he was subsequently interviewed by other detectives in mysterious circumstances – after which Trench was instructed to forget the matter, and to 'warn' his witness not to repeat the allegation, which he did – to such good effect that she subsequently denied telling him anything.

When Trench was approached by David Cook, conducting his own enquiry, he was torn between giving the facts he had, to assist a man whom he knew had been wrongly convicted, and loyalty to the Glasgow force. Cautiously, Cook approached an independant authority who wrote to the Scottish Secretary, Mr M'Kinnon Wood, and was advised that if Trench would make a written statement, he would give the matter his 'best consideration'. It was probably Trench's unassailable evidence that led to the enquiry – and to the officer's 'punishment'. Satisfied he had been authorised to co-operate with Cook, Trench gave him a full account of the incident. But his superiors regarded this behaviour as treachery, and later that year when the 'fuss' over the enquiry had died down, he was dismissed from the police with ignominy, forfeiting his pension. His appeal to the same Scottish Secretary who had invited his statement was ignored. Nor were his bosses satisfied with their revenge – their vindictiveness knew no bounds, and in 1915 both Trench and Cook were arrested on a trumped-up charge of receiving stolen goods over a year earlier. Both were detained for three months before being brought to trial, at which the judge directed the jury to acquit them and in the process even commended Trench for his honesty. The pity is that Trench and Cook were not compensated, or that the senior officers responsible for their harassment were not themselves named, and disciplined.

The war obviously diverted attention away from the injustice done to Slater, still languishing in prison, but in 1925 when he had served fifteen years, he smuggled out a note to Sir Arthur Conan Doyle asking him to try again. The creator of Sherlock Holmes wrote to the new Secretary of State for Scotland, asking him to look 'personally' into the case, while his fellow campaigner Sir Hubert Stephen published another article in which he wrote: '. . . no English judge would have allowed the case to go to a jury'. The joint plea fell on deaf ears, and the momentum was lost again, until 1927 when the first book on the subject was published – *The Truth About Oscar Slater*, by William Park, a Glasgow journalist.

The well-reasoned case argued by Mr Park revived the interest of the press, with several newspapers jumping on to the bandwagon - perhaps the most influential being the regular column in the *Daily News* by 'The Pilgrim' – although they outdid each other in their ingenuity in tracing original witnesses and obtaining suitably amended statements. When Mary Barrowman made a signed statement admitting she had been *bullied* into making a positive identification of Slater, and that she had been made to rehearse her statement every day for a fortnight, even the most loyal Government supporter must have thrown up his hands. Instead the Scottish Secretary, in November of that year, magnanimously announced that since Slater had now served eighteen and a half years of his sentence, he felt justified in authorising his release *on licence*!

The reaction of old campaigners like Sir Arthur Conan Doyle was to bombard MP's with a fact sheet on the case, demanding a public enquiry. Under tremendous pressure, the Government finally acceded to this demand, although at the preliminary hearing in June 1928 it was again stipulated that no attempt should be made to re-try the case, and that only new evidence would be permitted. Nevertheless, the assembled evidence was overwhelming, and on 20 July the appeal was granted, although only on the grounds of misdirection by the judge; it failed, in fact, on another issue – that the appellant had 'suffered prejudice by non-disclosure of evidence known to the Crown'!

Thus the decision was still grudging, and nothing was said about compensation for Slater's years in prison. After a question in the House of Commons the Scottish Secretary suggested that Slater might care to put in a claim! In fact, it was not until the following month that the Government had second thoughts and offered £6,000, which a weary Slater accepted. He lived the remainder of his life in relative anonimity, dying in 1948, leaving one remaining mystery – the identity of the mysterious 'A.B.', who was undoubtedly Miss Gilchrist's killer. The fact that he was obviously known to Helen Lambie, and that he had rifled through the dead woman's papers, suggests that he may have been a relative, interested to see how he might benefit from the old lady's will. More intriguing is the influence he had over the police, sufficient to persuade them to close the door on any further investigation into his movements.

5

THE ROLE OF THE DEFENCE

The Camden Town & Yarmouth Murders

The popular romantic image of a brilliant defence lawyer who not only saves the life of his innocent client, but actually unmasks the real murderer at the climax of the trial, is based more on the fictional hero, Perry Mason, the creation of Erle Stanley Gardner, than real life. There have, of course, been many exceptionally talented defence counsel, but the analogy of the eleventh hour triumph does not stand close inspection because the strategy of shifting guilt from accused to someone else is risky, and seldom attempted. Even in the dramatic case of Jessie M'Lachlan in 1862 where the defence were obliged to point the finger at the original police suspect who had become chief witness for the prosecution, the defendant was still wrongly convicted.

However, given the opportunity, defence lawyers may hedge their bets by implying in cross examination that the testimony of a witness is deliberately false – without actually accusing him or her of wrongdoing – if only to demonstrate the fallibility of the Crown case. This technique was used to perfection by the celebrated Edward Marshall Hall in his masterly defence of Robert Wood at the Old Bailey in 1907, in what was known as the Camden Town case, the murder of a young prostitute. Marshall Hall's handling of his brief, in which the defendant gave evidence on his own behalf – the first time with a successful outcome – remains a model for any aspiring lawyer, and the equal of any fictional counterpart.

Marshall Hall was unquestionably one of the great trial lawyers, securing a number of remarkable acquittals against the odds. But it should be obvious that although a criminal lawyer will try to represent a client to the best of his ability, inevitably his best work is seen when he is personally convinced of the defendant's innocence. Marshall Hall had no doubts about the likeable Wood, and did not rest until the jury shared that view, despite an occasionally hostile judge. The irony is that Marshall Hall's brilliance which saved Wood – a verdict that was hugely popular - may well have obscured the truth, because in a clinical assessment of the case, we cannot escape the fact that there were no other credible suspects.

Nevertheless, Wood was entitled to the benefit of the doubt. The evidence against him was circumstantial and found wanting, so the acquittal was justified. Yet Marshall Hall's equally impressive performance at the Old Bailey six years earlier in defending Herbert John Bennett, accused of the murder of his wife on a Yarmouth beach, was unsuccessful. Despite all Hall's efforts Bennett was hanged – but there is reason to believe that even though the trial was perfectly fair, he was not guilty. This theory, admittedly not supported by any firm evidence, cannot be lightly dismissed, and like an unhealed wound the case flared up again some eleven years after his execution when another woman was found strangled in Yarmouth on almost the same spot, in very similar circumstances.

Marshall Hall's courtroom strategy, his cunning cross-examination and eloquence in both those cases, demonstrate all that is best in the British legal system, despite the very different outcomes. We shall never know whether his own assessment of each client's character was justified, or whether he had the wool pulled over his eyes. Everyone, for example, liked the good-natured, gentle artist Robert Wood – so much so, that when he was arrested, his employers put up £1,000 (a considerable sum in those days) so that his solicitors could brief counsel of their choice without thought of cost. When he was acquitted there was public celebration, and even fears of 'retribution' against at least one prosecution witness.

Indeed, the case was interesting in that most of the main characters were likeable, including the murder victim, Emily Jane Dimmock, a twenty-three-year-old prostitute, and her common-law husband Bertram Shaw, a liberal-minded young man who had taken her off the streets on the understanding that she gave up her previous lifestyle. Phyllis, as she was known to her friends, was a tall, slim and attractive girl with a captivating personality, and Shaw fell in love, offering marriage once he had overcome the prejudice of his parents. There is reason to believe that his feelings were reciprocated, although Phyllis may well have been less than starry-eyed at the prospect of the dull existence respectability had to offer. It was Shaw's nightly absence (he earned £5 a week as a dining-car chef on the night train running between London and Sheffield) that dangled temptation before her increasingly jaded gaze. Left to her own devices while Bert was working, Phyllis would inevitably have gone out just for the company, and always popular with her clients, she decided it was somewhat pointless turning her back on easy money.

It is too easy to condemn her concept of morality. Undoubtedly she enjoyed the free and easy life, in which she could now afford to pick and choose whom she took back to their lodgings in Camden Town, but during the day she was the perfect wife – washing and ironing with an energy that even her future mother-in-law could not fault. Shaw remained blissfully ignorant until the September morning he returned from work to find her dead – naked on the blood-soaked bed, her throat cut so savagely that the head was practically severed. There was no sign of a struggle and the police doctor estimated that she had been killed several hours earlier, between four and six a.m. possibly in her sleep, although one arm tucked behind her back indicated she may have been held in position by her assailant.

Neither the landlady or her husband, living in the same building, had heard anything suspicious and the contents of the room seemed normal enough, although Mr Shaw was able to tell that a photograph album full of picture postcards had been moved and rifled. (Phyllis' hobby was collecting postcards, and there were examples from all parts of the world, mostly from admirers who knew of the interest.) Some of the contents had been scattered on the floor, and a few had been torn from the album. The possibility that the damage had been caused by the murderer searching for something incriminating, was not lost on the police, but the situation was confused by the loss of a few personal belongings, although other more valuable jewellery had been ignored – which meant that robbery was an unlikely motive. Shaw was the logical suspect, but his job ruled him out of police enquiries, and as soon as they investigated the girl's other life and began to interview her wide circle of associates, it was apparent Phyllis had taken a number of men home at different times.

The energy and resourcefulness of Scotland Yard in what was a routine murder investigation, counters the bungling image it had acquired in the Victorian years, fostered by writers like Conan Doyle. Murderers are far more likely to be caught by painstaking detective work than 'inspired' deduction, and the police diligently questioned hundreds of men and women who might have known the dead girl. Their first clue was from Phyllis' newest client, Robert Roberts, a ship's cook – which made him a potential suspect, since he had access to and expertise with a sharp knife. Having recently been paid off, and while waiting for his next voyage, Roberts was flush with money and fair game for prostitutes.

Phyllis had met Roberts on Sunday night in her favourite haunt The Rising Sun public house in Camden Town, and taken him home. Roberts also paid for her services on Monday and Tuesday nights, and admitted he would have returned for more on Wednesday night, if she had not spoken of a prior engagement. The police checked his alibi, but like Mr Shaw he had reliable witnesses to prove he was elsewhere at the time of the murder. However, as though compensating his interrogators he offered them another suspect – a mysterious 'Bert' – telling them that before leaving the girl's lodgings on Wednesday morning he saw two notes slipped under the door, one a private letter which, possibly to demonstrate the demand for her services, she let him read. The gist, he recalled, was a request that Phyllis meet the writer at the Eagle public house, Camden Town at 8.30 that evening. She had not elaborated, and he may not have paid that much attention to the message had she not then produced a postcard from one of the drawers. The card was unusual in that it was a hand impression of The

Rising Sun pub on the back of a printed woman and child illustration. The message read: 'Phillis darling, if it pleases you, meet me 8.15pm at the . . . [just the drawing] Yours to a cinder, Alice.'

According to Roberts she offered no explanation, but he got the impression that both letter and card had been written by the same person – despite the difference in names, and the fact that in the case of the card Phyllis's name had been mis-spelt. What was more significant to him was the similarity in style and the fact that both had been written in indelible pencil. He concluded his report of the incident by saying that the girl had burnt the letter in the fireplace and put the card back in the drawer.

Roberts' evidence had already been partly corroborated by the discovery by detectives of a partly burned letter in the grate; pieced together, the charred fragments comprised the basic element of such a request for an assignation. Before searching for the mystery letter-writer (it was no secret that Mr Shaw's christian name was Bert, but it was reasoned that he hardly needed to post a letter to the woman he regarded as his wife), the police decided to find the other half of the mystery – the postcard. It had obviously not been returned to the collection, but it later turned up by accident when Mr Shaw was emptying some drawers, and discovered it in the folded newspaper which had 'lined' the bottom. Roberts confirmed it was the one he had been shown.

However, their examination of the photo album had not been wasted, and the police found three other cards showing a striking similarity to the handwriting on the message from 'Alice'. When none of Phyllis's circle of friends could throw any light on them it was arranged for facsimiles to be reproduced in the major newspapers. One, the *News of the World*, offered its own inducement of a £100 reward to anyone who could identify the handwriting. The long arm of the press in 1907 was comparable to that of television today, and the police had high hopes that someone would recognise the handwriting. In the event, they were initially frustrated, although only through the quick reaction of the author/artist of the cards,

Robert Wood, who managed to get in first, and shut down the most likely 'leak'. In fact, he was only just in time to prevent a former girl friend, Ruby Young, from responding to the *News of the World* appeal (the envelope was actually addressed although not sealed on that Sunday evening when Robert called round and persuaded her not to mail it).

The middle-class and ostensibly respectable Ruby described herself as an 'artists' model', which meant that she was a better-class prostitute; but because of her background, she was discreet and anxious not to embarrass her family. Wood also came from a good home; his father was a skilled printer who had always been in well-paid work, although the size of his family meant that he was unable to give his children much of a start in their careers. Robert had immense potential as an artist but never received any training and considered himself fortunate to obtain a position as a junior designer in a glass factory. However, his ability was eventually recognised and in fourteen years with the same firm, his services were suitably rewarded. He supplemented a good income by freelance work as a cartoonist.

Wood was universally popular, and if his friends and associates realised his fondness for attractive women they conspired to keep it from his highly respectable father. At one stage, Wood and Ruby had been very close, and might even have married, but he had a roving eye and when Ruby and her mother moved out of the immediate area, there were other distractions. They drifted apart, and at the time of the murder had not seen each other for several weeks. Ten days after the discovery of Phyllis's body, Ruby must have been surprised to receive a telegram from Robert asking her to meet him at a familiar rendezvous. If she was expecting him to apologise for his absence and confess his undying love, she was disappointed; all he wanted was that if anyone asked, she was to maintain that they still saw each other every Monday and Wednesday nights. He offered no explanation, and surprisingly she did not demand one. When they met again he reminded her of her promise.

On seeing the postcard appeal, and in view of this recent

history, Ruby did not need to be a detective to realise that Robert knew something about the matter although she did not believe he could be involved. However, this time she was given an explanation. Confessing that he had no alibi for the Wednesday night of the murder, he admitted he had met the dead girl and had sent her the postcard. His explanation was that he had been with a friend in a public house when the girl had got into conversation with them. At one point, a boy pedlar had come in with a stock of postcards for sale. When the girl expressed interest, he persuaded her not to waste her money, because he had some more artistic cards he had recently obtained in Bruges, where he had been on holiday. He produced a selection he had with him and she chose one, asking him to inscribe it for her – jokingly suggesting that he sign it 'Alice'. He did not have a postage stamp but promised to post it later. By coincidence he saw her in the street the following day when she reminded him of his promise. He did not see her again.

Perhaps prompted by her pride, Ruby believed him and they worked out a detailed alibi for the murder evening; but for all his many qualities, it seems that Wood was a compulsive liar in matters relating to his private life. He had been seen in the company of Phyllis on several occasions, once by a friend only a few days before the murder, in a public house. The incident had stuck in his friend's memory because the girl had not been dressed for business (in fact, she had been wearing curlers and had even apologised for her appearance, explaining that she had come out in a hurry). At the time, Wood had claimed he was not stopping, yet had remained after him. Some days after the murder, Wood appealed to his friend to forget the girl's presence in the pub, suggesting that enquiries might be made, and he did not want to upset his father. The friend agreed. As far as he was concerned, Wood was incapable of such a savage murder; yet surprisingly, it did not occur to him to wonder about the girl's appearance, if her rush to leave home at short notice had not been to meet someone, and who that person might have been . . .

Ruby kept her promise not to communicate to the *News of*

the World, or the police – but it was a particularly tempting secret, and eventually she confided (in the strictest secrecy) to her best friend. However, her friend, faced with the same problem, decided to confide in *her* friend – in the strictest secrecy, of course! The latest recipient of the news was a journalist who went to see Ruby, drawing her attention to the possibility of being arrested as an accessory to murder! Ruby panicked and confessed to the police, who asked her to identify her former boy friend at an arranged rendezvous – and he was arrested. It is typical of Wood's ingenuous personality that it did not occur to him he had been betrayed, and in his statement he blithely trotted out the story he had arranged with Ruby, not knowing she had admitted the way it had been fabricated. Supported by other equally circumstantial evidence, the police now had a case. In an identity parade, Wood was picked out because of his peculiar way of walking, as the man who had been seen outside the lodgings of Emily Dimmock at five o'clock on the morning of her death.

Among the witnesses assembled by the police who claimed to have seen Wood with Phyllis, was a prostitute known as 'May'. However, her evidence was considered by the Crown to be unreliable, and in those circumstances she was not called. Nevertheless, the defence was granted access to her testimony, and it occurred to them that Robert Roberts' somewhat unlikely identification of Wood (on top of his damning evidence of the letter and postcard) might have been the result of a conspiracy between him and 'May'. Was it not possible that, as Wood had persuaded Ruby Young to agree a common story, that the ship's cook had not done the same to protect himself?

In the witness box, Roberts, after initially denying it, was forced to admit that he knew May, and that on the 'one' occasion they met, she had described Wood to him; that it was her description, not his own, he had passed on to the police. Having already established the witness's unreliability, Marshall Hall then dealt with the letter, raising some doubt as to the date of the assignation proposed by 'Bert', and then accusing Roberts of using the name 'Bert' to throw suspicion on Bertram Shaw. 'I put it to you that this fragment was never part of a letter which passed through the post . . . that the story of this long letter is an invention.' (The charred remains found by the police indicated two sheets of paper with writing closely spaced, on all four sides.) Although Roberts denied the allegation, he was so shaken by the time his ordeal was over that his evidence was practically worthless. And in answer to a whispered question from his old rival, Sir Charles Matthews, leading for the Crown, Marshall Hall's under-the- breath response: 'No. Most certainly I do not accuse him of murder . . .' was pitched high enough for the whole court to hear, and ponder over.

Marshall Hall's next significant assault on the credibility of the Crown case was on the testimony of the witness who claimed to have seen a man fitting Wood's description – or, at least, someone with the 'peculiar, jerky or twitching' way in which he walked – leaving Emily Dimmock's lodgings at about the time of the murder. At the preliminary hearing this witness's self-confidence was followed by indecision when challenged; and had been further shaken by Wood's solicitor, Arthur Newton, who had skilfully prepared a trap. He had heard the witness fix the time precisely, saying that shortly afterwards he had heard a clock strike five; also that it was a dark, drizzly and foggy morning, but that he could see the defendant clearly by the light of the electric street lamp: Newton had then produced a timetable chart proving that the electricity had been switched off at 4.37am.

At the trial Marshall Hall had already prepared a minefield for this witness by destroying the 'framework' for his evidence – the official police testimony relating to the lighting of the area. He demonstrated a series of glaring errors in the plans drawn up by the police, which at best showed them to be inefficient, at worst devious. The plans, for example, showed St Pauls Road where Phyllis lived, to be well lit from a row of lights from the overhanging railway sidings: unaccountably, they forgot to include a continuous row of houses which ran between the sidings and St Pauls Road, effectively blocking out any light. They also showed light from a railway bridge, omitting to show a nine-feet-high wall in the way.

In other words, the only artificial light of use to the witness was from the street lamps – which had been switched off. Now the witness admitted he had been mistaken, and that the meeting had taken place all of seven minutes earlier. But the significance of this sudden change of heart was not lost, and Marshall Hall did not labour the point, preferring to contrast the testimony of a 'drizzly, foggy' morning with the fact that the day before had been the hottest of the year, and that not a drop of rain had been recorded in London that morning. There were then a couple of important disclosures: firstly, that the witness had not originally identified the house he had seen the man with the peculiar walk leave, he had noticed the number in the newspapers. More to the point, his first statement had not even mentioned the walk, and when the defence asked to see the original statement, they were told it had been lost!

Hall's memorable turn of phrase, which never failed to impress a jury, is typified by such questions and answers as when the same witness tried to justify his claim that the man he believed to be Wood had been of 'stiff build with broad shoulders' – the defendant was in fact small, and quite frail. 'He is broader than me!' the witness insisted. 'Would you describe a bluebottle as an elephant, because it is bigger than a fly?' was the lawyer's response.

No worthwhile defence counsel would hesitate to challenge a judge if he feels his client is not receiving fair treatment but most, having made the point for the record, will not risk dicing with danger by pursuing the matter. Marshall Hall was fearless and had many blazing rows with the bench, sometimes to his cost. On this occasion he was justified in defending Wood's character when Mr Justice Grantham interjected a question out of the blue to a witness who had expressed the opinion that Wood was 'gentle and affectionate to a degree altogether out of the ordinary'.

The following passage is taken from *The Life of Sir Edward Marshall Hall,* by Edward Marjoribanks, Gollancz 1929:

. . .'Had you any idea of the life you have now heard he was

> leading – an immoral life?' The witness said he was unaware of anything abnormal, and Mr Justice Grantham then said, 'You had no idea he was leading the life we heard he was?' The witness replied in the negative, but Marshall was already on his feet. He saw that the judge already assumed that Wood had been Phyllis's lover, which was some way to assuming his guilt. Ruby Young had not yet given evidence, and there was as yet no evidence of his immorality. 'I do not understand your Lordship's question.' The judge then, lest there might be some misunderstanding, asked an even more objectionable question: 'Had you any idea he was living with such a woman as that?' Marshall assumed that the judge meant Phyllis Dimmock, as he probably did. 'My Lord,' he insisted, 'there is not one tittle of evidence . . .'
>
> The judge retorted severely. 'I am addressing the witness, and I must ask you not to argue with me.'
>
> Quite undaunted, he [Hall] had the last word. 'I want to point out,' he said, with a piercing glance, first at the judge and then at the jury, 'in the interests of justice, that there is not a particle of evidence that the prisoner ever had any improper intercourse with Emily Dimmock.'

The evidence of 'conspiracy' between Wood and Ruby Young was still the most damning, yet Marshall Hall's tactics were surprising. The unhappy girl had been portrayed as something of a monster by the press – a wanton temptress who had 'sold out' the young man who trusted her – and it was expected that he would destroy her in the box. Yet he was gentle, almost sympathetic before turning the false alibi to his client's advantage with one question: '. . . Have you ever thought, having regard to the evidence of Dr Thompson, who places the time of the murder at three or four in the morning that the alibi Wood arranged with you from 6.30 to 10.30 on the evening previous to the murder, would be a useless alibi for the murder, but a perfect one for the meeting of the girl?' The implication that if Wood had known the time of the murder he would not have left such an enormous gap was not lost on the jury.

The decision to call Robert Wood to give evidence was a calculated risk. He was practically a caricature of the unworldly artist whose attitude during the trial had been that of a detached observer, constantly sketching and showing little interest in the legal battle. It was as though he had declared 'I am innocent – I cannot take these allegations seriously'. Even Marshall Hall was exasperated at times by his refusal to come down from the clouds and give clear, unequivocal answers. The hostile Sir Charles Matthews fared no better. Wood walked, guilelessly, into every carefully prepared trap, and slipped out again just as effortlessly; at the end of the interrogation, prosecuting counsel was more exhausted than the prisoner but had proved nothing. A more calculating witness might have been cut to pieces by such ferocious cross-examination, and it was probably Wood's naîvete which pulled him through.

There seems little doubt that Wood's somewhat scatter-brained performance in the witness box did as much as anything to persuade the jury that he was basically an honest, gentle young man incapable of such a savage murder; that his only crime had been to lie about his meetings with Phyllis Dimmock – and then only to protect his father. Admittedly, the Crown evidence was inconclusive, but I believe it was this gut reaction more than what they heard in the closing addresses or the judge's summing up, that enabled them to reach their verdict in less than twenty minutes. The foreman's pronouncement of Not Guilty was received with a burst of applause in the court, quickly spreading to the crowd outside. It was, incidentally, the first successful outcome to a trial in which the defendant gave evidence on his own behalf since the passing of the Criminal Evidence Act of 1898. Public sympathy for Wood and his family, whipped up by the newspapers, was extremely high and conversely hostile to Crown witnesses, particularly Ruby Young, wrongly accused of 'selling' her former lover; she had to be smuggled from the court. Marshall Hall himself later commented: 'The scene, especially the cheering outside, was more like an election than the end of a criminal trial.'

Even the judge who at times had been quite hostile to the defendant, made it clear he believed that the Crown had not made out its case. Yet one cannot help speculating that Robert Wood was fortunate both in his legal representation, and in that atmosphere of near hysteria when the jury might have been 'conditioned' to react in his favour, because much of what Marshall Hall said was directed at the emotions, and tossed aside logic. In *Victorian Murders* (David & Charles 1988), I was able to demonstrate how a number of women accused of murder were acquitted by courts influenced less by the evidence than by the *mood* of society at the time. One wonders, for example, if the jury were not too easily swayed when Marshall Hall brushed aside the evidence of several Crown witnesses testifying that Wood had been on friendly terms with Phyllis Dimmock for as long as eighteen months (when he claimed to have known her only casually), as not to be believed because they were prostitutes and brothel-keepers. In fact, the jury were asked to accept *two* suspect assumptions – that only respectable witnesses could be trusted with the truth, and that a normally gentle and mild-mannered man was incapable of violent murder!

In his selection of *Famous Trials* (Viking Press 1984), the writer/barrister John Mortimer develops this point, posing a number of questions never put to Wood in court, and suggesting that a reassessment of the facts in a court today might have reached a different conclusion. However, my reason for featuring the Camden Town murder is to show how a brilliant lawyer was able to save the life of one client, and yet in another trial an equally impressive performance cut no ice.

Robert Wood and Herbert John Bennett had much in common – both were personable young men yet compulsive liars; the difference was that Wood was intrinsically honest and his lies were confined to his relationships with women of questionable morals, while Bennett was a petty crook who seemed to lie instinctively about everything. The latter was only twenty when he was charged with strangling his wife on a Yarmouth beach in September 1900. Not only had the Crown assembled a wealth of circumstantial evidence against him, but well before the trial, Bennett had been convicted in terms of public opinion by a vicious press campaign in which irresponsible reporting was compounded by speculation and even distortion – by the use in one case of a false moustache added to a photograph of Bennett, to illustrate how he might have looked in disguise! The damage was done so early that it influenced the evidence of many Crown witnesses.

Aware of Bennett's basic dishonesty, Marshall Hall was nevertheless convinced of his innocence of the charge of murder; indeed it was his client's cunning and expertise as a crook that persuaded him Bennett could not have behaved as stupidly as the Crown would have the jury believe. A further irony is that Hall knew, despite his evasiveness and apparent inability to come up with straight answers in the witness box, Wood's manner would nevertheless impress the jury; he did not have the same confidence in Bennett, but in the end he had no choice. He needed to call his client if only to corroborate the evidence of a last-minute witness of undoubted integrity who swore that he had been with the defendant in London at the time he was alleged to have been planning murder in Yarmouth. Such an alibi is the perfect defence, provided it cannot be challenged, and the only fly in the ointment was that Bennett had never mentioned the vital meeting to the defence team. The witness was undoubtedly honest, but Bennett was needed to corroborate the story, and he refused to go into the box.

Only three years after the passing of the Criminal Evidence Act of 1898, public attitudes had changed. Before that date, a defendant was not able to speak on his own behalf, so no significance could be attached to his silence; now it was already assumed that remaining silent meant he had something to hide. Bennett almost certainly *did* have something to hide, and Marshall Hall was fully aware of the fact when he urged him to go into the box and admit to everything he may have done or intended (outside of murder), and to trust in his ability to win freedom on the facts, and by destroying the Crown case. Instead, Hall was forced back on the defensive, and there were too many holes to plug. In the circumstances, the great lawyer may have been at fault in not over-riding the wishes of his client, or failing that, in deciding to use the witness without the defendant's corroboration.

Bennett was a complex personality. He had many redeeming features and, in moral terms, compares favourably with most convicted murderers. His father was a foreman in a cement factory, so that by working class standards the family was not in any way deprived. Although his education was limited, a natural intelligence suggests this may well have been due to an impatience with the system – a desire for the short cut, so obvious throughout his short life. As a child he sold newspapers, and by his early teens was already drawing a wage as a grocer's assistant.

He soon demonstrated his independence in a remarkably mature fashion. At sixteen he met Mary Jane Clarke, three years his senior, and found an excuse for developing the relationship by taking piano lessons from her. Music was not the only interest they shared, and in due course Mary was pregnant. Many of his contemporaries would have cut and run, but Herbert insisted on marrying her – defying his father to make it at the second attempt, and adding four years to his age so that the certificate described him as twenty-one. Since one of the witnesses also signed the register in a false name, there were almost certainly grounds for declaring the marriage void, which eliminates one of the so-called motives for later killing Mary, in order to marry the woman who had superseded her in his affections.

There can be little doubt the young couple were very close, because when the baby was still-born there was no suggestion of them parting. Initially they lived with Mary's grandmother, dependent on the young bride's tiny income as a piano teacher, but Herbert had never been short of ideas and now he exploited their common interest in music by buying and selling violins. Bearing in mind that late Victorian families were obliged to entertain themselves, young people were encouraged to play a musical instrument. The potential market was there but it would have taken years to make money by conventional means, and Bennett was in a hurry. Much more profitable to find a cheap fiddle at three or four shillings and pass it off as a Stradivarius which, with just a little attention might fetch several guineas. The couple were well matched in this respect; while Bennett masterminded the scheme, the pretty Mary was effective as the respectable clergyman's daughter in desperate straits and forced to sell the family's sole surviving heirloom. By moving about London to avoid awkward comebacks, the Bennetts prospered.

Shortly after his twentieth birthday, and a father for the first time, Bennett appeared to go respectable, opening a grocer's shop. Anyone who did not understand his outlook might have imagined he intended to cash in on his earlier experience learning the ropes. In fact, his career as a grocer lasted a week because the shop burned down. Fortunately, the Bennetts were insured! They received £200 from the building (about half of their inflated claim), and more than twice that amount for loss of stock – a handsome profit since much of that had been bought on credit, and Bennett had no intention of hanging around to pay his debts.

On 17 March, having left their two-year-old daughter with Bennett's father, the couple went to South Africa where the Boer War was in progress. The long round trip cost them over £100, yet they stayed only four days – arriving back in the UK on 9 May. No explanation for the trip was ever forthcoming and suspicions that they were spies for the Boers – highly unlikely in view of the shortness of their stay – were never substantiated. The young couple returned to new lodgings in south London, where there seemed to be a change in the relationship. At his trial, the landlady, Mrs Elliston, claimed the couple frequently quarrelled, that Bennett ill-treated his wife, and that the climax of this bad feeling was an argument provoked when Bennett threatened to leave her. Mary is reported to have retaliated: 'Herbert, I shall follow you for the sake of the child, and if you are not careful I will get you fifteen years.' Mrs Elliston told the court that Bennett's response was to express his wish that she were dead, and that, 'if she did not look out, she soon would be'.

Much was to be made of that threat by the Crown, but the couple were living in such a fantasy world that it was difficult to distinguish truth from make-believe. They had gone to Cape Town for no discernible reason as Mr and Mrs Hood, while on their return Mary sometimes passed herself as Mrs Hood, while he used the name Bartlett, as well as Bennett. Furthermore, when in the following month Mary rented a house in nearby Bexleyheath, paying a quarter's rent in advance, she provided a reference written by her husband under a different name. The threat of 'fifteen years' was understandably construed as blackmail, but for what it is impossible to say. The violin confidence trick, especially as a first offence, would have earned only a light sentence and was unlikely to have been implemented without exposing her own, equally criminal, involvement.

Nevertheless, Mary's house in Bexleyheath coincided with some form of amicable separation, since Bennett had taken lodgings in Woolwich (South London) near to the Woolwich Arsenal, where he obtained work as a clerk. That in itself was uncharacteristic of Bennett, unless he had some ulterior motive; he was a person who needed money to maintain his lifestyle. He was something of a dandy, said to change his collar and cuffs three times a day, and always travelled first class. If honesty held any attraction at all, he could have earned far more running a grocery business than as a tiny cog in a factory wheel. However, it is pointless to speculate over motives; whatever it was, he soon found an incentive to stay in that routine – through a workmate, he met and fell for a pretty young parlourmaid, Alice Meadows.

Although he continued to call on his wife and baby (claiming the visits were to a cousin and his wife), he courted Alice in London at least twice a week, and through correspondence, as though he were completely free of any ties. Although he lied to the girl about almost everything, his behaviour was never less than gentlemanly, and he made no effort to seduce her even when she agreed to spend a weekend in Yarmouth with him, and subsequently a two-week's holiday in Ireland. Bearing in mind his salary was barely thirty shillings a week, and that he was fully supporting Mary and the baby, one wonders how he could afford to conduct such an expensive courtship, especially in view of the fact that the journey to South Africa must have taken a chunk from the proceeds of his insurance swindle. The conclusion must be that there was another source of income which never came to light.

Whatever 'fiddle' Bennett was conducting, he had integrity. Although Alice had undoubtedly replaced Mary in his affections, he never made any attempt to wriggle out of his responsibilities. For a man of his deviousness it would have been simple merely to disappear. Not only did he stay in contact, but Mary knew where he lived. On one occasion in August, her next-door neighbour sent a telegram which read: 'Try come home M very ill'. When his landlady anxiously took the message to his office, he explained that his 'cousin' was ill. Dutifully he left at once for Bexleyheath on his bicycle, returning next day with the grim news that his cousin was not expected to live. (Usually the cousin had been called 'Fred'; this time he referred to 'she', but Bennett was never consistent or even constructive in his lies, because Mary's illness was obviously shortlived.)

At the end of the month Bennett gave Alice a ruby and diamond engagement ring, and they fixed the date for their marriage for the following June, another indication that his behaviour throughout – apart from the lies – continued to be reasonable. Their lifestyle was that of any other normal engaged couple; there was no suspicion of an obsessive passion such as might have compelled him to kill his wife rather than waste another day in separation. Judging by his record to date, Bennett would no doubt have taken bigamy in his stride, continuing to treat each wife correctly and without favour.

A few weeks after Bennett and Alice returned from Ireland, Mary told her neighbour that her husband was taking her and the baby to Yorkshire. As we have seen, Mary was as accomplished a liar as Bennett, and her journey was in fact to Yarmouth. The lies came in a flood. Using the name 'Mrs Hood', Mary arrived at the boarding house of Mrs Eliza Rudrum, claiming to be a widow and coming from York. On the first night, having put the baby to bed, she went out and returned late. Her tongue somewhat loosened by drink, she confided in Mrs Rudrum that she had been conducted to Yarmouth by her brother-in-law who was jealous enough to follow her about and was 'madly in love' with her. For the rest of the week she was in by nine, but on Friday after receiving a letter she had been expecting she went out and returned late, saying that she had been lost. In fact Mrs Rudrum's daughter, Alice, had seen her outside the house under an arch. She had heard a man's voice say: 'You understand, don't you? I am placed in an awkward position just now.' The window had been open and she distinctly heard the sound of a kiss.

On Saturday 22 September, Mary went out during the day and again, by herself, in the evening. She was wearing most of her jewellery, and there was a substantial amount of money in her purse. One cannot help wondering about the source of that money if she depended on her husband for rent and food. She was again seen by Alice Rudrum, this time at about nine in the evening outside the town hall. After that another witness saw her with a man he identified as Bennett. That identification is crucial because within another hour or so, Mary was dead – apparently killed within earshot of a nearby courting couple. The unwitting observers were a young man called Mason and his girl friend; they subsequently told the police that on a secluded part of the beach they had become aware of another couple about thirty yards away. The strangers were talking quite loudly before the woman cried out: 'Mercy, mercy!' followed by a moan. At that stage they got up and walked in the direction of the voices. As they passed, they noticed the man was on top of the woman; he looked up at them. Although the distance between them was only about five yards they could not make out his features. It did not occur to them that the woman was in trouble, and probably would not have done even had they noticed her skirt pulled up above her knees. All they remembered, in fact, was that the man was wearing a dark suit.

The witnesses were unfairly criticised by the judge at the trial for their 'miserable cowardice'; but they had merely jumped to the wrong conclusion. At six the following morning, Mary's body was found. She had been strangled with a mohair bootlace tied so tightly that the flesh had closed over it. Later that morning, by another strange coincidence, Mason, who had unconsciously witnessed the murder, was strolling on the same stretch of beach when he saw a man in a blue suit and cap apparently searching for something he had lost; he appeared to be agitated, but since Mason had no reason to imagine there was any connection with the earlier incident, his attention was soon distracted.

The police had little to go on. Judging from blood on her underclothes, the woman had been assaulted, but there was no suggestion she had been surprised by her attacker, and it was reasonable to think it may have been the outcome of a situation which had got out of hand. The bootlace had been tied with a reef knot followed by a granny knot which might have suggested the murderer understood knots and was therefore a seafarer, but that was a big assumption. Moreover there were no means of identifying the body; even after Mrs Rudrum had reported her lodger missing, the name 'Mrs Hood' meant nothing in isolation, especially as the only information given to the landlady had all been untrue. Indeed, the only information she could add was that Mrs Hood had been wearing a considerable amount of jewellery, but since the gold watch and chain was the only item apparently missing, robbery seemed a dubious motive. Coincidentally, Mary had been photographed that week while wearing the watch and chain – the police circulated copies but without success.

The only clue – a laundry number on the baby's clothing – was worthless without a town or even an area in which to start a search; the police did try, but a month later, the inquest verdict had to refer to an 'unknown woman' murdered by an 'unknown man'. Ultimately she was buried in a local churchyard, in an unmarked grave. However, in due course Mrs Rudrum recalled that the letter received by Mrs Hood on the day before her murder had had a Woolwich post mark. That single piece of information provided the breakthrough the police needed, enabling them to localise the search for the owner of their laundry mark. Tracing it to a Mrs Bennett at a Bexleyheath address they were able to establish something of her background, that she had been ill in August when her husband had been to visit her, and that she had received letters for him addressed to 'J.H. Bartlett'.

They were able to track down the husband because of a minor business transaction which had gone wrong, when an aggrieved associate was pleased to add to the police store of circumstantial evidence underlined by Bennett's apparent inability to tell the truth. The new witness explained that he had originally bought Bennett's bicycle. When they met in June, Bennett had said that his wife was an accomplished pianist, yet when he was invited to Bexleyheath in October to inspect a piano for sale, Bennett denied having a wife, taking the opportunity to mention that he was soon to be married. The man paid a deposit on the piano, but later decided he had been overcharged, and the pair quarrelled. It was he who arranged to meet Bennett, and identify him in order for a plain clothes inspector to make the arrest. When charged, Bennett said, 'I don't understand what you mean. I have never been to Yarmouth. I have never lived with my wife since January, as I found a lot of letters in her pocket from another man.'

Nothing is known of any letters from another man but the denial of ever having been to Yarmouth was foolish, since it was only a few months that he had stayed with Alice Meadows at the Crown and Anchor Hotel (in separate rooms), having first written to Mrs Rudrum, who had been fully booked. Local police enquiries revealed that the man who had stayed at the Crown and Anchor hotel with a woman friend in August, had returned alone on 15 September (the day of Mary's arrival in Yarmouth) leaving again the next morning. Although Mary had turned up on the Rudrum's doorstep alone, an unidentified man had been seen with her only minutes earlier, and she subsequently admitted having been brought by her 'brother-in-law'. Since the trip had been arranged by Bennett and it was undoubtedly his letter she was to receive later in the week, it seems likely that she was accompanied by her husband, but Bennett denied it, despite the fact that he had told Alice he could not see her on that date because he had to go to see his sick grandfather in Gravesend, another lie. The more crucial date was the following Saturday when he again cried off a meeting with his fiancée. The problem with a congenital liar is that one automatically assumes that *everything* he says is a lie; besides which, although a waiter stated that the guest he believed to be Bennett left on Sunday morning, catching the 7.20 to London, a friend of his future mother-in-law remembered speaking to him near her home in Stepney at least fifteen minutes before that train could have arrived at Liverpool Street station. But above all, it was Bennett's string of lies which made the Crown case so convincing.

On the Monday after Mary's arrival in Yarmouth he was telling people of the recent tragic death of his wife and baby in South Africa; later in the week he told the landlord of the house he rented for her that she was ill in Yorkshire and that he wanted to terminate the lease because he was going to America. At the same time Alice Meadows was encouraged to learn that he had obtained some of the furniture for their future home from his cousin in Bexleyheath, because she was going to South Africa. One cannot say for certain whether these were all deliberate lies, or whether it was all part of Bennett's fantasy world, because after his arrest a police search of his lodgings unearthed such unlikely articles as a revolver, a false moustache, wigs for a man *and* a woman, and – most incriminating of all – a watch with a long gold-link chain, assumed to have belonged to Mary Bennett. To compound his series of lies, Bennett then offered the clincher – two men whom he claimed could provide him with an alibi for the night of the murder; the problem was that his witnesses *had* met him at the place he named, but a week later than the one day that mattered. There is no suggestion that he had attempted to bribe these men, yet he could not have imagined that such a weak ploy would bear close examination.

By the time the newspapers had finished with him, the defence faced an almost impossible task. Although the trial was moved from Norfolk to the Old Bailey, many of the witnesses who had been interviewed by reporters posing as detectives, were incapable of distinguishing fact from conjecture, or from information originally fed to them as 'fact'. Experienced as they were, Marshall Hall and his colleagues believed that the one true statement Bennett *had* made was that he had not killed his wife, and they decided to contest every piece of evidence, working away at the whole fabric of the Crown case.

He began with the most vital piece of evidence – the watch and chain Mary had been given by her grandmother. It undoubtedly helped that Marshall Hall happened to have an interest in jewellery, and was on familiar territory. Examining the beach photograph under a magnifying glass, he realised the chain was different to the one found in Bennett's possession. Having checked his belief, he was able to call an expert witness who testified that the one in the photograph was a rope chain of the 'Prince of Wales' style, while the other was an old-fashioned link chain. In cross examination, the beach photographer had to agree that the chains were different, and it was not due to any optical illusion. The issue was contested by the prosecution, but Marshall Hall had done enough to counter the implication that the chain in Bennett's possession in itself connected him with his wife's death.

Marshall Hall's attention to detail also damaged the credibility of several witnesses, establishing that certain facts had been remembered only *after* the event, when there was a person in custody with whom to relate. The hotel waiter, for example, who thought he had recognised Bennett on 15 September, now admitted that on the third date he did not think it was the same person – the moustache being heavier – and had only identified him *after* the arrest when he had read an account in the newspapers.

As well as whittling away at the prosecution evidence, Marshall Hall was able to introduce a number of factors in his client's favour. Alice Rudrum had heard a man kiss Mary Bennett on Friday, but Bennett had been at work, with time-sheets to prove it; Mason and his girl friend had stated the man on the beach had been wearing a dark suit, and it would be proved that Bennett's only dark suit had been at the cleaners at the time; furthermore Mason had seen a man in a blue suit searching for something on the beach at a time when the prosecution claimed Bennett would have been on the train to London – and when a defence witness claimed he was already there. Hall was also able to prove that much of the background evidence, such as the suggestion that he and Mary had quarrelled, had been exaggerated out of all proportion, and even fabricated by distorted newspaper accounts of interviews with witnesses who had known the couple.

With his case looking much more promising, Marshall Hall was suddenly faced with a major problem of strategy. At the eleventh hour his solicitors had been approached by an independent witness, Douglas Sholto Douglas, a respectable business man who claimed that he had been in the company of Bennett at Bexley early in the evening of 22 September, which meant that Bennett could not have been in Yarmouth in time to murder his wife because the last train had left London at 5pm.

He had not come forward at the time of the preliminary hearing because he was in a delicate stage of negotiation over a business partnership. When the two men were re-introduced it was evident they recognised each other. But while it was apparent to all that Sholto Douglas was speaking the truth, Marshall Hall was worried by the fact that although this was the perfect alibi it had never been mentioned by his client who had even fabricated a different one. Corroboration, in his opinion, was vital, and as much as he feared Bennett's unreliability in the witness box, faced with such a deadly cross-examiner as Charles Gill for the Crown, Marshall Hall eventually came to the conclusion he would have to take that risk. Later, in a letter to his friend Sir Arthur Pinero, who had criticised his decision, he described a last-minute private confrontation with his client: '. . . I said to him this: "If you will only go into the box and admit *everything* except the actual murder, I can get a verdict, but of course you must admit that when you saw the papers the day after the murder you *knew* it was your wife, but that you were afraid to communicate for fear of losing Alice Meadows."

'His reply was: "I cannot say that, because I was not at Yarmouth on the 22nd, and I never knew that the murdered woman was my wife till I was arrested." I pointed out that this was hopeless, but he declined to give evidence at all . . .'

Marshall Hall had cross-examined Sholto Douglas throughout, and knew that he was an honest witness, but for various reasons suspected he may have made a mistake over the date. In the circumstances he made it doubly clear to Bennett the risk they were taking in calling him as a witness, asking him to deliberate carefully over whether they should rely on his evidence. Bennett insisted, and in the event Hall's fears were justified. Gill did not need to attack the witness's integrity; it was enough to suggest that without corroboration, everything rested on the man's memory of an incident he had not reported at the appopriate time, and of details of Bennett he could have unconsciously picked up from newspaper reports. He did not need to prove that the witness was mistaken, merely that the jury could not rely on the memory of one man, when no one was prepared to substantiate the story.

The point was seized upon by the judge, and without any doubt was a major influence on the jury. But before they could retire, the defence threw another bombshell into the proceedings. Marshall Hall had already embarked on his closing address, when he was obliged to call another witness, a newsagent from Lowestoft, incensed that the police had taken no action over a statement he had made earlier. This man now testified that four days after the murder, a man fitting the description of the original suspect – he had scratches on his face, wore a dark suit, and had a thick dark moustache – asked for the 'best account' of the Yarmouth murder. While he studied the paper, 'groaning as he read', the newsagent had noticed that one of his bootlaces was missing, and that the other was of mohair! The evidence caused a minor sensation, but it did little to detract from the incriminating material still hanging over Bennett, and it would not have taken the jury long to have dismissed the concept of a murderer not noticing that he was still a bootlace short four days after the murder.

Marshall Hall remained convinced of his client's innocence. Apart from the belief that Bennett was too cunning to have behaved so incriminatingly (in his summing up, he drew attention to the unlikelyhood of a person who had killed his wife, going back to the one hotel where he was known), he was convinced that the killer was a sex maniac. Why should Bennett, having tired of his wife, suddenly sexually assault her, and why then? Who was the man Alice Rudrum had overheard kissing Mary Bennett – and had they met again? However, despite his efforts, which included impassioned letters to the Lord Chief Justice and the Home Secretary – this was before the days of the Court of Criminal Appeal - Bennett was hanged at Norwich Gaol on 21 March 1901. As the black flag was hoisted, the flagstaff fell from its socket, which was taken as an omen of his innocence. After that, little thought was given to the Yarmouth murderer until 1912 when Dora May Gray was found strangled on the beach in almost identical circumstances; a case which was never solved. Could it have been done by the same man? We shall never know.

My own belief is that Bennett was not a murderer, and that given the unlikely theory he wanted to clear the way to marry Alice Meadows, he did not need to take Mary to Yarmouth, to a place where he was already known. This is supported by the fact that among Mary's few belongings in Mrs Rudrum's house, the police found the return half of a first-class rail ticket from London. If Bennett had murder in mind, he would have purchased Mary a single fare. In his interesting study of murder trials, *A Reasonable Doubt* (Cresset Press, 1960), Julian Symons supports the theory of Bennett's innocence, speculating that Bennett and his wife may have got together on another scheme to make easy money – blackmail, and that he had taken her to Yarmouth to meet a prospective victim. If he had intended to kill her, why wait a whole week during which she might have said something to give the game away? Symons suggests that Bennett might have gone back on the second Saturday for a planned 'showdown' – posing as the jealous brother-in-law Mary had mentioned – but underestimated the extent of the man's passion, having been kept at arms' length during the week, and arrived to find her already dead: something he did not think anyone would believe, which is why he stuck to his story of not having been in Yarmouth on the 22nd.

For all his brilliance, Marshall Hall made an error of judgement in not vetoing his client's insistence on calling Sholto Douglas. Defence strategy may rest on two opposite stances: the *positive*, in which the defence takes the initiative, relying on the overwhelming strength of its case; or the *negative*, in which there is not much to be done except to attack the validity of the prosecution case. The alibi, going on to the offensive, is unanswerable, but will backfire if there are any doubts thrown upon it, and this time it damaged the credibility of the defence at a time when Marshall Hall may have been on his way to gaining an acquittal by hitherto negative means – proving that so much of the Crown evidence did not bear close examination. They came so near, yet failed at the final hurdle. In a letter to a friend Marshall Hall insisted: 'It is discreditable to have been unable to convince the jury of the innocence of a man you, yourself, believe to be innocent.' Yet without Marshall Hall, the trial might have been over in a couple of days. Up until the verdict, we know that Bennett was impressed by what he heard; Robert Wood, of course, had even more reason to be so.

6

SCIENCE AND THE MURDERER

Girard, Waite, Hyde and Brinkley)

Scientific discovery gathered momentum during the Edwardian age, and it was inevitable that a few twisted minds would seek to capitalise on some of this emergent knowledge in areas for which it was never intended – such as murder. Doctors had always exploited their privileged knowledge of little known poisons, but now even the informed layman had access to such dangerous information. The first significant conclusion of the twentieth century was that there was a safer alternative to traditional poisons, and that was to harness the deadly weapons of nature, *germs*, which in times of plague had decimated whole cities. The concept – to infect the victim with a virulent bacillus so that death appeared to be from natural causes – seemed ingenious, yet it met with no greater success than 'old-fashioned' poisons. This was because, even with an apparently foolproof method of killing someone, murderers are usually caught through inadequacies in their psychological make-up, such as uncontrolled greed, over-confidence, and even plain stupidity.

Cultured germs as a weapon were used in this period by at least three murderers, although perhaps the most interesting had no medical or scientific training, apart from the fact his father had been a successful chemist. He was a French confidence trickster, Henri Girard who, despite a comfortable upbringing, showed no interest in a career and settled early on for being a petty crook. Specialising in insurance fraud, Girard had an attractive personality and was smooth enough to make a decent living from the gullibility of friends and acquaintances, but an extravagant lifestyle (he kept two or three mistresses at any one time) meant that he needed other, more substantial sources of income – such as life insurance. Having killed two people, he was caught through over-confidence, although an incriminating diary, full of names and dates, left no possible doubt as to his guilt. Nevertheless, he managed to escape the guillotine by literally taking his own medicine, managing to swallow some of his own germ cultures!

Having been expelled from various schools, he was able to purchase a commission in the army, but in 1897 he was discharged from the 10th Hussars for not paying his debts. Money was the dominating influence throughout his life. Having inherited some from his mother, and constantly borrowing from his wealthy father, he even resorted to stealing his half-sister's inheritance when his stepmother died and he undertook the financial arrangements. He then conveniently disappeared, as he did with so many of his 'deals' – most of them crooked. He was ambitious, and one of his schemes was to set up the Crédit Général de France to deal in lottery tickets and securities, but the money pouring in for re-investment actually remained in his own pocket, until the fraud was discovered. Fortunately for him the swindle was so complex that he escaped with a twelve months' suspended sentence. In fact, his 'wheeling and dealing' was such a tangled mess that, after his arrest, a one-hundred page report compiled by a financial expert failed to reach any clear conclusions as to the extent of his sources of income.

Girard needed extensive funds because of his lifestyle. Although his criminal activities were relatively trouble-free, his sexual relations were generally more complicated, and at one stage he was actually fined for adultery. Girard soon realised that the charisma and smooth talk he used instinctively to charm women would serve him well in a job: selling insurance, and once the idea had occurred to him, his instinctive dishonesty made him think of ways of maximising the potential income. It is not clear which came first: the decision to murder for profit, or the method of doing so, but it was in his middle forties that Girard suddenly developed an interest in bacteriology, buying books on the subject, and then laboratory apparatus to conduct his own experiments. Once he was familiar with the discipline, he was able to obtain quantities of typhoid cultures from wholesale chemists in Paris.

His first victim was a Parisian insurance broker, Louis Pernotte, whom he had cultivated as a friend (friendship helped him probe for personal details which would be useful later in completing application forms for life insurance). So persuasive was Girard, so sophisticated and apparently well educated, that the amiable but indecisive Pernotte was soon under his spell and by 1910, within a few months of their relationship, he had given him power of attorney over his estate. What he did not know was that his trusted friend – that enormous tower of strength – had also insured his life with two insurance companies for a total of 300,000 francs.

In 1912, totally trusted, Girard felt it was time to act and after a short visit to Pernotte's home, the broker, his wife and two children were suddenly taken ill with typhoid fever attributed to their somewhat primitive habit of drinking water from an earthenware vessel. Fortunately for them, the symptoms of the illness were evident to the family doctor and he was able to prescribe the necessary treatment. Later he was to comment on the uncharacteristic 'pureness' of the strain found in the water, almost as though it might have been cultivated in a test tube; but at the time there was obviously no cause for suspicion. Mrs Pernotte and the children soon recovered, but the intended victim made slower progress, and was still being treated for the illness when Girard called again.

Pernotte was relieved to see his friend, a familiar trusted face in whom he could confide not only his disappointment at the length of time it was taking to recover his health, but also the almost embarrassing admission that part of the treatment – injections of camphorated camomile – was uncomfortable . . . Girard was reassuringly sympathetic . . . why was that? Conscious of the presence of his wife, Pernotte admitted that he did not like injections; that the needle hurt! As he may have hoped, Girard, as always, had the solution to the problem – handling a hypodermic needle was merely a matter of technique and he could guarantee to be gentle – the patient would not feel a thing.

Knowing that he was totally above suspicion, Girard then put on a somewhat unconvincing performance, addressing Mrs Pernotte: 'Notice, Madame, that it is quite definitely your own syringe,' and before administering the injection, 'You observe that I have nothing in my hands'. It was not until years later that Mrs Pernotte had reason to reflect on those words, but at the time there were no grounds for suspicion, even when the patient died a few days later from what appeared to be a cardiac embolism.

Having drawn the substantial proceeds of his friend's two policies, Girard was encouraged to try again – but from now on encountered problems. He began by persuading a neighbour, M Godel to join him in a joint life insurance policy whereby, in the event of someone's death, the money would go to the surviving partner. In due course, Godel was taken ill with typhoid fever – but recovered, and for some reason was suspicious of his fellow policy-holder, sensibly refusing to see him again. After the outbreak of the Great War, Girard was conscripted and eventually selected one of his comrades, Émile Delmas as his next victim, managing to get hold of his papers so that he could filch the necessary insurance particulars. The incentive was 40,000 francs, but by now Girard was running short of funds. Delmas developed typhoid, but was taken immediately to an army hospital, and recovered.

After that failure Girard decided his cultures were too unreliable and to concentrate on mycology (the science of fungi), which he began with a supply of poisonous mushrooms, *Amanita phalloides*. To the concierge who remarked on how appetising the mushrooms looked, he admitted their poison content, and explained their presence by claiming that he was working on a new poisonous gas for the army. In the event he was just as unsuccessful with fungi as he had been with his cultures; two friends on whom he tried them were violently ill, but survived the experience.

By 1918 Girard appeared to be lowering his sights. No longer 'playing the field', he had actually succumbed to domesticity, marrying one of his mistresses, Jeanne Drouhin, although she maintained the pretence to some extent by retaining her own name and single status. In April of that year, well briefed by her husband, she developed a friendship with a war widow, Mme Monin, a milliner, who had no money but who could be insured with four different companies. The outlay could have been expensive, but in fact cost nothing because as an insurance agent Girard was entitled to the first premium as commission, and he got rid of her before the second premium was due. He got the information he needed by informing her that she was heiress to a fortune and that he needed to double-check personal details. On the pretext of ordering a hat, Mme Monin was lured to the Girard apartment where she was given a 'doctored' apéritif and hurriedly sent on her way. In the Metro, she was overcome with violent pains and dizziness and taken home in a taxi by a couple of gendarmes who then called a doctor, but this time the dose was sufficient and she died the next day.

A week later, Girard turned up at one of the insurance companies and received 20,000 francs, but his wife ran into problems. At two offices signing the receipt 'veuve (widowed) Monin, Jeanne Drouhin', in other words signing as the beneficiary, she was paid in full, but at the third – already suspicious about the death so soon after the policy had been taken – she was recognised as the woman who had originally posed as Mme Monin. The company refused to pay on the policy.

The post mortem revealed nothing to account for death, except the symptoms of mushroom poisoning. Linked to the suspicious circumstances of the insurance policies, the police decided to take Girard in for questioning, and it was while he was in custody that his premises at Neuilly were searched, and the research laboratory discovered. In addition to the apparatus and books, they found a box containing bacteriological cultures, including tetanus, anthrax and Eberth's bacillus; there were also capsules of strychnine and potassium cyanide. Despite his incriminating diary, the police took three years to complete their enquiries, largely because of the complexity of Girard's financial affairs. But the writing was on the wall in May 1921 when Girard decided to kill himself. His wife was subsequently tried and sentenced to life imprisonment.

Although they could not have been more different physically, Girard and Dr Arthur Warren Waite, twenty-eight-year-old American dentist, shared a common interest in the 'good life', which in their view meant wine, women and song, a regime which had to be supported by a considerable income. Neither were prepared to regulate their extravagances, or earn their money by conventional means, and both resorted to murder for what they might have regarded as business purposes. Girard was the archetypal Frenchman – a ringer for Charlie Chaplain's Monsieur Verdoux – small, neatly elegant and conscious of his appearance down to the trimmed and waxed moustache. Waite was tall and handsome, the 'all-American' college product who not only looked like the sporting hero but was in fact a competition standard tennis player.

In view of what we now know, Waite's good looks and charming manner seem too good to be true, almost a caricature of the fortune hunter; but when he married Clara Peck in 1915, he was considered such an eligible young batchelor that few people gave a second's thought to the fact that Clara's father, a retired druggist, was a millionaire. They seemed an ideal match, and John Peck and his wife were thrilled with their son-in-law. The fact that he had not yet established himself in a career (they knew he had qualified as a dental surgeon at Glasgow University, and gained some experience in South Africa) seemed of little consequence, and the arrangement was that until he had established himself in a practice, father-in-law would continue Clara's substantial allowance, and advance him any money he might need. In fact, Arthur so ingratiated himself with the Peck family that his noble career in medicine and his career prospects were far more important than his income. Aunt Catherine so admired him and respected his judgement in all matters that she entrusted him with £10,000 to invest on her behalf.

The Waites were soon ensconced in a New York mansion, provided by John Peck, and since Arthur had no intention of 'wasting' Aunt Catherine's money on investments, he already had a substantial personal income, which removed any incentive to start his career in dentistry. He occupied his spare time between social engagements in developing a genuine interest in bacteriology, becoming a willing pupil of the doctor he befriended, who happened to be in charge of the appropriate department at one of the better hospitals. In fact, he spent so much time there that on one occasion when Clara came to visit him, he deposited her in a waiting room until he had completed the 'operation' on which he was supposed to be engaged.

Always the perfect son-in-law, Waite insisted that the Pecks travel up from their home in Grand Rapids, Michigan to stay for a while. Despite his undoubted hospitality, the change of climate did not seem to agree with Mr Peck who was soon ill. Waite treated his father-in-law with throat and nasal sprays, but they seemed to have little effect (hardly surprising, since the spray contained tuberculosis bacteria), yet when the older man returned home he made a complete recovery. However, when Mrs Peck returned to New York to complete her broken holiday, it was her turn to be ill. Waite insisted on calling in another doctor to share his vigil. When the other man suggested the illness was not serious, Waite disagreed and expressed his fears that she was on the verge of death. His diagnosis was the more accurate, and she died on 30 January 1916, from what the two doctors agreed was kidney disease.

Apparently grief-stricken, Waite insisted on accompanying the body back to the Peck home where he announced that her last wish had been to be cremated. It did not occur to anyone to contest that statement. John Peck had been shattered by his wife's unexpected death, but agreed to return to New York to comfort his grieving daughter. He arrived in February and was almost at once taken ill.

Although he had no regular work, Waite contrived to leave home in the mornings and stay out for most of the day. More often than not he was with one of his regular girl friends, and eventually they were seen together, by a member of the Peck family, also a doctor. Waite sought to nip the threat in the bud by confronting the man and his woman companion, claiming that he was 'rewarding' a nurse who had worked particularly hard during an operation earlier that day. The story may have been acceptable to the relation who knew what tough work some operations could be, but his companion, with a woman's intuition, was not fooled by the obvious intimacy between Waite and his attractive 'nurse'.

Meanwhile, despite the presence of another doctor, John Peck's condition continued to deteriorate, and still no-one suspected anything, even when a nurse saw Waite on different occasions pouring 'medicine' into the patient's soup and tea to disguise the taste about which Peck had complained – it was the type of considerate behaviour they might have expected of Waite. The death certificate in March also gave the cause as kidney failure; in other words from natural causes. Although the body was sent to be embalmed in preparation for the journey to Grand Rapids, Waite warned the family that Mr Peck had also expressed the wish to be cremated.

However, there was just one member of the family who did not share the universal admiration for Waite – Clara's only brother Percival, who had now inherited half share in the $1 million left by their father. Already more than unhappy about the sudden deaths of his parents, his suspicions were confirmed by a telegram instructing him to demand an autopsy. The mysterious cable, signed 'K. Adams', which meant nothing to anyone, transpired later to have come from the young woman who had recognised Waite's attractive nurse as his probable mistress. Not only did he take the advice, but also employed a firm of private detectives to keep a watch on his brother-in-law.

The post mortem discovered a fatal dose of arsenic, and Waite first anticipated trouble when the undertaker asked Waite if he could be paid before the cremation. Waite wondered why he could not wait, and discovered that the undertaker feared that he might never get paid . . . in the circumstances. *What* circumstances? When Waite learned there was 'talk' of arsenic, he offered the undertaker $9000 to say that he had added arsenic to the embalming fluid, but the man lost his nerve and reported the attempted bribe.

Later that month, Waite tried to commit suicide by a

drug overdose, but recovered to face trial when he adopted an interesting ploy – claiming that he had a Jekyll and Hyde personality; that the 'Man from Egypt' inside him was the real murderer; that he was fond of the Pecks and wanted to save them (justifying his plea of not guilty) but the Egyptian was too powerful for him. The story was so wild by Edwardian standards that a body of opinion believed he must be speaking the truth. As part of that defence of insanity, he admitted premeditation and volunteered details of the murders, merely insisting that *he* had not been responsible. He told the court that he had killed his mother-in-law by implanting diphtheria and influenza germs in her food, and used the same methods on John Peck. When that did not seem to be working quickly enough he fell back on conventional poison, dosing him with eighteen grains of arsenic. Implying that he had not wanted to see his father-in-law suffer, he added: 'I gave him some chloroform and when he was unconscious I placed a pillow over his head, and kept it there until he died.'

His insanity tack dismissed, Waite was sentenced to die in the electric chair in May 1917. A few days before the execution, he was reading the Bible in his cell and told one of his guards: 'I was looking at the ten commandments and found I had broken all but one – the one about profanity. I have never been profane.'

People assume that, if only because of the years of study entailed, the person who qualifies as a doctor must be very intelligent. However, the number of medical men who have resorted to murder but come unstuck through their own shortcomings, demonstrates that the assumption does not bear close scrutiny. The American general practitioner, Bennett Clarke Hyde, who was forty when he implemented an ingenious scheme to make himself a millionaire, had more than his share of cunning, yet the way in which he carried out his plan was little short of stupid. Nevertheless, the foolish Dr Hyde may have had the last laugh – obviously guilty of three murders, he was convicted, yet through his wife's money he was able to escape justice.

Five years earlier, Hyde had married Frances Swope, niece

of Thomas B. Swope, the Kentucky colonel, famous as the founder of Kansas City, who had become a multi-millionaire through property. For all his faults, the Colonel was a shrewd judge of character and took an instant dislike to the latest member of the family, whom he recognised as a gold digger, and in his own down-to-earth language 'a sonofabitch'! But, worshipping money and power, Hyde set out to ingratiate himself, and over the years came to be accepted, if not liked. Hyde's incentive was that Swope was over eighty, and Frances might expect a small share in the Swope fortune of approaching $3 million. The more he thought about the prospect, the more he objected to being kept waiting, and then having to share. There was a frustrating clause that if any of the benefactors died, their share would go back into the pool.

The immediate stumbling block was Swope's executor, James Hunton, an elderly cousin but also a close and trusted friend of the Colonel. Hyde calculated that by getting rid of the executor he might persuade the old man to appoint him in his place; he may not be a favourite but was respected enough to have been appointed family doctor. His opportunity arose in September 1909, when the whole family were assembled at the Colonel's mansion at Independence, Missouri. As well as Colonel Swope, Hunton, Hyde and his wife, there were the Colonel's two batchelor sons, his brother's widow, and her three daughters.

When Hunton was suddenly taken ill with a fever, Hyde ordered him to bed, and although he was now the trusted family physician, insisted on calling in a second opinion, the man he had replaced, Dr Twyman, who agreed with his diagnosis of typhoid. The doctors, working together, did all they could but Hunton died two days later. Hyde's hopes of becoming executor were then dashed, so he decided there was no point hanging about. Almost overnight, Swope went down with the same fever. With excellent care he seemed to rally slightly but he eventually died two weeks later, on 3 October. Hyde attributed the cause of death to 'apoplexy'.

Through Frances' inheritance, the Hydes were now quite rich, but the doctor was not satisfied, and decided to get the entire fortune by wiping out all the other beneficiaries in one devastating 'plague' of typhoid. On Sunday 21 November, his mother-in-law gave a dinner party, after which all the guests were taken ill – except Frances. In view of the earlier outbreaks, typhoid was immediately suspected as the cause, and samples of the water from the household cystern sent for analysis, but no trace of any contamination was found. Some of the family were very ill, and the Colonel's son, Christopher actually died. Meanwhile, one of Frances' sisters the only member of the family who had not been at the dinner – was on her way back from a holiday in Europe, and Hyde considerately offered to go and meet her. She, too, was taken ill with similar symptoms after accepting a glass of water from her brother-in-law!

However, while the outside world regarded the calamity as an act of God, there were rumblings among the small army of nurses who had been recruited to take care of the houseful of patients; they had seen a number of suspicious goings on. Their spokesman confronted Mrs Swope and warned her that people were being murdered before their eyes. When she asked whom they suspected, she was told.

Although she found the allegation difficult to believe, Mrs Swope nevertheless confronted her daughter and son-in-law and, suitably offended, the couple left the house – which hardly helped their case because the survivors immediately began to get better! Mrs Swope now had no alternative but to approach a family friend, a former district attorney, and ask him to conduct an investigation into the events of the past months. As a result of his findings, the bodies of Hunton and Swope were exhumed, and traces of strychnine found.

Hyde was arrested, and released on bail of $100,000 put up by his wife, but at the trial the evidence was overwhelming. The police were able to prove that Hyde had borrowed typhoid bacilli from a colleague on the pretext of conducting experiments. Moreover, their medical experts demonstrated that once his victims were ill, and the cause established, he speeded up the process with poison, deliberately setting out to confuse the issue with conflicting symptoms produced by two very different poisons, strychnine and cyanide; the former acting on the nerves of the heart to produce convulsions, and the latter slowing the heart and congealing the blood. They also produced evidence that he had purchased cyanide on three occasions, for 'killing rats', while one of the nurses testified that she had seen Dr Hyde drop a capsule in the snow outside the house, and being suspicious had followed him out to pick it up; it had contained cyanide.

Such was the quality of the top lawyers engaged by Mrs Hyde that the trial dragged on for a month, and the jury was out for all of three days before arriving at the inevitable verdict, murder in the first degree, for which Hyde was sentenced to life imprisonment. However, money is a powerful motivator, and Mrs Hyde's lawyers left no stone unturned to get another hearing. There were two further trials, the first ending prematurely when a juror was taken ill, and the next where the jury failed to agree. Seven years were to elapse before the lawyers tried yet again, asking for a dismissal of the charges and the prosecution agreed! Hyde went free – his only 'punishment' was that his wife then divorced him. He died, still practising as a doctor, in August 1934.

Science was also being harnessed in the war against crime, the most significant development being the first workable system of recording fingerprints, introduced by Scotland Yard in 1901. Among the scientific landmarks in criminology was the trial in July 1907 of Richard Brinkley who poisoned two people (and almost certainly a third) with prussic acid concealed in a bottle of stout. Central to Brinkley's scheme was a fake will he had had drawn up; he claimed it had been signed by witnesses using the same supply of ink. But scientific evidence revealed that the inks had been different, and therefore could not have come from one source.

The Brinkley case, coincidentally, was also interesting because of the ingenuity of his original plan. A jobbing carpenter, Brinkley set about ingratiating himself with the owner of a house in west London at which he had occasionally called, Mrs Joanna Blume, a seventy-seven-year old German born widow, who lived with her young grand-daughter. Although his initial excuse was to help out with odd jobs, Brinkley's visits became more social, calling in to see her four or five times a week while her grand-daughter was at work. He would greet her affectionately, and call her 'Granny'.

In view of his declared interest in the welfare of old people, it was no surprise to Mrs Blume when he announced his generous plan to take a number of them on a day's outing to the seaside; she was only too pleased to add her signature to the list of names he was compiling. What she did not notice, however, was that the paper thrust in front of her had been neatly folded over; the part she could not see was her will and testament. In ignorance, she had with one squiggle of the pen cut off her intended beneficiary, her grand-daughter, and left everything – the house and contents, and her money (a little under £1,000) – to Brinkley. The will was witnessed by two associates, Henry Heard and Reginald Parker (who, since Brinkley was almost illiterate, had drawn up the will), both taken in by the same ruse of the seaside outing, and signing over a folded blank sheet of paper.

Two days later, Mrs Blume was dead. It was very sudden and unexpected, but the authorities do not normally have any cause to suspect foul play in the case of a person of that age. The situation is recalled by Mr S. Ingleby Oddie, then deputy coroner of the area, in his memoirs, *Inquest* (Hutchinson, 1941). The pathologist, having found no signs of natural disease, nevertheless decided that death had been due to apoplexy (cerebral haemhorrhage). Since such deaths, happening so quickly, were invariably due to very large haemhorrhages in the brain, while Mrs Blume's had been very small, Mr Oddie remembers that he was not entirely happy – yet in the absence of an alternative solution and the pathologist's assurance it was a natural death, the jury were directed to bring in the appropriate verdict.

The verdict left the way clear for Brinkley to realise his 'inheritance', but Mrs Blume's grand-daughter went to consult a solicitor. There was no doubt the old lady's signature was genuine, but the solicitor agreed that the fact the will had been signed only two days before her death, and the fact that everything had been left to a stranger, gave them grounds for contesting it. They entered a *caveat*, calling on Brinkley to prove the validity of the will. Brinkley, having raised some ready cash by selling or pawning odd items of Mrs Blume's possessions, was unprepared for that reaction and now behaved with unbelievable naïevité.

Faced with the problem of persuading his two witnesses to support the lie that they had signed Mrs Blume's will in her presence – possibly countering any reluctance to commit perjury with an appropriate bribe – he chose instead to call on Mrs Blume's widowed daughter (the girl's mother) suggesting an arrangement in which, if she agreed to have the litigation dropped, he would marry her! As though expecting her to swoon at the prospect, he further encouraged her with the promise that he was prepared to move in with her there and then. If there was the faintest possibility of her even considering his proposal, it would have been dashed by his further magnanimous offer to make love to her young daughter occasionally!

Plan B was to get rid of the witnesses to the will, starting with Mr Parker. However, his unexpected friendly overtures were met with increasing suspicion, and at one stage Parker told a friend that if anything happened to him the police need look no further than the carpenter. But Brinkley's desperation made him doggedly persistent, and Parker could not get rid of him, feeling relatively safe as long as he did not eat or drink anything Brinkley might have contaminated. He certainly had no intention of sampling the bottle of oatmeal stout Brinkley had brought to 'celebrate' the purchase of a bulldog Parker had obtained for him. The bottle was left on the table while the two men went out to inspect the dog, and in their absence Parker's landlord, Mr Beck and his wife and daughter arrived and fancied a drink. A mouthful was enough to kill Mr and Mrs Beck, although their daughter recovered in hospital after several days. The symptoms in all three cases were of prussic acid poisoning.

On advice from Parker, the police arrested Brinkley and charged him with the double murder. At the trial, he was caught out in blatant lies, as well as being linked to the purchase of prussic acid. However, when Parker insisted he had unknowingly witnessed the will (ie having written his name on a sheet of paper with the top folded over), with ink borrowed in a public house, it might have been a question of his word against that of Brinkley – who claimed it had been witnessed in the presence of Mrs Blume, at her home. A bottle of ink was obtained from that public house and Parker asked to repeat his signature, and with the help of a tintometer to analyse the constituent parts of the ink, the Crown was able to demonstrate that the two inks were the same. Furthermore it was possible to prove that the signatures on the will had been completed with *three* distinctively different inks. Asked for an explanation, Brinkley claimed that Mrs Blume had actually had three types of ink in the house, and for some reason all three had been used. But in a search of the house, only one had been found; what had happened to the other two? Tamely, Brinkley asked the court to believe he had given them to a little girl.

Brinkley was found guilty and hanged at Wandsworth prison in the following month. Meanwhile, the body of Mrs Blume had been exhumed but nothing found to change the original verdict of natural causes, although this may well have been because prussic acid is such a volatile substance.

7

UNSOLVABLE PUZZLES

The Gorse Hall, Bingham and Luard murders

My reference in earlier chapters to the unreliability of eye-witnesses was not intended as a criticism of the people involved. We have to accept the fact that the human eye is less efficient than the camera, and when suddenly put to the test, a startled individual often has only a split second, possibly in poor light, to register his or her impression. But even when the conditions are good, positive identification does not necessarily lead to conviction – nor should it, in certain circumstances.

In what has become known as the Gorse Hall murder in 1909, the first suspect arrested by the police was confidently identified by *four* witnesses, yet the Crown case did not stand up at the trial. Five months later, a second man, remarkably similar in appearance, was apprehended – the only time in British legal history that two people have been charged with the same murder. This man was also picked out in a line-up, although not with the same conviction – but the defence played on the fact that the witnesses had been wrong before, and this element of doubt was enough for a second acquittal. The murder remains unsolved, with just a glimmer of suspicion that the witnesses may have known more than they admitted – including the victim who, in his dying breath after a lengthy struggle, denied that he had known his assailant.

The murdered man, George Henry Storrs, was killed at his isolated manor house, Gorse Hall at Dunkinfield near Stalybridge, Cheshire, ostensibly by an intruder, in circumstances pointing to attempted robbery. However, since the intruder had behaved threateningly on a previous occasion, and both times announced his presence with considerable recklessness, robbery does not seem a likely motive. Afterwards, it was said that Mr Storrs had no enemies, but his reputation as a tough, self-made millionaire suggests he may not have attained his eminent place in society, from humble origins, without upsetting a few people en route.

The first indication that the intruder was no ordinary burglar was the manner of his initial appearance in September of that year. The house was set in grounds so imposing that the Lodge gates were a mile away. Facing the gates was a local mens' club – the only sign of civilisation in a barren area which consisted mainly of disused quarries. Storrs and his wife were sitting with their niece, Marion Lindley, in their drawing-room one evening after dinner, when they were disturbed by a noise in the shrubbery outside the French windows. The curtains were drawn, so it was a disembodied man's voice which threatened: 'Hold up your hands, or I'll shoot!'

Although they could not see anyone – and it was unlikely the man could see through the curtains – there seemed little doubt he was addressing them. Before they could react there was the sound of a gunshot, and then of breaking glass. This time Storrs leapt to his feet, drew the curtains and looked out. It was apparent from the gun in the man's hand that he had used the butt to smash the window. The men stared at each other for a few moments, and then the stranger made off into the night. Mrs Storrs held on to her husband's arm to prevent him from giving chase.

As a result of their unnerving experience, Storrs installed an alarm bell powerful enough to be heard in Stalybridge, and the police agreed to post a local constable in the grounds every evening. The twin deterrent seemed to work because there were no further incidents for almost a couple of months until November, night of the local elections, when Storrs agreed that the officer on duty should be released to assist his colleagues with their extra duties. We do not know if the gunman had been watching the premises, but significantly in the absence of the guard he struck again. This time he entered through the kitchen, frightening the cook, Mary Evans, with the threat: 'Not a word! Speak and I will shoot!'

Terrified, the woman reacted in a way he could not have anticipated – ignoring the gun, and fleeing from the kitchen, through the hall, into the living-room to warn her employer. Mr Storrs was playing Patience; his wife and Marion Lindley (who had been with them since she was a few months old and was more like a daughter) reading and sewing. Hot on the heels of the cook was the housemaid, Eliza Cooper, who had also had a good view of the gunman. She had barely reached the apparent sanctuary of the living-room when Mr Storrs thrust the women aside and confronted the intruder, now in the hall. Perhaps he was too accustomed to authority to worry about the small matter of guns, because he did not hesitate. At just under fifty, the building contractor may have been past his physical peak, but he was almost six feet tall and heavily framed – apparently more than a match for the stranger, who was much smaller.

At that stage, most burglars would have turned on their heels to escape, or endeavoured to restore the 'authority' imposed by the gun. For what must be obvious reasons he would try to say as little as possible – all of which makes this man's reaction: 'Now I've got you!' (unmistakably a threat) so uncharacteristic. One wonders what else he might have said had not Storrs closed with him, and they began to fight. Although much smaller, the gunman was wiry and reasonably strong, judging by the struggle he put up as Mr Storrs concentrated on trying to wrest the revolver away.

In view of Storrs' physical advantages, it must have seemed evident to the women that the gunman was no longer a serious threat, because Mrs Storrs did not hesitate to join in and grab the gun. Still confident, her husband instructed her to go to the landing to sound the alarm, while at last the others sprang into action, the two servants hurrying out to the nearby stables above which the remaining servant, coachman John Worrell lived with his wife. Miss Lindley, although aware of a long bladed knife in the man's pocket, followed them out to use the telephone at the club opposite the Lodge gates, or hoping to meet anyone responding to the loud noise of the bell. It is a measure of confidence in the millionaire that all four women were prepared to leave the men fighting, instead of trying to assist him. In the event, it was the knife Miss Lindley had seen which made all the difference, and Mr Storrs was stabbed fifteen times. Even so, he retained enough strength to subdue his assailant, push him into the scullery and lock the door – effectively trapping him – before his strength gave out and he collapsed.

Almost twenty minutes after the break-in, Marion Lindley returned having collected several men, including a police constable (she was fortunate that the club had been full of members gathered to hear the election results). However, understandably, they concentrated their attention on the dying man, unaware that his assailant had escaped through a window. To a question from one of the newcomers, Mr Storrs claimed he was unable to describe the man with whom he had been fighting for at least fifteen minutes, although whether that was because he was in a state of shock, or dying, is not clear. He was certainly bemused, concerned by the somewhat surprising fact that his wife had not returned, and yet remarkably unconcerned about the whereabouts of his attacker. However, he was quite clear when he answered 'no' to the police officer's question about the man's identity. It was clear he did not know him . . . or was it? One theory is that he knew the man – possibly an illegitimate son – and that he did not have a clear conscience.

Despite the chaotic outcome, the police were able to issue the following description: 'About 25 to 27 years of age, 5ft 6in in height, thin features, very fair to pale complexion, slight moustache, very light. He is supposed to be dressed in a brownish mixture cap, and dark tweed suit. He has the appearance of a working man.' Accompanying the description was a £100 reward, later increased by the family to £500, but to no effect.

About two weeks later there was a second tragedy at Gorse Hall when the coachman, John Worrall, hanged himself – according to the coroner's jury because he was broken-hearted by his employer's death. The police did not link the two deaths, and there does not seem to be a connection as Worrall was in his flat at the time of the break-in. However, one cannot help wondering if there was not more to it; it is unusual, to say the least, for a servant to commit suicide through grief in such circumstances. Meanwhile, police issued the description (very similar to that of the original 'wanted' notice) of a man called Cornelius Howard – without explaining his possible connection with the case.

Howard, having a criminal record, was easier to find, and he was arrested in Oldham, about five miles away, using the name John Ward. He was, in fact, a thirty-one-year-old cousin, the black sheep of the family, to whom Storrs had not spoken for eleven years and whom Mrs Storrs had not even seen in the eighteen years of her marriage. Bloodstained socks had been found in his pocket, and stains – possibly blood – on his clothing; his trousers were torn and his legs bruised; he also had a cut or scratch on his hand. At the identification parade, scrupulously fair in that the eight other men in the line-up were all similar in appearance, Howard was the one picked out. At that stage, Mrs Storrs was not positive, but at the inquest her doubts vanished. 'That man looked at me in just the same way as he looked at me in the hall when I took the gun from him. He identified himself!'

The other three were more confident from the start, apart from a couple of minor features. Marion Lindley and Mary Evans had been slightly worried that Howard had no moustache (in fact, the police had found a barber who claimed he could identify Howard as a man who had come in for a shave on the day after the murder, and had his moustache removed). Originally, Miss Lindley's reaction was 'Yes, I feel positive, except that the man had a moustache,' but at the coroner's court she added: 'I say this is the man unless he has a double, exactly like him'. In any case, any qualms about the absence of a moustache had been offset by the certainty of the young women that '. . . the eyes, cheeks and forehead are the same'.

However, black as it appeared for the accused, Howard insisted he had been nowhere near Gorse Hall; that he had been staying at a Huddersfield lodging house from 16 October to 11 November except for two days when he had been in Leeds. His alibi for the night of the murder was that he had been playing dominoes with the landlord of the 'Ring o' Bells' public house, in the presence of several other players. The police, in view of their eye witnesses, may have been complacent because they seemed to disregard the alibi, suggesting that if the game had taken place at all, it was on a different night. But at the trial they had a shock, because the landlord remembered the evening particularly as the date of the local elections. The case fell apart when the defence produced other witnesses to confirm that Howard had been in Huddersfield earlier in the evening.

Since Mrs Storrs and Marion Lindley had been convinced that the murderer was the same man who had fired the shot and smashed the window two months earlier, Howard had to be acquitted when it was revealed that at that time he had been in Wakefield prison on remand, before facing a charge of housebreaking. In fact, it is not known whether the murderer was the same man because an examination of the revolver grabbed by Mrs Storrs revealed that it could not be fired – the hammer and spring were missing; yet the gun used on the earlier occasion had been working.

Howard – having been such an obvious suspect – despite the fact he had not been identified by his dying cousin – it is a tribute to the persistent detective work of the police that they did not throw in the towel. A year after the murder, the gun was traced to an ex-serviceman who was then living – of all places – very near Gorse Hall. The fact that the new suspect, twenty-eight-year-old Mark Wilde, had a record of violence was encouraging; indeed, at the time of his arrest he had just finished a two-month prison sentence for jealously wounding a man who had flirted with his girl friend – with a long one-edged knife, which could have been the one used on George Storrs. Detectives investigating the case had their hopes raised each day as their enquiries unearthed more and more incriminating evidence. On the night of the murder he had returned to his mother's house at ten o'clock with his face bleeding, and with blood on his shirt and scarf. His explanation was that he had been in a fight outside a public house in nearby Ashton. At the trial, the judge asked if he knew the name of the man who had picked the fight with him, and whether he had seen him since. But he answered 'no' on both counts, despite the importance of corroboration.

The Crown produced three former army colleagues who insisted that the distinctive revolver (as well as being broken, it was a particularly cheap and unusual model) had belonged to Wilde and that they had handled it in his presence, but while he admitted to owning two other guns, he denied possessing the exhibit in question.

But juries do not work on the basis of probability, and a murder suspect has to be 'tied' to the scene – which now hinged on the issue of identification. The assurance of the four women witnesses in identifying Cornelius Howard now worked to the detriment of the prosecution case. There was a marked similarity in the appearance of the two men, and Wilde's counsel had asked Howard to attend as a defence witness. He was not needed as three of the women admitted they could not be sure – no more than that he Wilde *resembled* Mr Storrs' assailant – but Howard was used as a trump card when Mrs Storrs said she 'thought' she could identify him (Wilde). Howard was then asked to stand up, and she was reminded of her claim at the previous trial that he had the same 'staring eyes' as the man who attacked her husband. Did she still believe that? Her admission that she had been mistaken before now ruined her more qualified identification of Wilde.

My own feeling is that Mark Wilde, thus able to capitalise on the collapse of the Howard trial, may have been lucky to go free, but this has to be qualified by inconsistencies in what happened on the night of the murder. Wilde did not know the Storrs family. If he had been motivated by theft, what had the murderer meant by his initial threat: 'Now I have you!' – hardly the sort of remark made by a burglar . . . Why did Mr Storrs suddenly appear to lose interest in his assailant, suggesting the possibility that he knew him, and did not wish to pursue the matter – which would support rumours of a skeleton in the family cupboard, such as an illegitimate son denied recognition . . . why did John Worrall commit suicide, an implication that the murderer might have been someone close to *him*. Questions, now unanswerable, and thus mere speculation.

While a jury cannot be too influenced by laws of probability when judging someone of murder, any police investigation understandably leans heavily on such considerations, especially in cases of pre-meditated murder. One of the first questions is inevitably: which person in the victim's circle had a motive and opportunity? The enquiry proceeds, and when everything points to the most likely suspect, the question must be asked: Who else might fit the bill? When there is no-one else, the police would feel confident of a conviction. But very occasionally the evidence does not add up, and identity of the real murderer remains a mystery.

When he died in January 1911, James Hodgson Bingham had been caretaker and official guide to Lancaster Castle for over thirty years. Built by the Normans on the site of a Roman encampment, Lancaster Castle has a fascinating history, having been besieged several times, on the last occasion by Cromwell during the Civil War. More recently it housed the Lancaster assizes. As such, the post carried a certain prestige and the family was pleased when Bingham's son James Henry Bingham was appointed to succeed him. When Henry took up residence, he invited his sister Margaret to be his housekeeper. To general dismay, the hitherto healthy young woman was suddenly taken ill, and died within the week.

Henry Bingham needed to look no further than his other sister, Edith, to replace her, and she agreed to join him in an official capacity. Unfortunately, Edith was not cut out for the more mundane domestic chores, and neglected them – a situation which led to an 'atmosphere' and arguments when she ignored her brother's demands that she should 'mend her ways'. The outcome of this hostility was that Bingham announced he would have to replace her, and that her successor, a Mrs Cox Walker, would be in charge of domestic affairs as from 14 August.

However, on the previous Saturday, Henry Bingham was taken ill after eating a beef steak prepared by Edith, but it was no ordinary stomach upset, and he died on the Tuesday. A post mortem revealed that death had been caused by arsenic poisoning, and as the logical suspect, Edith was arrested and committed for trial at the assizes – which happened to be the Bingham home. Suspecting that arsenic had been obtained from weed-killer used extensively in the Castle grounds, the police now became suspicious of the two earlier deaths. The bodies of Edith's sister and her father were then exhumed, and both found to contain traces of arsenic. She was then charged with all three murders.

As I suggested, one could excuse the police for taking it for granted that Edith was a murderess; *three* poisonings at the same location within the space of less than nine months made it almost impossible to lay guilt on any other person. At the trial in October (proceeding initially with the charge in relation to her brother), the Crown case was impressive. Another brother, William Bingham, testified to the tension caused because of Edith's lack of interest in her household duties, but more sinister was evidence that Edith was in danger of losing her fiancé because of her pretensions to grandeur she had claimed to *own* the property from which she had been dismissed, presenting her with the further problem of trying to explain her absence from the Castle. The prosecution case was therefore based on motive, opportunity, and access to poison, through weed killer used by the Castle gardeners.

However, Mr Wingate Saul, leading for the defence, reminded the court of the law with respect to murder, ie it was up to the Crown to prove that arsenic had been *wilfully* administered – in other words, not merely how it had come to be in Henry Bingham's organs. Arsenic might have got into the food accidentally, he postulated, but more to the point, there was nothing to connect Edith Bingham with access to arsenic whether in weed-killer, or any other form. Although dealing primarily with the charge in respect of Henry, he went on to suggest there was equally no evidence in the case of the other deaths – not even any evidence to suggest that Mr Bingham senior had taken food prepared by the prisoner just before he was taken ill. In the case of Margaret, it was difficult to see how arsenic could have been introduced into her food at breakfast (after which she was struck down), without affecting the others eating the same food.

Mr Justice Avory drew the attention of the jury to these significant points, and they were out for only twenty minutes before returning a verdict of 'not guilty'. In view of the way in which its case had collapsed, the Crown decided not to offer evidence on the others, and Edith Bingham was formally found not guilty. On the evidence, Edith Bingham had to be declared innocent, but my own reaction is that no-one else could have committed the murders in the circumstances you have heard; that the police were too complacent and did not prepare a proper case. The irony is that if she had not quarrelled openly with her brother, she would never have been charged. Either way, the deaths of three members of the Bingham family remain unsolved.

Murder without apparent motive presents an extra dimension of complexity, because – short of rounding up every suspicious character in the neighbourhood – the police have no 'launch-pad' for their investigation. Motive introduces suspects, and suspects are an integral part of the jigsaw puzzle they need to piece together. When there are none, the investigation has no guidelines; like a mathematical puzzle, the formula is essential to the solution. This is one reason why the murder of Mrs Caroline Luard, at an isolated spot between Seal and Ightham, near Sevenoaks, in August 1908, remains unsolved, and offers little scope even for speculation. In fact, because there were no suspects, fingers were pointed at her most unlikely killer – her husband Major-General Charles Edward Luard who eventually chose to commit suicide rather than endure such unjustified allegations in the midst of his grief.

Admittedly, even the most loving of husbands have resorted to murder in a moment's aberration, but it was physically impossible for General Luard to have shot his wife – an observation made clear by the coroner, although it failed to stop wagging tongues. Malicious gossip seldom has any foundation, and is usually sparked by the sort of cynicism which, for example, disparages any 'establishment' ruling, such as the Scottish 'not proven' verdict. 'Of course he/she was guilty – they just couldn't *prove* it!' Similarly, 'It *must* have been the General; who *else* could it have been?' The rumours took no account of the General's character, or the couple's circumstances and lifestyle.

Having retired to Ightham Knoll after a distinguished military career in the Middle and Far East, Charles Luard, at sixty-eight, was undoubtedly content with his new life as a country gentleman and a county councillor. His pension was sufficient to employ two maids and a cook, and they lived well within their means, so there were no financial worries. He seemed to want little more than a regular round of golf (his handicap was fourteen), and the company of friends in the Sevenoaks social circle, predominantly couples of a similar background. However, Caroline, ten years his junior and his constant companion throughout his career, remained his closest friend. Remember, these were the days before women were considered to have a separate identity, and they were regarded everywhere as an inseparable loving pair.

The Saturday afternoon on which Mrs Luard was killed – 24 August – had begun innocently enough. She was expecting a friend to tea, but since the preparation could be left to the servants, there was time for an hour or so at one of her favourite haunts in the nearby Fish Pond Woods. The location was a little known summer-house (a large wooden bungalow with a verandah) called 'La Casa', owned by a rich neighbour. Almost hidden by dense undergrowth, it was situated on the brow of a hill, so offering fine views of the surrounding countryside, and she would often visit the area to pick wild flowers. To get there on this occasion she accompanied her husband part of the way to his golf club at Godden Green, a regular three mile walk which usually took him an hour.

It was a beautiful summer's day, and they set off at a leisurely pace until the village of Crown Point, where the road split and they went their separate ways. It was now three o'clock and the General stepped out, arriving at his club at half-past three. Since he had only come to collect some clubs (the Luards had been invited to spend the week-end away), he remained only to chat for ten minutes, before setting off on the return journey. En route, the local vicar offered him a lift in his car, but General Luard, who enjoyed walking, was content merely to put his clubs in the boot. However, further down the road the vicar returned and repeated his offer; this time the General took advantage of an empty seat, enabling him to get home by 4.30pm.

He was surprised that Caroline had not yet returned, especially as their guest, Mrs Stewart, wife of a retired local solicitor was already waiting. In those days, formal tea was a ceremony not to be delayed, especially as Mrs Stewart had to leave promptly because she was expecting a guest of her own, so the General took over as host. Then, having decided to go and look for his wife, Luard was accompanied as far as the wood by Mrs Stewart who then had to leave to meet her guest. He took the cross-country route by which he expected Caroline to return. It was now 5.30pm and he must have been getting apprehensive.

At the deserted summer house, he found his wife lying face down on the floor of the veranda, at the front of the wooden building. As he rushed forward, fearing she might have fainted or even suffered a heart attack, he saw a large pool of blood under her head. Then it became obvious she had been shot twice at close range through the head – a third 'wasted' bullet had ploughed into the ground at the front of the verandah. Mrs Luard's arms were stretched in front of her, her right glove having been pulled off; it lay nearby almost inside out – and the four rings she always wore were gone. Even more startling, the pocket of her dress had been cut away, and the purse she kept there was also missing.

A doctor's examination revealed that the first shot had entered the cheek below the left eye, penetrating upwards; the second had been fired behind her ear while she was lying face down, in what appeared to be a deliberate *coup de grâce*. Her straw hat found nearby had a dent on the crown where the material had been crushed, leading one doctor to speculate that someone had crept up behind and struck her over the head with a heavy object. His theory was that the assailant had then shot her the first time before she hit the ground. The second doctor disagreed, arguing that the blow to the head had been caused when she fell and struck a post on the veranda. This seems much more likely. Apart from the fact that there was no blunt instrument in sight, why should Mrs Luard's assailant have bothered to shoot her when another blow would have been sufficient to kill?

Because of the value of at least three of the rings – family heirlooms (one consisted of one large and two small diamonds; another was a twin setting of sapphire and diamond; the third a large opal and the fourth a solid gold band wedding ring) robbery seemed to be the motive, although the use of firearms seemed somewhat uncharacteristic, especially in such an isolated spot, in the depth of the woods. Eighty years later, in a more 'sophisticated' age one speculates about other possibilities. Since the odds of bumping into an itinerant tramp – one who happened to be a thief, and carrying a handgun – are so great, could Caroline Luard have known her killer, someone able to approach closely without alarming her? Even an arranged assignation? As unlikely as it seems from what we know of her, a woman in her late fifties is not too old for a 'relationship' with another man. If there ever was such a person he kept a remarkably low profile.

Initially, the police assumed they would get their first lead when the jewellery was sold, but it never was – eliminating money as the motive. Scotland Yard were called in to supervise the case – it was only two years since Scotland Yard's services had been available to provincial forces (most of which did not have a plain-clothes unit) by request and since the Chief Constable of Kent was a personal friend of the Luards, he would not have dragged his feet. But when all their enquiries were frustrated, it was appreciated that as Mrs Luard's body was not discovered until 6pm, little under three hours since she had been shot, the killer might have caught a train from Sevenoaks or Wrotham stations and been anywhere, including London where he could simply disappear. There were a couple of false alarms, the first when a crank walked into Bow Street police station and confessed, and the other when a note in the pocket of a coat was found, with a pair of boots, by the lake in Regents Park. Addressed to 'Dear Father', it read: 'I can bear the suspense no longer. The Ightham affair has preyed on my mind. I fired the shots while the devil was in me. By the time you get this I shall be beyond human aid.' It was signed 'Your affectionate son, Jack Storm'. The lake was dragged but no body found. Clutching at straws, the investigators even called in bloodhounds – as had the desperate London police at the time of Jack the Ripper – but any scent they may have picked up at the site of the murder eventually disappeared in the thick undergrowth.

So the rumours began, and poison pen letters were received not only by the police, but the distraught General. What the writers did not know, or chose to ignore, was that apart from the fact that Charles Luard was clearly no murderer, he could not have been at the scene of the crime at 3.15pm, the time of death estimated by the doctor. This time was supported by the evidence of two witnesses, both of whom heard the shot and noted the time, despite the fact that shots in the heart of the country are commonplace. One was the gardener on the estate bordering the grounds of Ightham Knoll, who was little more than quarter of a mile away.

Little over five minutes later General Luard was actually seen by another witness about a mile and a half from the scene of the shooting, and a twenty-minute walk away. At 3.25pm he was spotted arriving at Godden Green links and five minutes later at the club house. After that, all his movements were corroborated by independent witnesses. Whether to demonstrate their thoroughness or simply to prove the General's innocence, the police double-checked every aspect of his statement. They retraced the footsteps of both husband and wife, and found his timings to be exact to the minute. At the inquest he had to produce the three revolvers he owned, so that it could be clearly demonstrated they had not been the murder weapons. The servants were obliged to testify to the Luards' excellent relationship.

General Luard decided to move to London. On the night

before he was to meet his son, an army officer serving in South Africa who had returned because of his mother's death, he stayed with his friend, Colonel John Warde (an MP and brother of the Chief Constable), and after breakfast in his room he wrote farewell notes to his son, his brother-in-law, and to his host. To all he referred to the poison pen letters, and to the pressures on him, and to his friend these poignant words: 'I am sorry to have to return your kindness and long friendship in this way, but I am satisfied it is best to join her in the second life at once as I can be of no further assistance to anyone in this world. Now in the last day or two something seems to have snapped. The strength has left me, and I care for nothing but to join her again.' Then he jumped under a train and was killed instantly. His death was no less murder by persons unknown, than that of his wife.

Even the scope for speculation is limited by the absence of clues, but in *A Reasonable Doubt* (Cresset Press 1960), Julian Symons suggests that the volume of malicious mail written anonymously was unusually large, almost amounting to a campaign, and that this may well have been the work of the murderer who had a grudge against the Luards. He supports the theory with the argument that Caroline Luard had not attempted to escape from her attacker, which implies he (or she) was known to her. In fact, the vendetta hypothesis was explored at the inquest, but no-one appeared to be aware of anyone who even disliked such a popular couple. It is possible, of course, that a person with such a twisted mind was cunning enough to conceal his hatred in public, but certainly there was no apparent motive, and I would have thought such enmity would, in any case, have spilled over and warned someone. On the other hand, why did the murderer cut out the pocket of Mrs Luard's dress when he/she could have simply put a hand in to remove the purse? As a 'keepsake' perhaps?

The theory has no basis in fact, yet is no weaker than the more common suggestion that the murderer may have been John Alexander Dickman, hanged two years later at Newcastle for shooting a colliery wages clerk to steal his wages satchel containing £370. The evidence against Dickman was entirely circumstantial and he went to his death protesting his innocence – which would have been ironic justice if he *had* been responsible for Mrs Luard's death, but the allegation has little foundation. There were rumours that Dickman knew Mrs Luard, and had forged a cheque purported to be hers, but apart from the fact that a gun was used in both killings there is nothing to link Deadman with 'La Casa' on that fateful day two years earlier.

8

IT HELPS TO BE RICH

Roland Molineux and Albert Patrick

Although, in general, the law is free of corruption in Britain and the United States, there is little doubt that a guilty person can sleep more easily if he or she has a personal fortune to cushion the blow. It is common knowledge that money can unlock prison doors, but even when trial proceedings are above reproach, wealth is invaluable in stonewalling and delaying the wheels of justice, and in establishing a climate of opinion in favour of the defendant, even to the extent of an acquittal or pardon. You have already heard how Dr Bennett Hyde, supported by his wife's money, managed to escape retribution; but the two most glaring examples of the power of money and its influence on the legal system are the cases of Roland Molineux and Albert T. Patrick, two well-heeled killers who got away with murder at the beginning of the century, in relation to poisonings which took place in New York, within a stone's throw of each other.

No-one would dispute the fact that Molineux was guilty (except perhaps on a technicality) of two murders, so I offer no apology for making certain statements without corroborating evidence, particularly regarding his first victim, Henry Barnet, the less dramatic of the cases. Molineux, a spoilt rich boy now in his late thirties, had been trained as a chemist, but did not have the same business aspirations as his contemporaries, preferring the prestige role of an officer of the exclusive Knickerbocker Athletic Club, of which Barnet was also a member, which then stood on the corner of Madison Avenue and 45th Street. The son of a Civil War general, Molineux was status conscious, and although his position meant little, the connection was important to a snob like him because club membership was restricted to gentlemen of means, and primarily graduates of the Ivy League colleges.

In 1898 Molineux was interested in Blanche Cheesborough, a New York socialite, and was incensed when he suspected Barnet was muscling in on his territory. Nothing specific was said although Molineux made his feelings apparent. Suddenly, in November, Barnet was afflicted by a mystery sickness and died within a few days. Death was attributed to natural causes. Nineteen days later Molineux and Blanche were married. That might then have been the end of the story, except that the bridegroom suffered delusions of grandeur which made him ultra-sensitive. Already jealous of the popularity of the club's athletic director, Harry Cornish, Molineux challenged him to a weight-lifting contest – and lost.

As a result of his loss of face, and his unsporting reaction to defeat, the two men quarrelled and Molineux tried to persuade the committee to sack his rival. His demand fell on deaf ears, and since he had made it clear he could not work with Cornish, he had no alternative but to resign. His new job was as superintendent of a firm manufacturing colours, which gave him access to potentially dangerous chemicals.

A few weeks later, on Christmas Eve, a small package addressed to Harry Cornish arrived at the club; it had come from the New York general post office, literally around the corner. The contents, a small blue bottle of Bromo-Seltzer, gave an excuse for considerable leg-pulling because of the implication that the anonymous well-wisher expected Cornish to eat and drink to excess over the festivities. Who was it, the members speculated, who knew Harry's habits so well? In fact, Cornish, not expecting to need the seltzer, left the bottle in his office, and on Boxing Day another member, Harry King, had an upset stomach and decided to make use of his friend's unused Christmas present. But the seltzer had to be taken in water, and infuriatingly (so he thought) the water cooler was not working, so he put the bottle back.

As it turned out, King had a lucky escape, because Cornish took the bottle home where he was looked after by a relative, Mrs Katherine Adams, and her married daughter. When Mrs

Adams complained of a violent headache, he prepared a glass of the Bromo-Seltzer, although she only took a few mouthfuls, complaining of the bitter taste. Cornish obligingly sipped the drink. They were both sick, but Mrs Adams had drunk much more, and within half an hour she was dead. Cornish recovered, but was unwell for several days.

The news that the Seltzer had been mixed with cyanide of mercury caused a sensation, and when another doctor realised that Cornish's symptoms were almost identical to those of another club member who had died only a few weeks earlier, the newspapers latched on to the story. One published a facsimile of the address on the Christmas package – what they described as the 'poison label' – and the secretary of the Knickerbocker Club recognised the handwriting as that of a former officer and member. With this revelation, the newspapers clamoured for police action, although the authorities seemed strangely reluctant to react; finally Molineux, accompanied by his legendary father and a family lawyer, gave himself up, ingeniously volunteering any information or assistance that might be relevant. He had nothing to hide, he insisted, freely admitting his quarrel with Cornish and the reason for his resignation from the club.

Whether impressed by his story, or by the power and authority of his father, the police seemed happy to release him, but the general furore led to the exhumation of Barnet's body, and the discovery that he had died from the same cause as Mrs Adams – cyanide of mercury poisoning. At this stage, in February, Molineux was arrested, but a grand jury threw out the indictment. However, by now the police had changed their minds and he was re-arrested before finally coming to trial, in November 1899.

Over the next three years, trying to bring Roland Molineux to justice cost the state of New York $200,000 (a considerable sum then), but this must have been matched by General Molineux who was financially ruined in the process. The tactics, with no expense spared, were to contest everything, to fight every inch of the way – it took twelve days just to select a jury – and the defence objected to all and sundry, examining 504 men and women before they were satisfied.

However, the prosecution evidence was overwhelming. Fourteen handwriting experts agreed that the writing on the package was that of Molineux. Testimony was given that the silver presentation holder which contained the bottle of seltzer had been purchased at a store next to Molineux's business in Newark; that the distinctive blue writing paper (with three silver crests entwined) accompanying the present, had been seen in his office; that one of the chemicals to which he had access in his work, some of which had recently been purchased, was prussian blue, from which cyanide is made.

As his lawyers had contested every allegation, the court was stunned when no evidence was offered in Molineux's defence, although it should have been obvious there was nothing they could say. Even so, when the jury retired, in February 1900, it took them eight hours to reach a verdict of guilty, and he was sentenced to die in the electric chair. The sentence hung over Molineux's head for eighteen months while his lawyers explored every avenue to save him. Despite the weakness of his case, in October 1901 the Court of Appeal ordered a retrial. By the time he faced a second jury, four years had elapsed since the poisonings; the story had been virtually forgotten, and the lawyers were able to paint a sympathetic picture or an innocent victim of media prejudice and police stupidity.

Leading the defence attorneys was the authoritative former state governor Black, who was allowed far too much scope by the judge, falling back on wild allegations (he actually accused Harry Cornish, who had no possible motive, of poisoning Henry Barnet), and calling suspect witnesses, such as a young woman who claimed to have been in the general post office when she saw a man (not Molineux) mail a package bearing the name 'H. Cornish' and the Knickerbocker Club address. No-one bothered to ask her why she had not offered this evidence at the original trial. This time it took the jury only four minutes to acquit Molineux, to emotional applause that 'justice' had triumphed over the bigoted police and the newspapers.

Molineux survived to become a professional writer and

his first book was about his experiences in prison, *The Room With the Little Door*. In addition to a number of articles and features he produced a more unlikely title in *Vice Admiral of the Blue*, about Nelson and Lady Hamilton. After his wife divorced him, he married the woman who had collaborated with him in writing the stage play, *The Man Inside*. However, he did not escape unscathed emotionally. Mental problems resulted and he was committed to an asylum in 1913, dying there four years later.

Only a few hundred yards away from the Knickerbocker Club on Madison Avenue was a large, red-brick apartment house known as 'The Berkshire', the New York home of the oil and property millionaire, William Marsh Rice, who was eighty-four years old at the start of the new century. A few years earlier, Rice's estranged wife had died and left her money – under Texan law she was entitled to half her husband's fortune – to her family. Rice contested the will, insisting that as he had moved to New York where the state inheritance laws were different, her bequest was invalid.

With several million dollars at stake, the court battle dragged on interminably, with lawyers on both sides being the main beneficiaries. Increasingly suspicious of the jackals surrounding him, the old man looked around for someone he could trust, and finally appointed twenty-three year old Charles F. Jones to be his secretary. Jones had no particular qualifications for the considerable responsibility entailed, but he had a pleasant equable temperament and Rice became attached to him, taking him more and more into his confidence, and giving him greater authority so that he was, in fact, the old man's personal assistant.

If he had been so inclined, Jones was in a position to throw his weight about (as Rice became more of a recluse he relied more and more on his young assistant for all relatively routine matters), but he lacked personal initiative, was gullible, and easy to influence. He was flattered by, rather than suspicious of the attentions of a new friend, the worldly Albert T. Patrick, who had actually been one of the lawyers representing the estate of the late Mrs Rice and might well therefore have been regarded as the 'enemy'. A short, fat man whose only distinguishing feature was a neat Van Dyke beard, Patrick had a strong, persuasive personality and Jones began to appreciate his advice.

When Patrick learned that Rice had made a new will, leaving the bulk of $3 million to the William Rice Institute, a college in Houston which had been founded by the old man, he commiserated with Jones about the 'unfairness' of it all. The young man agreed that he should have been entitled to something in return for his loyalty, but did not see what could be done about it. Patrick did – produce a new will! He could draft the document, and all Jones had to do was provide Rice's signature, which was no problem since he had already written it (on Rice's authority) on thousands of letters. The secretary was shocked by the idea, but he was under Patrick's influence and the lawyer wore away at his resolve so that when he produced the will and thrust it under Jones' nose for signature, in a weak moment Jones put pen to paper. He was a little perturbed that half the money would go to Patrick, but since he would be entitled to a substantial bequest, and the rest divided among the family (there were no children of Rice's two marriages), it was not likely to be too contentious. However, he had not counted on Patrick's greed. Having once been compromised, he was now putty in the lawyer's hands, and a month later he tamely forged his employer's signature on a re-drafted will which did not apportion specific sums of money or property, but appointed Patrick as sole executor. When he protested that as the millionaire's faithful secretary and confidant, he was not even mentioned, Patrick's excuse seemed reasonable – he claimed it was better that way, but 'don't worry, I'll look after you'.

Now totally involved in the conspiracy, Jones was given the task of forging two dozen or so letters, purportedly from Rice, making it seem that the lawyer had done some excellent work on his behalf and was now a trusted confidant. The next stage would be to forge cheques, and they prepared the way with a 'dummy run', sending forgeries to genuine recipients, which could be explained away if necessary.

Having done all the groundwork and established himself as a close associate, Patrick decided that old man Rice had outlived his usefulness, and was now an encumbrance; furthermore, since he was quite a sick man, it was hardly a crime to help him on his way. Jones resisted the idea initially, but at every stage in the plot, he had become further committed, and as Patrick exerted his authority he crumbled under the pressure. All he had to do was to see that his employer took the mercury pills the lawyer had prescribed – in small doses. The symptoms were similar to indigestion and Patrick made certain that a long-standing family doctor was brought in immediately to monitor the illness. Cunningly, the supply of poison was controlled, so that the patient's deterioration was very gradual, and the blissfully ignorant doctor, reminding everyone of Rice's advanced years, warned them that his heart was becoming weaker.

By September 1900, Rice was very ill, but Patrick, who had made a study of the properties of mercury, suddenly realised that in the unlikely event of a post mortem, traces of the poison might be found in the organs, and called a halt. It seemed obvious that the millionaire was not long for this world, and had Patrick been patient he would have waited for nature to take its course. However, taken off his mercury diet, the old man began to recover, and Patrick's greed then overcame his better judgement. Realising that no-one would be very surprised if Rice suffered a relapse and suddenly died, Patrick decided on the use of chloroform as a short cut. Again, it was to be Jones' responsibility since he was the only person who had constant access to the patient's bedroom, and although he baulked at the prospect he was by now completely under Patrick's influence. In fact, the lawyer had planned everything down to the last detail; Jones had only to follow instructions. Even so, he was understandably nervous, and must have had the fright of his life when the front door bell rang!

A Sunday (23 September) had been chosen because there would be no business calls to disturb him, but what they had not reckoned with was a surprise visit from two elderly ladies, long-time friends of Rice, who had called to cheer up the invalid with presents of cake and wine. They were later to testify of their surprise at not receiving a reply, as they could hear someone moving about inside the apartment. In fact, administering the chloroform was the least of Jones' problems, since his employer was too weak to resist; he was more concerned with getting rid of the evidence – a sponge soaked in the chloroform and enclosed in a towel, both of which were burned before he opened all the windows to get rid of the pungent smell. Only when everything was back to normal, did Jones ring Patrick and the doctor to break the news.

The doctor was not surprised by what he had considered inevitable, and signed the death certificate without a second thought. A letter from the dead man (forged by the conspirators) requesting that his body be cremated immediately was of little interest – his concern was with the living. As it happened, this was one of Patrick's few oversights. The cremation was intended to avoid any possibility of a post mortem, but officers at the crematorium pointed out that they needed twenty four hours to get the ovens to the correct temperature.

Next day, soon after the banks had opened for business, a friend of Patrick presented a cheque for $25,000 made out to Albert T. Patrick, although on the back it had been *endorsed* Albert T. Patrick. The clerk recognised the familiar signature of William Rice, but could not honour the cheque with a faulty endorsement. His caution seemed to be justified by the man's apparent nervousness. Within minutes the stranger returned with the correct endorsement, but the clerk was not satisfied and drew the unusual mistake to the attention of one of the bank directors, Eric Swenson who telephoned the millionaire to double-check. He was assured by Jones that the cheque was legitimate, despite the original mistake in the recipient's name. Normally, Jones' assurance would have been enough, but instinct made Swenson insist on speaking to Mr Rice. It was only then he was told that the millionaire had 'passed away' the day before. In the circumstances, Swenson decided on his own authority to cancel the cheque.

Patrick refused to take the snub lying down, at once calling at the bank in his capacity as executor of the Rice estate. He demanded that the relatively small amount be paid, pointing out that it would take months for the deceased's affairs to be settled, and he was not prepared to wait. However, Swenson objected to the lawyer's tone and refused to be browbeaten. When he enquired about the cause of Rice's sudden death, Patrick's answer: 'Baked bananas' seemed almost flippant. He pressed for an explanation and was informed that the old man liked baked bananas, although he knew they gave him indigestion; on the day of his death he had eaten *nine* – the implication being that he had died because of his own greed.

Swenson refused to budge and was so disconcerted by the lawyer's manner that when Patrick had gone he called the district attorney. The resulting investigation revealed that during the morning *three* 'normal' cheques totalling $215,000 had been presented, plus another for $25,000 on a different bank. The signatures on all four were *identical*, as though they might have been traced over a single specimen. Detectives interviewing Patrick found him suspiciously glib, and started to dig deeper. They were intrigued by the reaction of one man who had been Rice's personal lawyer for many years, and who only knew Patrick as an attorney representing the estate of Mrs Rice in the contentious battle over her will; he could not believe that the millionaire would have appointed him executor of his own estate. A post mortem was now carried out and traces of mercury found in the organs, together with a congestion of the lungs caused by 'a gas or vapour'; Jones had used too much chloroform.

When they were arrested, Patrick remained calm, confident that he had covered his tracks, but feared Jones was weak enough to crack under pressure. In adjoining cells, while awaiting trial, he pretended to confess his fears to the younger man. 'It's all up – we're done for!' Passing his penknife through the bars, he whispered: 'You go first . . .' Jones was found lying in a pool of blood, but was rushed to hospital where his life was saved. After that, it was not difficult for the district attorney to persuade him to turn State's evidence. In 1902, with Jones' testimony in addition to other documentary evidence, Patrick was found guilty and sentenced to die in the electric chair.

However, as I said at the outset, big money is a powerful ally, and Patrick had a wealthy benefactor – someone he may have helped in the past, or someone who was expecting some future reward – who ensured that no legal effort was spared to obtain his freedom. He was in the Death House for four years and seven months, and within two weeks of the electric chair when, in 1906, the Court of Appeal granted a stay of execution. Finally, in December of that year the governor of New York State commuted the sentence to one of life. That might have been the end of the story, but Patrick was nothing but a battler. Supported by apparently unlimited funds, the protests and appeals continued, until November 1912 when a new state governor granted a free and unconditional pardon. How that was accomplished is something of a mystery, but it is a reasonable bet that most other people in that position would have died in prison. Patrick not only went free, but lived on in comfort for another twenty-eight years.

Bibliography

Adam, H. L., *Murder By Persons Unknown*, London 1931
Archer, F., *Killers In the Clear*, W. H. Allen 1971
Bresler, F., *Scales of Justice*, London 1973
Camps, Dr F., *The Investigation of Murder*, M. Joseph 1966
Duke, W., *Six Trials*, London 1933
Jacobs, T. C., *Cavalcade of Murder*, London 1955
Kershaw, A., *Murder in France*, Constable 1955
Laurence, J., *Extraordinary Crimes*, London 1931
Logan, C. B., *Guilty Or Not Guilty*, London 1933
Marjoribanks, E., *Famous Trials of Marshall Hall*, Penguin 1950
Mitchell, C. Ainsworth, *Science and The Criminal*, Pitman 1911
Oddie, S. Ingleby, *Inquest*, Hutchinson 1941
Pearson, E. L., *Murder At Smutty Nose*, USA 1926
Roughead, W., *Classic Crimes*, Cassell 1951
Shore, W. T., *Crime And The Detective*, Gresham Publ. Co. 1921
Speer, W. H., *Secret History of Great Crimes*, London 1919
Symons, J., *A Reasonable Doubt*, Cresset 1960
Thompson, C. J., *Poison Mysteries Unsolved*, London 1937
Young, Filson, *Notable British Trials*, Hodge & Co. 1920

INDEX

Abberline, Chief Insp., 43
Abinger, Edward, 60–1, 67–8, 71
Adams, Arthur, 74–6, 78
Adams, Dr J., 80
Adams, Mrs K., 146–7
Antimony, 44–5
Arsenic, 42, 122, 137
Avory, Mr Justice, 138

Bacteria, 115–17, 119–21, 123–4
Baderski, Lucy, 43
Baker, George, *see*, George Smith
Barnet, Henry 145–8
Bartlett, Mr & Mrs, *see* Bennett
Bath, 26
Beck, Mr, 127
Bell, Charlotte, 47
Bennett, Herbert, J., 88, 99, 102–13
Bennett, Mrs, 106, 109–12
Béron, Leon, 60–73
Bexley, 1-3–4, 106–8
Bingham, Edith, 136–8
Bingham, J. Henry, 136–7
Bingham, Margaret, 136–7
Bingham, William, 137
Bishop, Cecil, 46
Bishops Stortford, 40
Black, Governor, 148
Blackpool, 24
Blatch, Miss, 27
Blériot, 7
Blume, Mrs Joanna, 125–8
Booty, Emily, 34–35
Borrowman, Mary, 76–80, 85
Bournemouth, 39
Brighton, 15
Brinkley, R., 125–8
Bristol, 16–17, 19, 21, 23, 26
Brixton Prison, 30
Brodski, E. & J., 63
Bruges, 93
Burnham, Alice, 24, 26–7

Camden Town, 49–50, 53–4, 89, 99
Camps, Dr. F., 12
Capetown, 102
Castlin, Alfred, 66
Chapman, George, 42–5
Cheesborough, Blanche, 146
Chelmsford Prison, 39
Chacago, 40–2
Chloroform, 122, 151
Clarke, Mary Jane, 101
Clavering, 36
Clifton, 19
Cook, David, 83–4
Cooper, Eliza, 131
Cornish, Harry, 146–8
Cranwell sisters, 38–9
Crédit Général de France, 115
Criminal Defence Act 1898, 61
Crippen, Cora 47–57
Crippen, Dr. H. H., 8, 25, 46–58
Crippen, Otto H., 47
Crossley, Mrs, 25
Crown & Anchor Hotel, 107
Cyanide, 147–8

Darling, Mr Justice, 60–1, 64, 69–70
Deitch, Mrs N., 67–8
Delmas, Emile, 117
Dew, Chief Det. Insp., 53–6
Dickman, John A., 143–4
Dimmock, Emily Jane, 88–95, 97–9
Dougal, Samuel, 31–40, 42
Douglas, D. Sholto, 110, 112
Doyle, Sir A. Conan, 60, 79, 83–5, 90
Drouhin, Jeanne, 117–8

Eagle Public House, 90
Edinburgh, 59
Edward VII, 7
Elliston, Mrs, 102
Elmore, Belle, *see* Cora Crippen
The Era, 52
Evans, Mary, 130, 133

Fish Pond Woods, 139
Flitterman, Eva, 64–5
Freeman, Sarah, 18–19

George V, 7
Gilchrist, Marion, 74–86
Gill, Charles, 110–11
Girard, Henri, 114–19
Glasgow Police, 60, 73–4, 78–9, 83–4
Glasgow University, 119
Godden Green, 139, 142
Godel, M., 117
Gorse Hall, 129, 132–4
Grantham, Mr Justice, 42, 96–7
Grapel, Dr F., 44–5
Gravesend, 107
Gray, Dora May, 112
Greaves, PC., 64

Harrison, Mrs, 50–1
Hastings, 15
Hayman, Edward, 66–7
Heard, Henry, 126
Herne Bay, 21
Hoch, Johann, 40–42
Holland, Camille, 35–39
Hood, Mr & Mrs *see* Bennett
Howard, Cornelius, 133–35
Hunton, James, 123–24
Hyde, Bennett C., 122–25, 145
Mrs Frances Hyde, 122–25
Hyocine, 56–7

Ightham Knoll, 139, 142

James, Charles Oliver, 225–6
Jones, Charles F., 149–53

Kendall, Captain, 55–6
King, Harry, 146
Klosowski, S., *see* Chapman
Knickerbocker Club, 145, 147–49

Lambie, Helen, 74–86
Lancaster Castle, 136
Leicester, 14
Leschziner, *see* Slater
Lindley, Marion, 130–34
Lloyd, John, *see* George Smith
Lofty, Margaret, 26–27
Los Angeles, 53
Love, George, *see* George Smith
Luard, Caroline, 138–44
Lusitania, 77, 80

MacBrayne, D., 80
Mackamotzki, K., *see* Cora Crippen
M'Lachlan, Jessie, 87–8
March, Maud, 44–5
Margate, 23
Marjoribanks, Edward, 96
Marshall Hall, Edward, 13, 28–30, 56, 94–113
Martinetti, Paul, 58
Mason, Mr, 105–6, 109
Matthews, St. Charles, 95, 98
Meadows, Alice, 103–4, 107–8, 110, 112
Mercury, 151

Mitchell, Det. Sgt., 53–5
Moat Farm, 36–40
Molineux, Roland, 145–48
Monin, Mme., 118
S.S. *Montrose*, 54–5
Morrison, Steinie, 59–73, 77
Mortimer, J., 99
Muir, Sir Richard, 57, 67–9, 71
Mundy, Beatrice, 19–23, 28–9
Music Hall Ladies Guild, 51, 53

Neil, Det. Insp. a., 27–8
Neuilly, 118
le Neve, Ethel, 47, 50–8
Newton, Arthur, 95
News of the World, 92–3
New Jersey, 41, 47–8
New York Police, 78
Norwich Prison, 112

Oddie, S. Ingleby, 57–8, 71, 126
Old Bailey, 108

Palmer, E. C. (The Pilgrim), 82, 85
Palmer, Dr. W., 28
Park, William, 85
Parker, Reginald, 126–28
Patrick, Albert, T., 145, 149–54
Peace, Charlie, 61
Peck, Clara, 119–20
Peck, John, 119–22
Pegler, Edith, 17–19, 21, 23, 25–6, 30
Pentonville Prison, 58
Pernotte, Louis, 116
Pernotte, Mrs 116–17
Pinero, Sir A., 110
Prussic Acid, 125
Pyper, Inspector, 78

Reavil, Alice, 25–6
Rice, William M., 149–53
Ripper, Jack the, 42, 46
Rising Sun, The, 90–1
Roberts, Robert, 90–1, 94–5
Robinson, John, *see* Crippen
Rose, George, *see* George Smith
Roughead, William, 60, 79, 82

Sando, *see* Slater
Saul, Mr Wingate, 137
Scotland Yard, 90, 125, 141
Scrutton, Mr Justice 28
Shaw, Bertram, 88–91, 94
Shearman, M., 28, 30
Shoreditch Empire, 65
Slater, Oscar, 59–60, 74–86
Smith, F. E., 57
Smith, George Joseph, 11–30, 32, 34, 40, 46
Smith, Madeleine, 74
Southampton, 18
Southend, 19, 21
Southsea, 24–5
Spilsbury, B., 29, 57
Spink, Mrs Isabella, 43–4
Stalybridge, 130
Stein, Morris, *see* Morrison
Stephen, Andrew, 66, 73
Stephen, Sir H., 85
Stepney, 108
Stewart, Mrs, 140
Storrs, George H., 129–35
Storm, Jack, 142
Strathclyde, Lord, *see* Ure
Swenson, Eric, 152–53
Swope, Frances, 122–24
Swope, Thomas, B., 122–23
Symons, Julian, 72, 112, 143

Tagger, Moses, *see* Morrison
Taylor, Bessie, 44–5
Thornhill, Caroline Beatrice, 15–16
Thompson, Dr, 97
Trench, John, 84
Tunbridge Wells, 23
Turner, Cora, *see* Cora Crippen
Twyman, Dr, 123

Ure, Alexander, 80–2

Victoria, Queen, 7–8

Waite, Dr Arthur W., 118–22
Wakefield Prison 134
Walker, Amelia, 41
Walker, Julia, 41
Walker, Mrs Cox, 136
Wandsworth Prison, 128
Ward, John, 133
Ward, Col. J., 143
Wensley, Chief Det. Insp. F., 63–4, 67, 72
Weston-super-Mare, 21
Weymouth, 19
White, Sarah, 35–7
Wilde, Mark, 134–5
Willcox, Sir W., 57
Williams, Henry, *see* George Smith
Wood, Robert, 87–8, 92–113, 118–21
Woolwich Arsenal, 103
Worrell, John, 131–35
Wright Brothers, 7

Yarmouth, 88,99–100, 103–4, 107–8, 110–12
Young, Filson, 58
Young, Ruby, 92–4, 97–8

Ruth Ewertowski

Und wenn dir ein ZIEGELSTEIN auf den Kopf fällt

Rudolf Steiner lesen

Freies Geistesleben

1. Auflage 2011

Verlag Freies Geistesleben
Landhausstraße 82, 70190 Stuttgart
Internet: www.geistesleben.com

ISBN 978-3-7725-2490-5

Umschlaggestaltung: Patricia Hagel
Druck: Freiburger Graphische Betriebe
Printed in Germany

INHALT

Vorwort 7

Zucker und die unschuldige Egoität 9

Und wenn dir ein Ziegelstein auf den Kopf fällt 15

Je spiritueller der Mensch,
umso ruhiger die Erde? 22

Wiedergeburt versus Genforschung
Über Weihnachten und Golgatha 31

Die Doppelgängerbegegnung:
eine Eintrittskarte in die geistige Welt 41

Die Heimatlosigkeit des Eingeweihten 48

Schöpferische Wirkungen und
Nebenwirkungen des Verzichts 56

Glaube ist Zusammenhang
oder: Warum Rudolf Steiner glauben? 63

«Wir wären nicht Menschen ... wenn nicht
das Weltenall fortwährend in uns erstürbe» 71

Trauerzug und Vogelgrippe
Karma oder Zufall? 80

Die Schwelle erleben
Die wahre und die falsche Gestalt des Todes 87

Die Sünde des Intellekts 98

Das Jüngern des Ätherleibes 105

Aus dem Leib wird der Kopf 112

Umgestülpt
oder: Anders denken lernen, als man denkt 120

«Haarsträubender Idealismus»?
oder: Geliebte Pflichten, gelassene Rechte und
das soziale Hauptgesetz 127

In der Mitte der Zeit: das Ich 135

Die Religion der Götter 144

Glaube, Liebe, Hoffnung
Fähigkeiten der Wesensglieder 151

Anmerkungen 161

Vorwort

Es gibt Tage, die wie nichts dahingehen und an deren Ende der fahle Geschmack bleibt, zwar viel «gewirtschaftet», aber nichts Wesentliches erlebt, getan oder gedacht zu haben. Man ist dann wie halb verhungert. Am Abend solcher Tage bitte ich manchmal meinen Mann noch um «einen Gedanken», gewissermaßen als Wegzehrung für die Nacht, und bin froh, wenn er einen hat, möglichst kurz und anregend, gerne auch experimentell, vor allem aber so, dass ich für Kopf und Herz etwas mitzunehmen habe.

In diesem Sinne dachte ich mir, einmal eine Sammlung anzulegen, aus der man an solch schiefen, aber auch an anderen Tagen schöpfen kann: eine Sammlung von Gedanken, die ich bei Rudolf Steiner fand, die mich in der Lektüre innehalten ließen, die im Notieren und Anverwandeln neue und eigene Wege gehen, die dem Verstehen eine Aufgabe, manchmal eine Herausforderung sind und vielleicht erst viel später zu angemessenen Erkenntnissen führen. Es geht also nicht um ein Steiner-Referat, sondern um einen verstehenden und natürlich auch subjektiven Umgang mit geisteswissenschaftlichen Inhalten. Manchmal ist der Hintergrund etwas persönlich Erlebtes, manchmal ein Gedanke eines anderen Autors. Dass dabei vieles offen bleibt, liegt in der Natur des Experiments.

Was hier als Sammlung abgedruckt ist, war ursprünglich eine Serie unter dem Titel «Steinerlese» in der Zeitschrift *Die Drei*. Es sind Gelegenheitstexte. Die meisten aus der ursprünglichen Serie wurden überarbeitet, manche weggelassen, andere sind dazugekommen. Der Blickwinkel auf die Gedanken Steiners mag manchmal ungewohnt sein. Vielleicht ist nicht alles für den «Anfänger» unmittelbar zugänglich, so wie Steiner ja überhaupt nichts für Anfänger ist, man aber doch irgendwann mit ihm anfangen muss. Allmählich kommt man dann hinein, und irgendwann ist man so drin, dass man sich über nichts mehr wundert. Jetzt den Anfängerblick wiederzuerlangen, scheint mir wichtig für das Ungeheuerliche, was Steiner zu sagen hatte und was einen immer wieder wunder nehmen darf.

Ruth Ewertowski

Zucker und die unschuldige Egoität

Als ich vor bald siebzehn Jahren zum ersten Mal der Anthroposophie und mit ihr auch Anthroposophen begegnet bin, habe ich mich darüber gewundert, dass man bei gemeinsamen Mahlzeiten zwar nie Alkohol, wohl aber Süßes in ziemlichen Mengen zu sich nimmt. Ja, eine solche Sorglosigkeit im Umgang mit dem Zucker bei ansonsten doch ernährungsbewussten Demeter-Käufern fand ich merkwürdig. Muss man sich, wenn man kein Glas Wein trinkt, in Sachen Genuss irgendwie anders schadlos halten?

Warum der Alkohol der geistigen Entwicklung schadet, habe ich dann bald bei Rudolf Steiner gelesen: Hatte er in früheren Zeiten einmal seine Aufgabe gerade im Zusammenhang mit der Individualisierung des Menschen, so wirkt er spätestens seit unserer Zeitrechnung in vieler, besonders in spiritueller Hinsicht den «Errungenschaften» des Ich entgegen. Er dämpft das Bewusstsein und schafft geradezu ein «Gegen-

Ich», das dem in der Moderne anstehenden bewussten Schritt in die Welt des Geistes entgegensteht.

Um den Zucker habe ich mich dann nicht weiter gekümmert. Er schien ja auch nicht «verboten». Erst als mir jemand aus gesundheitlichen Gründen riet, auf Zucker ganz zu verzichten, wurde er interessant. Zwar hatte ich gehört, er solle das Ich stärken, aber ich hatte eigentlich mehr den Eindruck, dass eine gewisse Ich-Stärke dazu gehört, ihn wegzulassen. Ja, Zucker ist doch eher ein Genuss- und Suchtmittel, das, wenn man es mit einer Steuer belegen würde, die Finanzmisere des Gesundheitssystems lösen könnte. Das brächte nicht nur viel Geld, sondern würde, bei Konsumverzicht wegen des Preises, auch viel Gesundheit bringen und so wieder Geld sparen.[1]

Nun gibt es bei Rudolf Steiner viele Stellen, an denen er sich zum Thema Zucker äußert, und er äußert sich nicht selten positiv. Doch muss man sehen, dass sein Blick dabei nicht auf die physische Gesundheit geht. Was er über den Zucker sagt, gehört nicht ins Apotheken- oder Reformhausblättchen, sondern betrifft die seelisch-geistige und wohl auch die moralische Entwicklung des Menschen und der Menschheit. Es ist aus esoterischer Perspektive gesprochen. Das heißt nicht, dass es weniger konkret wäre. Die geisteswissenschaftlichen Wahrheiten finden an manchen historischen und sinnenfälligen Phänomenen ihre Bestätigung. So weist Steiner darauf hin, dass mit der Entwicklung der Bewusstseinsseele die Ich-Kraft des Menschen besonders hervortritt, und diese nun wird äußerlich materiell durch den Zuckergenuss unterstützt. Die Epoche der Bewusstseinsseele beginnt mit dem, was man nach der Periodisierung der Historiker die Neuzeit nennt, also im 15. Jahrhundert. Und eben in dieser Zeit, der Zeit der großen Entdeckungen, kommen auch die Zuckerproduktion und der Zuckerhandel auf.[2]

Die Bewusstseinsseelenepoche ist die der vollen Entwicklung des Ich. Rudolf Steiner nennt als Repräsentanten dieser Epoche das Volk der Engländer, und dieses schreibt ja tatsächlich als einziges Wort seiner Sprache das Ich groß. Dem entspricht, so Steiner, der hohe Zuckerkonsum in jenem Land, der zu seiner Zeit etwa ein Fünffaches von dem betragen haben soll, was in Russland an Zucker verzehrt wurde.[3] Die Ausprägung der Ich-Tätigkeit und der Egoität verhält sich proportional dazu.

Würde man den Völkern Temperamente zuordnen, wie man das bei Individuen tut, so würde man vermutlich das sanguinische Temperament den Engländern mit ihrem Humor und ihrer Spielfreude attestieren und das melancholische dem russischen Volk, das einen Dostojewski, einen Tolstoi, einen Tschechow mit ihren so schwermütigen Dichtungen hervorgebracht hat. Nun kommt Steiner im Rahmen seiner pädagogischen Hinweise auf das melancholische und sanguinische Temperament zu sprechen, und zwar im Zusammenhang mit dem Zuckerthema. Dabei findet sich das, was auf der charakterologischen Ebene von Völkern zu beobachten ist, jetzt auf der Ebene des Individuums wieder, nun freilich nicht als bloße Beobachtung, sondern als pädagogische Maßnahme, denn es geht hier ja um die Erziehung des Kindes. So wäre es hilfreich, einem melancholisch gestimmten Kind in bestimmten Mengen Zucker anzubieten, weil der sich dämpfend auf die Leber, das Organ der Schwermut, auswirkt, während es umgekehrt bei einem sanguinischen Kind gerade gut sein kann, die Lebertätigkeit durch Zuckerenthaltung anzuregen.[4] Es geht also darum, durch die Nahrung auf die seelisch-geistige Entwicklung Einfluss zu nehmen und ausgleichend zu wirken. Und eben diesen Aspekt gilt es auch bei einer esoterischen Entwicklung zu berücksichtigen.

In einer gewissen Hinsicht ist es wohl erlaubt, das melancholische Temperament als das anzusehen, das den Tiefen der Seele und der Welt des Geistes mehr zugetan ist als das eher an der Sinneswelt orientierte sanguinische. So darf man vermutlich auch der Zuwendung zur Geisteswissenschaft eher eine melancholische Disposition unterstellen.

Wo nun aber eine größere Bereitschaft oder auch innere Notwendigkeit vorliegt, den Weg in die Welt des Geistes einzuschlagen, muss gleichzeitig das Gebot der Selbstlosigkeit beachtet werden. Rudolf Steiner sieht jedoch auf eben diesem Weg auch Gefahren, jene Gefahr zum Beispiel, dass das Ich seinen Zusammenhang mit der Erde verliert, dass der Mensch in seinem Geistesstreben nicht nur selbstlos, sondern auch träumerisch und phantastisch wird. Dabei gewinnt dann das luziferische Element die Oberhand. Deshalb, so Steiner, könne man an dieser Stelle dem Zucker «eine Art Lobrede» halten. Denn der Zucker gebe – wohl auch durch seine kristalline Struktur – eine innerliche Festigkeit, eine Art «natürliche Egoität», derer es als Gegengewicht zu einer falschen Selbstlosigkeit und einem Verlieren der Persönlichkeit bedürfe. Mit dem Zuckergenuss wird «eine Art unschuldige Egoität» – so der schöne Ausdruck Steiners – geschaffen, die den Betreffenden davor bewahrt, sich bei seiner moralischen Entwicklung in der Selbstlosigkeit zu verlieren.[5]

Der Zucker als eine die Persönlichkeit stärkende Substanz hat in dieser Betrachtung eine ganz andere Bedeutung als das gesundheitsgefährdende Genussmittel, auf dessen Konto eine ganze Reihe von Zivilisationskrankheiten gehen. Er hat eine geistig-seelische Qualität, die einem luziferisch gearteten Selbstverlust entgegenwirkt und einer angemessenen Selbstbehauptung dient. Wer ihn aus diesen Gründen braucht, wird vermutlich seinen speziellen Nutzen daraus ziehen. Zu unterscheiden gilt es aber zwischen dieser geistigen Wirksamkeit der materiellen Substanz Zucker und ihrer physischen. Von Karies und manch anderen schädlichen Folgen bleibt gewiss niemand verschont, der um seiner «unschuldigen Egoität» willen nascht.

Und wenn dir ein Ziegelstein auf den Kopf fällt

«Und wenn dir ein Ziegelstein auf den Kopf fällt, bist du ganz sicher, dass es nicht doch bis zu einem gewissen Grade deine eigene Schuld war? Dass du die Möglichkeit seines Falles nicht vorher erwogen, war das nicht ein Mangel an Voraussicht? Und ist es gänzlich auszuschließen, dass es nicht vielleicht dein eigener Schritt war, der den Stein lockerte? Oder gingst du nicht am Ende schon in der unbewussten Absicht vorüber, das Haus zu erschüttern, von dessen Dache er dir auf den Kopf fiel?»

Nein, dieses Zitat stammt nicht von Rudolf Steiner. Es ist ein Aphorismus aus dem *Buch der Sprüche und Bedenken* des österreichischen Schriftstellers Arthur Schnitzler, das 1927 in Wien erschien. Eine der Parallelstellen bei Steiner lautet: «Sagen wir, uns fällt ein Ziegelstein auf den Kopf. Wir können zunächst die Ursachen nicht einsehen, aber wir stellen uns einen Menschen vor, der dieses Ziegel-auf-den-Kopf-Fallen in folgender Weise hervorruft: Er läuft zunächst auf das Dach und zieht dort den Ziegelstein so weit los, dass er nur ein klein wenig zu warten hat, bis er herunterfällt; dann läuft er rasch hinunter, und der Ziegelstein trifft ihn. Und so machen wir es mit bestimmten Ereignissen, von denen wir durchaus wissen, dass wir sie nicht selber herbeigeführt haben nach unserem gewöhnlichen Bewusstsein, die uns sogar sehr gegen unseren Willen kommen.»[6]

Der Band von Arthur Schnitzler, in dem die so erstaunlich ähnlichen Sätze vorkommen, enthält Aphorismen, die vor allem in den Zwanzigerjahren, aber zum Teil auch schon in den Neunzigern des 19. Jahrhunderts in verschiedenen Zeitungen veröffentlicht worden waren. Es steht zu vermuten, dass Steiner und Schnitzler unabhängig voneinander auf den gleichen Gedanken kamen, denn es gibt keine Hinweise darauf, dass beide füreinander irgendeine besondere Bedeutung gehabt hätten, auch wenn Steiner gelegentlich ein Drama von Schnitzler bespricht.[7] Für beide ist der Gedanke vom Ziegelstein, den man selbst gelockert hat, damit er einem auf Kopf oder Schulter fällt, eine Auseinandersetzung mit dem Zufall, doch sind die Grundstimmungen des Denkens dabei jeweils sehr verschieden.

Weitere prominente Stellen im Werk Steiners, die diesen Gedanken entfalten, finden sich in den Vorträgen vom 9.2.1912 und vom 20.2.1912.[8] Sie handeln jeweils von karmischen Zusammenhängen. Die Aufforderung, sich einen «künstlichen Menschen» vorzustellen, der etwas tut, was einem selbst unmittelbar nur schadet, und der man aber doch selber ist, ist als Experiment gedacht. Dieses Gedankenspiel kann aber nach und nach eine Wirkung auf unser seelisches Erleben entfalten. Gibt man dem Gedanken Raum und wendet man ihn noch auf andere Begebenheiten an wie etwa auf eine Krankheit oder einen verpassten Zug, so verliert er allmählich seine ursprüngliche Fremdheit. Das, was einem zuvor wie von außen begegnet ist, wird zur eigenen Sache. Das Widerstrebende beginnt einem irgendwann bekannt vorzukommen, und man erlebt sich schließlich gar als Selbstgestalter seines Schicksals – vielleicht sogar mit einer gewissen Entspannung oder Erlösung.

Freilich bedarf es bei der Bildung jenes künstlichen Menschen schon auch einer recht ordentlichen und sich selbst überwindenden Anstrengung. Es gibt genug Gelegenheiten, das auszuprobieren, und als Anthroposoph kann man einen anderen Anthroposophen geradezu damit ärgern, ihn in einer entsprechenden Situation an diese Gedankenübung zu erinnern. Das tat ich einmal, als mein Mann ziemlich entnervt bei winterlichen Straßenverhältnissen und penetrantem Schneefall viel später als erwartet abends nach Hause kam. Nach Bibliotheksdienst mit vertrackten Computerproblemen und einem anschließenden Arbeitskreis, bei dem man für diesmal über ein gewisses Gerede nicht hinauskam, was immer anstrengender ist als richtige Arbeit, wuchs sich die sonst viertelstündige Heimfahrt zu einer Stunde aus. Ein schneeglatter Berg hatte den Verkehr zum Stocken gebracht und manche Autofahrer auch auf wieder ebener Strecke nur noch Schritttempo fahren lassen. Und dann stand auch noch einer vor der Garage, mit auswärtiger Nummer. Also nichts mit schnell ins Warme, Tee trinken und entspannen.

Nun stell dir vor, du selbst hast dieses Auto hier geparkt, vielleicht damit du endlich Kontakt zu all deinen Nachbarn aufnimmst, indem du erfragst, ob sie eventuell einen auswärtigen Besuch haben. Wer weiß, was daraus wird. Der Ärger wird sich durch die Zumutung dieser Vorstellung wahrscheinlich erst mal nicht gleich besänftigen lassen, im Gegenteil. Gelingt es aber doch, diesen Gedanken zu erwägen, welche Ruhe kann sich dann einstellen und welche Gelassenheit gegenüber dem, was einem so querkommt!

Bei Steiner ist dieser Gedankenprozess ein «Hilfsprozess», der eine Umwandlung in uns begleitet und schließlich zu jenem lebendigen Gefühlseindruck führt, dass auch das Widrige noch etwas mit uns zu tun hat. Dieser Prozess lässt uns wiedererkennen, was uns vorher fremd war und macht uns mit uns selbst bekannt. Fortgeschrittene führt er womöglich gar in eine frühere Inkarnation. Er bringt gewissermaßen eine Lösung oder Erlösung, die letztlich in der Erkenntnis von Sinn liegt. Alles gehört in einen organischen Zusammenhang, der, wenn er als solcher erlebt wird, ein Gefühl sowohl der Gelassenheit wie der Geborgenheit mit sich bringen kann.

Wenn zwei das Gleiche sagen, muss es noch nicht das Gleiche sein. Auch bei Schnitzler gilt es sich vorzustellen, dass der Ziegelstein, der mich verletzt, von mir selbst so gelockert wurde, dass er auf mich herabfällt. Doch sowohl das Umfeld, in dem dieser Aphorismus steht, wie auch sein Duktus selbst, lassen auf eine ganz andere Denkungsart schließen. Schnitzler – ursprünglich Arzt, dann Schriftsteller und gut mit Siegmund Freud und dessen psychoanalytischer Methode bekannt – denkt nicht wie Steiner aus karmischen Zusammenhängen und dem spirituellen Interesse an der Sinnhaftigkeit des Lebens und der Menschheitsentwicklung heraus, sondern im Hinblick auf die verborgenen Hintergründe und Ambitionen psychischer Verfassungen. War es nicht dein eigener Schritt, der den Stein gelockert hat, und zwar in unbewusster Absicht? –, so fragt Schnitzler und meint damit die damals eben erst gemachte psychoanalytische Entdeckung der unbewussten Zielstrebigkeiten der Seele, die auf raffinierte Weise ihre eigentlichen Zwecke bemäntelt, indem sie die Mittel zu ihrem Erreichen so darstellt, als könnten es gar nicht ihre wirklichen Zwecke sein. Denn wer lässt sich schon einen Ziegelstein auf den Kopf fallen? Das tut nur jemand, der seinem Leben mehr oder weniger entschieden ein Ende setzen will, dies aber – auch vor sich selbst – nicht zugeben mag. Er verbrämt seine Absichten, indem er den Zufall für das verantwortlich macht, wofür er selbst nicht verantwortlich gemacht werden will.

Eine solche psychologische Sichtweise hat eine umgekehrte Ausrichtung als die Steiners. Sie enttarnt die Raffinesse einer Pragmatik, die sich selbst verbergen will. Während Steiner nicht enttarnt, sondern offenbar zu machen sucht, was das Geistige sowohl in der individuellen wie auch in der Menschheitsgeschichte ist. Steiners Blick geht nicht auf die Zwecke, sondern den Sinn, nicht auf Entlarvung, sondern auf

Beheimatung in der Welt, die in sich, eben wegen der zu machenden Sinnerfahrung, keinen Grund zur Depression enthält, während eine solche bei Schnitzler wohl der eigentliche Hintergrund des vermeintlichen Unfalls ist.

Je spiritueller der Mensch, umso ruhiger die Erde

Anders als in früheren Jahrhunderten ist man heute zu Recht empfindlich, wenn ein Zusammenhang zwischen einer Naturkatastrophe und einer menschlich-moralischen Verfehlung oder Schuld unterstellt wird. Was man einst als Gottes Strafe ansehen mochte, wie das Heinrich von Kleist in seiner ganzen Fragwürdigkeit in der Novelle *Das Erdbeben in Chili* zum Thema gemacht hat, ist für das Allgemeinverständnis heute meist schlicht eine Naturkatastrophe mit rein natürlichen Ursachen. Natur und Moral sind geschieden. Auch die Theodizee-Frage, die noch Voltaire aus Anlass des Erdbebens in Lissabon von 1755 in seinem *Candide* zu einer bissigen Antwort auf Leibniz´ Idee von der «besten aller Welten», die Gott schuf, herausforderte, also die Frage, wie Gott das alles zulassen konnte, wird so kaum mehr gestellt. Naturkatastrophen folgen Naturgesetzen. Nur insofern der Mensch etwa an der Klimaerwärmung «schuld» ist, können sie auch auf menschliches Handeln zurückgehen. Das aber ist als «Umweltfaktor» in seiner Komplexität nicht unmittelbar moralisch.

Rudolf Steiners Perspektive ist eine andere: Erdbeben, Vulkanausbrüche etc. haben karmische Konsequenzen und okkulte Hintergründe. Sie sind Ausdruck geistiger Sachverhalte und spiegeln den Entwicklungsstand der geistig-moralischen Verfassung der Menschheit. Dabei ist aber auch Steiner weit davon entfernt, einen ursächlichen Zusammenhang zwischen einer moralischen Verfehlung aufseiten des Menschen und einer strafenden Aktivität geistiger Wesen in Naturkatastrophen zu behaupten. Ein Erdbeben oder ein Vulkanausbruch bedeutet ebenso wenig eine Schuld der Betroffenen, wie auf der anderen Seite das Wohlergehen Unschuld oder gar Verdienst bezeugt. Doch kann ein Erdbeben karmische Bedeutung haben. Wenn dabei etwa eine ganze Menschengruppe einem vernichtenden Schicksal zum Opfer fällt, so kann dies die Voraussetzung für eine gemeinschaftliche Entwicklung sein, zu der es ohne die Katastrophe nicht gekommen wäre. Steiner ist sich bewusst, dass solche Aussagen in der Öffentlichkeit auf wenig Gehör stoßen, formuliert sie aber mit Entschiedenheit: «Denn dasjenige, was hier auf Erden wenig Anklang findet in unseren Seelen, etwa der Satz: Ich wähle mir ein großes Unglück, um vollkommener zu werden, weil ich sonst unvollkommen bliebe gegenüber dem, was in meinem vergangenen Karma liegt, – dieses Urteil, das wie gesagt, wenig Anklang findet innerhalb des Erdenlebens, es ist da, es ist als ein vollgültiges Urteil da, wenn wir in dem Leben zwischen dem Tod und einer neuen Geburt stehen. Da suchen wir auch einen Vulkanausbruch, da suchen wir auch ein Erdbeben, um auf dem Wege des Unglückes den Weg zur Vollkommenheit zu finden.»[9]

Nun spricht Steiner aber nicht nur von der zukünftigen Vervollkommnung der Opfer einer Naturkatastrophe durch diese, sondern auch davon, was sich Negatives in ihr ausdrückt: Naturerscheinungen lassen Diagnosen über Geisteshintergründe zu. Die Wesenheit, die Steiner hinter einem Erdbeben oder Vulkanausbruch ausmacht, ist Ahriman.[10] Und die Geisteshaltung, die ihm entspricht, ist die des Materialismus. Mit dem Heraufkommen des Materialismus häufen und vergrößern sich diese Naturkatastrophen. Was die Zahl der Vulkanausbrüche betrifft, belegt dies Steiner am Beispiel der vor allem im 19. Jahrhundert zu beobachtenden Häufigkeit der Vesuvausbrüche.[11] Eine Katastrophe von so ungeheurem Ausmaß wie die in

Südostasien Ende des Jahres 2004 mag in diesem Sinne für unsere Gegenwart sprechend sein.

Ahriman und der Materialismus. – Die Gefahr bei einer solchen diagnostischen Zuordnung liegt in einer Hypostasierung der Katastrophe und einer Schuldzuweisung. Diese Gefahr besteht. Merkwürdig ist nur, dass sich eine ganz andere Perspektive auf das Phänomen ergibt, wenn man beide von Steiner genannten Aspekte zusammendenkt, also zum einen den möglichen Sinn der Naturkatastrophe in der Vervollkommnung der Betroffenen und zum anderen die Katastrophe als Ausdruck einer materialistischen und unspirituellen Gesinnung. Also, was ein Ausdruck für die Verhaftung an die Welt der Sinne ist, ist möglicherweise zugleich die Ursache für eine Spiritualisierung in der Zukunft anderer Menschen.

Für die unmittelbar Betroffenen sind es in der Hauptsache zwei Arten von Beziehungen, in denen ihr Schicksal zu einem Erdbeben oder Vulkanausbruch stehen kann. So spricht Steiner zum einen von denen, die durch eine solche Katastrophe ums Leben kommen, und zum anderen von jenen, die in dieser Zeit geboren werden. Beide Menschengruppen verhalten sich wie komplementär zueinander: «Es stellt sich heraus, dass die Menschen, welche bei einem solchen erschütternden Ereignis zugrunde gehen, abgesehen von allen ihren übrigen karmischen Veranlagungen, durch Tatsachen karmischer Art mit Seelen an dem Ort, wo ein Erdbeben stattfindet, zusammengeführt werden. Alle Seelen, die durch solche Erschütterungen zugrunde gehen, finden dadurch die Möglichkeit, einen letzten Punkt zu überwinden, der ihnen in ihrem Karma noch im Wege liegt, um von einem Materialisten zu einem Idealisten zu werden und zur Erkenntnis des Geistigen zu kommen. Diejenigen, die unter solchen Umständen geboren werden, sind dagegen merkwürdigerweise Seelen, bei denen eine bestimmte Anziehungskraft zu Trieben, Instinkten und Leidenschaften besteht und die zu richtigen Materialisten geboren werden. Diejenigen, die unter dem Einfluss eines solchen Ereignisses geboren werden, entwickeln sich zu Materialisten, und zwar zumeist zu praktischen, zu solchen, die es im Leben in Bezug auf ihre Moral sind. Es hängt die Naturkraft mit dem zusammen, was die Menschen als ihre Kraft im Devachan entwickeln, und die Kräfte, welche als Reaktion von Feuer- und Fruchterde bei solchen Katastrophen auftreten, haben einen inneren Bezug auf solche Seelen, die bestimmt sind, im nächsten Leben eine praktisch-materialistische Gesinnung zu haben. Es sind also die unter den Auspizien von Vulkanausbrüchen geborenen Seelen die eigentlich materialistischen, die ungläubigen Menschen, diejenigen, die nichts von einem geistigen Leben wissen wollen.»

Wie der Tod unter den Umständen einer Naturkatastrophe in der nächsten Inkarnation der Betroffenen zu einer Spiritualisierung führt, so kündigen auf der anderen Seite die Geburten im Umfeld der Katastrophe eine Steigerung des Materialismus an. Das ist merkwürdig: Einerseits ist die Katastrophe eine Chance zur Hinwendung zum Geistigen, andererseits ist sie gerade Ausdruck einer zunehmenden Abwendung. Die Beziehung dieser beiden gegenläufigen Tendenzen zueinander ist äußerst rätselhaft, prekär und sicher auch befremdlich. In ihr liegt aber der Knotenpunkt einer Kulmination. Auf dem Gipfel der materialistischen Entwicklung kann sich der Knoten lösen oder noch fester zuziehen. – Wodurch wird diese Krisis entschieden?

Für viele heute gewiss schwer verständlich ist Rudolf Steiners Aussage, dass, je mehr es gelingt, den universalisierten Materialismus zu überwinden, desto weniger solche Katastrophen auftreten werden: «Es besteht nämlich diese Anziehung zwischen dem Materialismus und dem, was in der Feuer- und Fruchterde vorhanden ist, so dass unsere Erde ruhiger und harmonischer werden wird in demselben Maße, wie die Menschheit vom Materialismus frei wird.»

Soll eine Zuwendung zur Welt des Geistes tatsächlich ein Erdbeben verhindern können? – Möglicherweise liegt genau in der Skepsis, mit der diese Frage gestellt wird, der Entscheidungspunkt der Krisis. Denn dieser Skepsis liegt die radikale Trennung von Natur und Geist, von Natur und Moral zugrunde. Man hat den Zusammenhang bestritten und vergessen. Man hat ihn zu Recht kritisiert, was die eingangs genannte Idee von der Strafe Gottes betrifft. Das heißt aber nicht, dass er nicht besteht.

Was ist denn eigentlich «Materialismus»? Kaum jemand wird sich heute selbst als «Materialist» bezeichnen, und die Mehrzahl der Menschen versteht sich wohl auch mit Recht als moralisch, auch wenn sie nur die Welt der Sinne gelten lässt. Materialismus, das muss nicht einfach eine Haltung sein, die keine Moral mehr kennt, weil sie alles zur Materie erklärt hat. Es ist vielmehr jene Geisteshaltung, für die es keine Verbindung zwischen natürlicher und moralischer Welt mehr gibt. Sicher, die naiv gebaute Brücke zwischen diesen Welten, die die Natur nur als das Instrument göttlicher Strafe oder Belohnung ansah, musste abgerissen werden. Eine echte und tragfähige Brücke ist hingegen nur schwer zu errichten. An ihr wird aber zum Beispiel überall da gebaut, wo man versucht, die Verwandlung des Moralischen in das Natürliche im Durchgang durch die Welt zwischen Tod und neuer Geburt zu begreifen.

Wäre es nicht möglich, dass eine behutsame Erforschung der Beziehung zwischen Naturerscheinungen und ihren geistig-moralischen Hintergründen und Auswirkungen, eine Forschung jenseits von allen Schuldzuweisungen, hier zu jener Spiritualisierung führen könnte, die die Erde beruhigt? Eine solche Aufgabe stellt sich vor allem im Hinblick auf ein zunehmendes Verständnis des Karmagesetzes, denn dieses ist nicht zuletzt das Gesetz der Verbindung beider Sphären, wie sie sich zum Beispiel in der Verwandlung bestimmter moralischer Ambitionen in der einen Inkarnation zu gewissen physischen Merkmalen in der anderen zeigt oder eben in der Einwirkung von Naturereignissen auf eine künftige seelisch-geistige Verfassung. Das Karmaprinzip ist das Gesetz einer Metamorphose, dessen Verständnis ein außerordentlicher Schritt auf dem Weg zu einer Spiritualisierung wäre. Für eine solche Zuwendung zum Geist ist die Materie alles andere als bedeutungslos. Geist ist nicht einfach das Gegenteil von Materie, sondern das, was sich selbst und das Andere, die Materie, in ihrem Zusammenhang begreifen kann. Dem Materialismus ist eine geistige Welt fremd; die Geisteswissenschaft aber kann die Materie zu verstehen versuchen.

Natürlich kommt es nicht nur auf das Verstehen an, sondern auch aufs Handeln, und somit hat z.B. die Spendenbereitschaft, die der materiellen Not nach einer Naturkatastrophe Abhilfe schaffen will, eine enorme Bedeutung, aber sie allein genügt nicht. Zudem ist sie fast immer allein vergangenheitsbezogen, und zwar auch im Hinblick auf den Wiederaufbau. Was die Zukunft betrifft, hat auch weniger ein ausgeklügeltes Frühwarnsystem eine echte Rettungsbedeutung als eine noch ganz andere «Spendenbereitschaft»: eine Bereitschaft, sich aus den gewohnten Denkmustern zu lösen und Natur und Moral wieder in eine Beziehung zueinander zu setzen, damit die Erde nicht immer wieder auf unerhörte, weil ungehörte Weise erbeben muss.

Wiedergeburt versus Genforschung
Über Weihnachten und Golgatha

«Zweimal geboren müssen wir sein, das eine Mal durch die Kräfte der Natur, das andere Mal wiedergeboren durch die Kräfte des Christus Jesus.»[12] – Die Menschwerdung ist eine Aufgabe, die nicht schon mit der Geburt am Anfang des irdischen Lebens vollendet ist, sondern erst mit unserer Wiedergeburt. Im Unterschied zur ersten, zur natürlichen Geburt muss man für die zweite Geburt selbst erst empfänglich werden, denn sie ist eine Geburt mit Bewusstsein, während die physische Geburt für den Geborenen ein bewusstloses Geschehen ist. Voraussetzung für die zweite Geburt ist nicht zuletzt ein Verständnis für das Weihnachts- und das Golgathamysterium.

Im gewöhnlichen Bewusstsein nimmt heute das Weihnachtsfest weit mehr Raum ein als das Osterfest. Zum einen ist es gefälliger, zum anderen sind Tod und Auferstehung naturgemäß kaum zu begreifen und haben zudem auch etwas Beängstigendes. Man wendet sich deshalb gerne vor allem dem freudigeren, dem leichteren Ereignis des natürlichen Geburtsfestes zu. Schon der 6. Januar als Fest der Epiphanie, der Erscheinung Christi auf Erden, als Geburt Christi im Leib Jesu im Augenblick der Jordantaufe ist für das Vorstellungsvermögen nur schwer zu fassen, weshalb er in der westlichen Welt ziemlich aus dem Blick geraten ist. Im Mittelpunkt steht der 24./25. Dezember mit der Geburt Jesu. Allein in der Ostkirche wird auch heute noch der 6. Januar als Christgeburt gefeiert.

Als kirchlicher Feiertag ist der 25. Dezember erst seit dem Jahr 336 in Rom belegt. Auf dieses Datum wurde der Geburtstag Jesu, dessen genaue historische Datierung faktisch gar nicht anzugeben ist, festgelegt. Am Vortag des 25. Dezember beginnt die Sonne wieder zu wachsen. Diesen Sonnenbezug nahm man für Christus, die neue, die eigentliche Sonne, zu Recht in Anspruch, jedoch unter Vernachlässigung des eigentlichen Inkarnationsgeheimnisses.

Einen noch ganz anderen Schritt in der Entfernung vom eigentlichen Geheimnis der Christgeburt stellt das Aufkommen eines Weihnachtssymboles dar, das heute so selbstverständlich zum Weihnachtsfest gehört, dass man sich kaum vorstellen kann, dass es einmal nicht dazu gehörte: der Weihnachtsbaum. Steiner weist wiederholt darauf hin, dass dieser kaum zweihundert (heute dreihundert) Jahre alt ist.[13] Goethe hat ihn übrigens erst 1770 in Straßburg kennengelernt, und so gehört seine Erwähnung im *Werther* 1774 wohl zu den frühesten literarischen Zeugnissen dieses Symbols.

Es geht Steiner nicht darum, uns die Freude am Weihnachtsbaum zu verderben: «Er [der Weihnachtsbaum] stellt uns die schöne, die liebenswürdige, sympathische Seite desjenigen dar, was auch in einer anderen Weise, in einer weniger anmutigen Weise uns in der neueren Menschheitsentwickelung vor die Seele tritt.» Es geht um Entwicklungstendenzen innerhalb der Bewusstseinsgeschichte, für die das Aufkommen dieses Baumes symptomatisch ist.

Der Weihnachts- oder Christbaum hat seinen Ursprung im mittelalterlichen Krippenspiel. Vor dem eigentlichen Krippenspiel fand das Paradiesspiel statt, in dem gezeigt wurde, wie durch Adam und Eva die Sünde in die Welt kam, von der die Menschheit durch Christi Kreuzestod befreit wurde. Zu diesem Spiel gehörte ein immergrüner Baum als «Paradiesbaum» (auch Adamsbaum), der mit Äpfeln geschmückt war. Wenn heute am 24. Dezember, dem Adam- und Evatag, die Kerzen am Weihnachtsbaum angezündet werden, so können das Immergrün des Baumes und die Lichter als Hoffnung auf ein Leben über den Tod hinaus verstanden werden; zugrunde aber liegt, freilich ins Unbewusste abgesunken, der Bezug zum natürlichen, paradiesischen und bewusstlosen Ursprung des Menschen. Es geht also nicht um das eigentliche Geburtsmysterium Jesu Christi und damit auch nicht um unsere zweite Geburt, sondern um den natürlichen Menschenursprung, seinen physischen Beginn, um die «Geburt» der Menschheit im Paradies. Auch darin liegt Sinn, denn die Erinnerung an die Paradiesessituation und ihren Verlust ist der Grund für das Weihnachts- und Ostergeschehen. Nur zeigt sich hier eine doppelte Bewusstlosigkeit: zum einen nämlich die Täuschung über das Symbol des Baumes – der «Christbaum» hat seinen Ursprung eben nicht als Christus-, sondern als Paradiesessymbol –, und zum anderen hinsichtlich der impliziten Sehnsucht nach Rückkehr ins Paradies und einer «Natürlichkeit», in der die Geburt ein physisches Ereignis und eben nicht die Vollendung der Menschwerdung in der Wiedergeburt ist. Steiner sieht in dieser Hinwendung den Anachronismus einer einseitigen Zuwendung zu dem, was er hier «Jahveprinzip» nennt, das mit allem natürlichen Dasein bis hin zur Blutsverwandtschaft und zur Volkszugehörigkeit zusammenhängt. Seine Aussagen über Jahve sind im Übrigen vielfältig und zum größten Teil ganz anderer Art. So gibt es in Steiners Vortragswerk auch die Bemerkung, dass sich Jahve und Christus gar nicht grundsätzlich voneinander unterscheiden.[14] Hier aber wirft er ein Licht auf tendenziöse weltanschauliche Positionen seiner Zeit. So sei Jahve der Gott, «der, wenn man sich mit ihm allein verbindet, dem Menschen niemals das volle Menschtum geben kann. Denn er gibt dem Menschen das Bewusstsein seiner natürlichen Geburt, allerdings mit ihrem geistigen Einschlag von Kräften, die nicht bloß natürlich sind, aber er gibt dem Menschen nicht das Bewusstsein von seiner Wiedergeburt, die er sich erwerben muss durch etwas, was ihm nicht durch natürlich-sinnlich-physische Kräfte gegeben werden kann. Und so sehen wir denn, wie abgelenkt worden ist die neuere Menschheit von dem Christus Jesus, für den es keinen Unterschied gibt der Klassen, keinen Unterschied der Völker, keinen Unterschied der Rassen, für den es nur ein einziges Menschtum gibt, wie abgelenkt worden sind die Gedanken, die Empfindungen der neueren Menschheit zu dem, was durch das Mysterium des Geborenwerdens des Christus Jesus schon überwunden war: zu dem hin, was nur zugrunde liegt den natürlichen Kräften der Menschheitsentstehung, die zusammenhängen mit der Menschheitsdifferenzierung in Klassen, in Völker, in Rassen.»

Auch dort, wo in unserer westlichen Gesellschaft eine Aufteilung in Klassen, Völker und Rassen weitestgehend überwunden ist, bleibt doch die Frage nach der natürlich-sinnlich-physischen Herkunft des Menschen, die die Unterschiede zwischen den Menschen ausmacht, diskussionsbeherrschend präsent. Sie ist nur subtiler geworden, ohne sich in der Sache, in der Zugangsweise geändert zu haben. Denn die Ursprungsfrage stellt sich auf Gebieten, deren Forschungsmethoden und Instrumentarien nur um ein vielfaches verfeinert wurden, ohne sich – z.B. gegenüber der Erforschung der Erbgesetze – im Prinzip geändert zu haben. Sie stellt sich in der Genforschung und der Neurophysiologie. Aus diesen Disziplinen ergibt sich zwar kein Zugehörigkeitsgefühl wie etwa das zu einem bestimmten Volk, wohl aber das Sich-berufen-Können auf eine durch Gene oder physiko-chemische Prozesse bedingte Anlage und Verfassung, aus deren natürlicher Gegebenheit sich Verantwortung erledigt. Oder es wird auf der anderen Seite ein Bewerber auf eine Stelle aufgrund eines durchgeführten Gentests, der bestimmte Krankheitsanlagen ausmachen lässt, zurückgewiesen. Auch das ist eine Art Rassismus.

Wir begegnen hier einer Persiflage jenes Satzes aus der *Theosophie*, dass jeder Mensch eine Gattung für sich ist. Steiner verwendet den Gattungsbegriff dort als Metapher und bezieht sich auf die Zusammengehörigkeit jedes Einzelnen mit sich selbst, insofern er seine eigene geistige Existenz, auch physisch, beerbt. Bei der Gen- und Hirnforschung wird der Gattungsbegriff aber wörtlich genommen und erklärt die spezifische Fixierung des Einzelnen durch genetische und neuronale Faktoren, die ihn immer schon aus jeder Verantwortung entlassen haben, wie sie ihm umgekehrt aufgrund seiner physischen Bedingtheit auch nicht zutrauen, über diese hinauszuwachsen.

Genforschung und Neurophysiologie sind die Gebiete, die heute die Ursprungsfrage stellen. Dass auch sie dabei dem «Jahveprinzip» folgen, wie es Steiner im Zusammenhang eines Missverstehens des Weihnachtsmysteriums herausstellt, wird deutlich daran, dass man auf höchstem Bewusstseinsniveau zurückstrebt in einen Zustand der Bewusstlosigkeit, nämlich den der stofflich bedingten Ausrichtung unseres Denkens und Handelns, in dem unser Bewusstsein nur das abkünftige Phänomen neuronaler Prozesse ist.

Jenes «Keiner kann anders, als er ist» (Wolf Singer) bestätigt das Jahveprinzip des rein natürlichen Ursprungs in vollem Umfang. Aus ihm folgt, dass unter Berücksichtigung aller gegebenen Umstände alle Ereignisse voraussagbar sind. Das aber heißt letztlich auch, es gibt nichts Neues mehr. Es gibt nur neue Kombinationen einer außerordentlichen Vielzahl von Variablen, Variablen im Genom, in der Sozialisation, in der Umwelt, aber keine Wiedergeburt. Gerade aber die Wiedergeburt ist das Neue, das Offene, das Unerwartete, das Schöpferische, mit dem ein Anfang gesetzt wird, der bedingt und unbedingt zugleich ist, so wie Christi Geburt, Passion, Tod und Auferstehung. Wiedergeburt, das bedeutet die radikale Änderung des natürlichen Menschen, das Anders-Können als man ist, mit dem sich das Menschsein immer neu vollendet. All dies ist mit dem Begriff der Initiation gemeint: einen Neuanfang setzen.

Für diesen Neuanfang waren die Hirten und die Könige auch zur Zeit von Jesu Geburt offen: die einen am Anfang der Heiligen Nächte in ihrem Gang zur Krippe, dem eigentlichen Weihnachtssymbol, die anderen am Ende dieser Nächte, deren letzte mit der Jordantaufe zusammenfällt. Ihre Hinwendung zu den Zeichen der Natur auf der Erde und im Himmel bezog sich nicht auf Gene und mathematische Abstände von Himmelskörpern, sondern auf das, was in unserem Innersten und im Kosmos gleichermaßen zu finden ist.

Wenn die Naturwissenschaft heute versucht, den Dualismus von Geist und Materie dadurch aufzuheben, dass sie jede seelisch-geistige Regung auf komplexe Substanzverhältnisse zurückführt, so verengt sie unsere Bewusstseinskapazität auf eine mechanistische Kausalität, mit der die Freiheitsfrage «überwunden» ist. Das ist ein Rückfall in das, was Steiner das Jahve-Prinzip nennt, dessen Defizienz heute von vielen Menschen, ja gewiss sogar von manchem Gen- und Hirnforscher selbst, verspürt wird, die aber gegenüber der komplexen und dichten Argumentation dieser Wissenschaften auch ohnmächtig macht: Man will Bedrohtes retten – die Freiheit, die Liebe, das Christliche –, weiß aber nicht wie, weil das Kausalitätsprinzip der Stofflichkeit alles im Griff zu haben scheint. Was es aber nicht erfasst, was ihm prinzipiell verborgen bleibt, das sind alle Metamorphoseverhältnisse. Metamorphosen aber sind es, die die Beziehung von Geist und Materie ausmachen. Die Inkarnation Christi darf als ein Inbegriff dieser Beziehung angesehen werden. Das Geburtsgeheimnis, das Weihnachtsmysterium und das Mysterium von Golgatha beinhalten die Verwandlung des Geistigen ins Natürliche und des Natürlichen ins Geistige. Die zweite, die geistige Geburt spricht von einer vollständigen Verwandlung des Menschen, die im Unterschied zu allen Ursache-Wirkungs-Verhältnissen nicht durch die Vergangenheit erklärt, sondern nur im Blick auf die Zukunft verstanden werden kann, die sie eröffnet.

Die Doppelgängerbegegnung: eine Eintrittskarte in die geistige Welt

Der Doppelgänger begegnet dem Menschen an der Schwelle zur geistigen Welt. Er hat bekanntlich mit dem Hüter der Schwelle zu tun, aber wie? Er scheint mit ihm identisch und doch auch wieder nicht.

Hilfreich für eine Klärung des Verhältnisses zwischen beiden kann die simple Frage nach der Zahl sein: Wie viele Doppelgänger gibt es? – Es gibt annähernd 7 Milliarden, also ebenso viele, wie es Menschen auf der Erde gibt, denn jeder hat seinen eigenen. Aber gibt es auch 7 Milliarden Hüter der Schwelle? – Das hört sich doch so merkwürdig an, dass man hier nachdenken muss. Es gibt zwei Hüter der Schwelle: den kleinen und den großen. Der kleine ist eine wesenhafte Funktion des individuellen Doppelgängers, während der große ein Vorbild ist und etwas mit Christus zu tun hat. Der kleine Hüter, um den allein es hier geht, ist nicht von sich aus schon ein Schattenbild, aber als ein solches tritt er auf, wenn er mit dem Doppelgänger vereint ist. Der

Doppelgänger, der auch der Hüter ist, ist ein Schwellenphänomen. Vor allem als solches ist er – im Unterschied zu anderen Bedeutungsvarianten – ein Thema der Anthroposophie, denn sie ist die Wissenschaft von der Schwelle, also Einweihungswissenschaft.

Wenn der Mensch auf dem Weg zur Einweihung seinem Doppelgänger begegnet, so ist das Ausdruck eines entscheidenden Fortschrittes, den er auf diesem Weg gemacht hat. Ja, er ist dann bis zur Schwelle und wohl auch schon zu einem ersten Einblick in die geistige Welt gekommen. Zugleich aber und paradoxerweise begegnet er eben genau hier seiner eigenen Schattenseite. Er sieht sich in seiner ganzen Unzulänglichkeit genau in dem Moment, in dem er über sich selbst hinausgewachsen ist. Das geht mit einem Seelenschmerz einher, denn der Doppelgänger ist so schrecklich und hässlich, dass man sich seiner schämen muss. Die Scham gehört zu den unvermeidlichen Begleitumständen der Doppelgängerbegegnung.

Schämt man sich auch des Hüters der Schwelle? – Wohl nicht, denn er ist eine ehrwürdige Gestalt. Hier liegt, neben dem Zahlenverhältnis 1 : 7 Milliarden, ein weiterer bedeutsamer Unterschied: Man schämt sich des Doppelgängers, nicht aber des Hüters, und dennoch gehören beide unmittelbar zusammen.

Rudolf Steiner hat das Verhältnis von Doppelgänger und Hüter selbst nirgends ausdrücklich geklärt, aber dem Kapitel «Die Erkenntnis der höheren Welten» in der *Geheimwissenschaft im Umriss* lässt sich doch einiges Aufschlussreiche entnehmen. Hier spricht Steiner auch im Besonderen von dem Schamgefühl, das gegenüber dem Doppelgänger aufkommt. Dieses Gefühl scheint mir von zentraler Bedeutung. Steiner erklärt nämlich mit seiner Hilfe, warum wir unseren Doppelgänger gewöhnlich gerade nicht sehen: Drängt uns die Scham normalerweise dazu, etwas vor anderen zu verbergen, so geht die Scham über den Doppelgänger noch darüber hinaus: Sie verbirgt sich selbst, und damit verbirgt sie eben auch unsere Schattengestalt.

Vor diesem Hintergrund lässt sich das Verhältnis von Doppelgänger und Hüter der Schwelle auch noch folgendermaßen interpretieren: Der Doppelgänger, der uns verborgen bleibt, weil wir uns seiner allzu sehr schämen, nämlich so, dass das Gefühl der Scham ihn uns verhüllt, dieser unsichtbare Doppelgänger ist der Hüter der Schwelle. Das heißt, der Schatten, den wir selbst nicht sehen, nicht sehen wollen, nicht sehen können, ist der Hüter, der uns nicht einlässt. Sehen wir aber unseren Doppelgänger, so tritt der Hüter zur Seite und gewährt den Eintritt. Dann darf der Initiand, der Einzuweihende berechtigt die geistige Welt betreten. Man kann das auch so sagen: Solange wir unseren je eigenen Doppelgänger nicht sehen, ist er der Hüter der Schwelle, der uns für unreif befinden muss und uns die geistige Welt verschließt, weil wir noch nicht in der Lage sind, uns dort wirklich orientieren zu können. Denn wir würden all unsere Schattenseiten für objektive Gegebenheiten in dieser Welt halten und sie dort bekämpfen und damit nicht in uns selbst, also nicht dort, wo sie tatsächlich überwunden werden müssen. Zugleich bewahrt uns der Hüter damit aber auch vor dem Anblick dessen, was wir noch nicht aushalten können, nämlich unseren eigenen Doppelgänger. Für den aber, der dazu in der Lage ist, seinem Anblick standzuhalten, wird der Hüter zum Wegbereiter in die geistige Welt.

Über diese Situation an der Schwelle kann nur im Allgemeinen gesprochen werden. Denn kein Mensch kann konkret von einer eigenen Doppelgängererfahrung in diesem Sinne berichten. Wenn Goethe in *Dichtung und Wahrheit* davon spricht, dass er nach dem Abschied von Friederike Brion in Sesenheim sah, wie er sich selbst zu Pferd entgegengeritten kam, so war dies kein Doppelgängererlebnis im Sinne einer Begegnung mit dem Hüter der Schwelle. Es war, was die Psychologie eine «Heautoskopie» nennt – eine Wahrnehmung des eigenen Leibes als eine identische Gestalt außerhalb der eigenen Person. Bergsteiger können eine solche Wahrnehmung bei großer physischer Anstrengung kurz vor dem Gipfel haben. Auch Nahtoderlebnisse, bei denen der Betreffende sich etwa auf dem Operationstisch liegen sieht, beziehen sich auf die Leiblichkeit und nicht die eigene innerseelische Wahrheit. Eine solche Begegnung hat nicht jene moralische Qualität des Doppelgängererlebnisses an der Schwelle, das stets mit einem Gefühl der Scham verbunden ist und letztlich auf die Regung des Gewissens zurückgeht.

Wenn aber nun doch jemand von einer seelisch-moralischen Doppelgängerbegegnung berichten würde? Ja, dann darf man wohl seine Zweifel haben: Natürlich mag derjenige zu einer unangenehmen Selbsterkenntnis gekommen sein. Aber ist er wirklich durch den Abgrund seiner Existenz gegangen? Ist er wirklich dem begegnet, was ihm in seinem tiefsten Inneren peinlich ist – peinlich im Scham- und Schmerzenssinne des Wortes? – Ich glaube, wir hätten bei einem «Doppelgänger-Erlebnisbericht», also bei einer Art «Bekenntnis», allen Grund zu dem Verdacht, dass ein solches Geständnis mehr Alibifunktion hat, dass allenfalls ein Zipfelchen des eigenen Doppelgängers gesehen wurde, der verdünnte Schatten des eigentlichen Schattens. Denn ein wirkliches Doppelgängererlebnis lässt sich nicht veröffentlichen. Es bleibt im Verborgenen, ja muss da bleiben. Es ist etwas, was sich nur tief im Innersten der menschlichen Seele abspielen kann. Jede Veröffentlichung hätte da geradezu etwas Exhibitionistisches und damit eben etwas Schamloses. Scham aber gehört zu den geistigen Erkenntnisbedingungen. Man kann nicht das veröffentlichen, dessen man sich schämt. Das wäre unnatürlich. Die konkrete eigene Doppelgängererfahrung ist unaussprechlich. Es ist eine Begegnung, die jeder mit sich selbst abmachen muss. So liegt es in der Sache begründet, dass wir keine direkten Erfahrungsberichte einer solchen Begegnung haben können. In solchen läge vermutlich auch immer schon ein Bestreben nach Entlastung oder vielleicht sogar nach Anerkennung durch diejenigen, denen davon erzählt wird, weil man ja etwas ganz Schlimmes durchgemacht hat und dadurch irgendwie ausgezeichnet ist.

Rudolf Steiner hat sachgemäß sein eigenes Doppelgängererlebnis nirgends beschrieben. Wir dürfen aber davon ausgehen, dass er als der größte Eingeweihte unserer Zeit eines gehabt hat, auch wenn wir uns einen Doppelgänger Steiners nicht vorstellen können. Erst die Doppelgängerbegegnung, das Aushalten dieser Konfrontation führt legitim über die Schwelle zur geistigen Welt. Sie ist gewissermaßen eine Eintrittskarte in die Welt des Geistes, und die ist teuer. Wer diesen Preis nicht zahlt, also «umsonst» die Schwelle überschreitet, schaut vielleicht auch in die geistige Welt, aber nur dadurch, dass er sich bei seinem Eintritt am Hüter der Schwelle vorbeigemogelt hat. Ein legitimer Einlass durch den Hüter der Schwelle ist nur möglich, wenn eine Doppelgängerbegegnung bestanden wurde. Insofern dürfen wir diese Begegnung zu einem Kriterium, einem Prüfstein für die Wahrhaftigkeit von Aussagen über die geistige Welt machen. Trauen wir einem Menschen zu, dass er seinen Doppelgänger gesehen hat? Oder tritt er uns noch mit einem großen Schatten gegenüber, von dem er selbst nichts weiß? Wenn wir den Eindruck haben, dass jemand seinen Doppelgänger selbst noch nicht gesehen hat, dann sind seine Aussagen über ein Jenseits der Schwelle nur mit Vorsicht zu genießen. Denn dann hat er die Selbsterkenntnis noch nicht geleistet, die die Voraussetzung dafür ist, frei von Täuschungen die geistige Welt zu erforschen.

Die Heimatlosigkeit des Eingeweihten

Es gibt Orte und Gegenden, die einen besonders anziehen, und andere, in denen man nicht dauerhaft leben möchte. Die meisten Menschen haben so etwas wie eine äthergeografische Sympathie oder Antipathie. Sie ist ein Teil ihres Seelenlebens: ein Gefühl für die vorhandene oder fehlende «Heimatpotenz» einer Landschaft, der Luft und der Art, wie sich die Wolken bilden, der Menschen dort und ihrer Sprache, ihres Witzes oder ihrer Melancholie. Es sind sehr subtile und sehr individuelle Faktoren, die so etwas wie Heimat ausmachen und irgendwie zum Charakter eines Menschen gehören.

Für Rudolf Steiner hat nun aber gerade die Heimatlosigkeit einen Wert, der in geisteswissenschaftlicher Hinsicht von großer Bedeutung ist. Sie ist nämlich in einem gewissen Sinn die Voraussetzung für das richtige Verhältnis zur geistigen Welt. Der Eingeweihte, so Steiner, muss ein heimatloser Mensch sein. «Ohne dies Prädikat kann niemand im wahren Sinne des Wortes die Einweihung erlangen.» Und das heißt: «Ein Mensch darf keine Spezialsympathien in der geistigen Welt entwickeln, die ähnlich sind jenen Spezialsympathien, die der Mensch hier in der physischen Welt für einzelne spezielle Gebiete und Zusammenhänge hat.»[15] Die Bindung an Familie, Volk, Staatsgemeinschaft, Landschaft, Luft und Wetter hat ihr unbenommenes Recht in der physischen Welt. Heimat ist noch kein negativer Begriff, weil Heimatlosigkeit eine Qualität des Eingeweihten ist. Sie gehört der Sphäre der Persönlichkeit an, darf aber in der geistigen Welt nicht aufrechterhalten werden, weil es hier darum geht, jede Spezialisierung, jede Bevorzugung zugunsten einer Objektivität zu überwinden, die jedem Menschen als Individuum, jedem Ding in seinem Wesen und jedem Geist als solchem gerecht wird. Diese Heimatlosigkeit ist über alles Urteilen erhaben. Sie ist, als eine Grundhaltung, objektiv und meint etwas ganz anderes als die Heimatlosigkeit eines Vertriebenen oder die Entwurzelung des nervösen Zeitgenossen. Die Heimatlosigkeit des Eingeweihten ist nie schon durch die Umstände gegeben, sondern will immer erst errungen sein und ist insofern eine Auseinandersetzung mit den eigenen Bindungen und persönlichen Bedürfnissen.

Doch gibt es auch Phänomene, die uns von sich aus in eine Objektivität führen und aus der Sache heraus einen Übergang von der Heimat zur Heimatlosigkeit ermöglichen. Es gibt Erfahrungen in der Sinneswelt, in der Natur oder der Kunst, die uns etwas aufs Intensivste erleben lassen, ohne uns zu binden. Es sind die Erfahrungen mit der *Schönheit*. In der Begegnung mit dem Schönen wird jene Sachlichkeit erfahrbar, die der Eingeweihte auch allem anderen gegenüber mitbringt. Das Schöne hält auf Distanz, man kann es betrachten, ohne es haben, ohne es «essen» zu wollen. Man will, dass es da ist, muss es aber nicht für sich haben. Schönheit ist eine Berührung des Seelisch-Leiblichen, die zugleich eine Erfahrung des Geistigen ist. Im Betrachter kann sie von außen eine Objektivität und ein freudiges Genügen bewirken, wie sie der Eingeweihte in seiner Heimatlosigkeit von innen selbst erzeugt. Dieses Genügen, das alles andere als Gleichgültigkeit ist, ist das Gegenstück zu dem Verlangen, einer Sache habhaft zu werden, sie so zu besitzen, dass sie einem nicht mehr genommen werden kann. Das gilt auch für das Habhaft-Werden im Streben nach Beweisen. Das Schöne ist nicht beweisbar. Es hat eine andere Daseinsqualität und schlägt auch damit eine Brücke zur geistigen Welt, die ja ebenfalls jenseits der Beweisbarkeit liegt. Eigenartig treffend, wenn auch zunächst außerhalb des gewöhnlichen Empfindens, ist von daher Steiners Beobachtung, dass heimatlose Seelen ein Ungenügen an der bewiesenen Welt erleben,[16] der allein ja vom herkömmlichen Standpunkt aus Objektivität zukommt.

Nun ist es eine gängige Auffassung, dass gerade das Schöne nichts Objektives ist, sondern eine bloße Geschmacksache. Geschmacksachen aber sind im Grunde Angelegenheiten von Sympathie und Antipathie, und wo nur das Sympathische, das Gefällige als «schön» befunden wird, hat man es weniger mit dem Schönen als mit dem Kitsch zu tun. Dass gerade auch die «Heimat» nicht selten unter Kitschverdacht steht, hat vielleicht seinen Grund darin, dass man eine sympathische Behaglichkeit absolut setzt, in der ja tatsächlich mancher Heimatfilm schwelgt, der allein auf Wohlbehagen und Selbstgenuss des Zuschauers angelegt ist. Der Heimatkitsch ist aber kaum weniger weit von der wahren Heimat entfernt als die Entwurzelung. Weder Heimat noch Schönheit hat etwas mit der Sättigung durch «Geschmacksachen» zu tun. Die Schönheit deshalb nicht, weil in ihr die Objektivität des Geistes enthalten ist, und die Heimat nicht, weil sie im Grunde stets auf Heimatlosigkeit bezogen ist. Ja, Heimat kann nicht ohne die Fremde erlebt werden.

Die Bewusstwerdung der Heimat ist immer eine irgendwie melancholische Empfindung, der schon ihr Verlust eingeschrieben ist und die deshalb über das Seelisch-Leibliche hinausgreift und eine Sehnsucht ist. Unterwegs zum Geistigen hat hier das Ich eine Quelle der Selbsterfahrung, und zwar im Schmerz der Loslösung vom Seelisch-Leiblichen. In ihm dämmert ein Geistiges auf.

Das Ich ist der Vermittler des Geistes, der stufenweise realisiert wird: Wahre Heimat birgt tief in sich einen Vorgriff auf die Heimatlosigkeit, die in der Schönheit schon ein Stück weiter verwirklicht ist. Gleichwohl ist auch die Erfahrung der Schönheit noch ein Übergang zur letzten Heimatlosigkeit des Eingeweihten, die die volle Realisierung des Ichs ist, die Loslösung, die Freiheit. Emil Bock hat einmal bemerkt, dass die Heimatlosigkeit wesenhaft zum Ich gehört. «Das Ich ist allein, einsam und heimatlos, es löst den Menschen aus dem Mütterlich-Tragenden der Welt heraus und wirft ihn auf sich selbst zurück. ... Das Ich ist der innere Sohn im Menschen, der Menschensohn, und das Schicksal des Menschensohnes ist die Heimatlosigkeit, durch die er allein sich selber und die Freiheit finden kann.»[17]

Die Heimatlosigkeit des Eingeweihten bekommt niemand geschenkt. Sie ist ein angenommenes Schicksal, mit dem der Eingeweihte seine Objektivität und Freiheit gerade in der Auseinandersetzung mit der Heimat erringt. Diese Qualitäten gehen erst aus dem Schmerz der Loslösung hervor. Insofern sind Heimat und Heimatlosigkeit dialektisch aufeinander bezogen, und das Abschiednehmen gehört als ein wesentlicher Bestandteil dieser Dialektik zur Ich-Findung – und damit auch zur Anthroposophie. Der Anthroposoph, der mit seinem Anthroposoph-Sein einfach nur eine bestimmte Zugehörigkeit anstrebt und sich sicherheitshalber nur in «unseren Kreisen» bewegt, ist kein Anthroposoph. Das «Wer nicht verlässt ...» gilt auch hier. Prinzip der Heimatlosigkeit des Eingeweihten ist die beständige Überwindung, und das ist im Grunde schon ein Stück Kamaloka zu Lebzeiten.

Doch kann auch die Heimatlosigkeit als eine höhere Form der Beheimatung gedacht werden, dann nämlich, wenn sich der Horizont der Heimat allumfassend erweitert. Das ist wie mit dem Egoismus, der, wenn er die ganze Welt umfasst, nicht mehr egoistisch ist. Wenn sich die Liebe nicht mehr auf den unmittelbar heimatlichen Umkreis beschränkt und sich ausdehnt über den Erdkreis, findet eine Umstülpung statt, in der sich der Übergang von der physischen zur geistigen Welt vollzieht. Das Zerrbild davon ist die rein aus wirtschaftlichen Interessen betriebene Globalisierung. Ihr steht eine liebende Weltbeheimatung gegenüber, zu der sich die Menschheit langsam hin entwickeln kann. Für Rudolf Steiner ist dies zugleich die Entwicklung hin zum Geistselbst: «Nach und nach erst, aus den kleinen Gemeinschaften heraus, können sich die Menschen hinentwickeln zu einer großen Liebesgemeinschaft, wie sie sich konkret gerade durch die Einpflanzung des Geistselbstes entwickeln wird. So musste der Eingeweihte gleichsam vorausnehmen, wozu die Menschheitsentwickelung wieder drängt: alle Schranken zu überwinden, zu überbrücken, den großen Frieden, die große Harmonie und Brüderlichkeit auszubilden. Der Eingeweihte muss in seiner Heimatlosigkeit schon von vornherein immer die gleichen Keime aufnehmen zu der großen Bruderliebe. Das wurde symbolisch angedeutet in alten Zeiten dadurch, dass geschildert wird, was der Eingeweihte alles für Wanderungen durchgemacht hat, zum Beispiel bei Pythagoras. Warum wurde das geschildert? Damit er mit seinen Gefühlen, die innerhalb der inneren Gemeinschaft ausgebildet werden, allem gegenüber objektiv werde.»[18]

Heimat und Heimatlosigkeit treffen hier in dem Ethos zusammen, das Martin Heidegger einmal mit dem «Wohnen» gleichsetzt. Und wohnen im hohen Sinne ist immer auf ein aktives und nicht nur «gewohntes» Beheimaten bezogen, welches, im Unterschied zur vergangenheitsgegründeten Heimat, stets unterwegs ist und an der Zukunft baut.

Schöpferische Wirkungen und Nebenwirkungen des Verzichts

Nicht immer führt die größte Willensanstrengung zu den größten Ergebnissen. Natürlich, wer etwas in der Welt erreichen will, muss sich anstrengen. Aber von nicht geringerer Bedeutung als die Wirkungen des Willens sind die des Verzichts, nur fallen sie meist nicht auf, denn sie sind in einer ganz anderen Sphäre angesiedelt, nämlich in der des Geistes, ja, wenn man so will, des «heiligen» Geistes, der das Heil, das Ganze angeht.

Die größten geistigen Wirkungen gehen aus dem Verzicht hervor. Man denke zum Beispiel an jemand, der auf sein Recht verzichtet: Hätte Michael Kohlhaas, dem schweres Unrecht geschehen ist, darauf verzichtet, sein Recht in dieser Welt durchzusetzen, so hätte dies unweigerlich eine ungeheure Wirkung in der geistigen Welt gehabt. Der in dieser Welt nicht erfolgte Ausgleich hätte in jener ein enormes Potenzial freigesetzt, das dem Grad des Vergeltungsbedürfnisses entsprochen hätte. Ein solches Verzichten hat wenig mit einer Willensanstrengung zu tun, wie man sie z.B. für eine Diät oder sonst eine Askese braucht, denn diese zielt meist noch auf ein Ergebnis in der sinnlichen Welt und ist in jedem Fall selbstbezogen. Ein Verzicht, der ohne äußerliche Wirkung und Anerkennung bleibt, hat eine ganz andere, eine geistige Qualität, in der ein schöpferisches Potenzial für die Entwicklung des Menschen und der Menschheit liegt.

Von der ungeheuren Wirkung des Verzichts spricht Rudolf Steiner in einer der Sternstunden seines Vortragswerkes, nämlich im dritten Vortrag der nur fünfteiligen Reihe über *Die Evolution vom Gesichtspunkte des Wahrhaftigen*.[19] Steiner betrachtet hier nicht die natürlichen, sondern die moralischen Hintergründe der Weltentwicklung durch die vier Entwicklungszustände unserer Erde hindurch.

In der Sonnenverkörperung der Erde kommt es zu einem außerordentlichen Verzicht in der Hierarchie der Cherubim: Ein Teil dieser hohen Wesenheiten verzichtet nämlich darauf, jenes Opfer anzunehmen, das ihnen die Throne, die Geister des Willens, darbrachten. Durch jenes Opfer der Throne entstand zu Beginn der Weltentwicklung die Zeit, die Entwicklung überhaupt erst möglich macht. Die Annahme des Opfers nimmt auch die Verhältnisse der Zeit an. Später verzichtet dann ein Teil der Cherubim auf die weitere Annahme dieses Opfers, damit nicht nur Zeit sei, sondern auch Ewigkeit, denn offenbar gab es die «vor» der Zeit noch nicht. Zeit und Ewigkeit sind dialektisch aufeinander bezogen, so wie das Planmäßige und das Außerplanmäßige, wie Notwendigkeit und Freiheit.

Der Verzicht der Cherubim hat bedeutende Konsequenzen für den Menschen, und zwar nicht unmittelbar im Sinne des mit dem Verzicht beabsichtigten Zieles, sondern indirekt, nämlich im Hinblick auf die Genese des Bösen und der Freiheit.

Die Tat des Verzichts ist die Tat, die in den Verlauf der Evolution das Unvorhergesehene einlässt. Der Verzicht gehört nicht in den gesetzlichen Ablauf der Dinge. Hätten die Cherubim nicht verzichtet, so wäre nichts weiter geschehen als das, was jene Entwicklung ausmacht, die quasi mechanisch nach und nach all das entfaltet hätte, was ursprünglich im Keim angelegt war. Ja, der Verzicht ist im Grunde schon eine Ungesetzlichkeit, denn mit ihm bleibt eine sonst selbstverständliche Erfüllung aus.

Der Verzicht der Cherubim bewirkt, dass die ihnen zugedachte Opfersubstanz nicht an den Ort ihrer

Bestimmung kommt. Was geschieht mit ihr? Dieser Substanz, so Rudolf Steiner, bemächtigen sich nun Wesen, denen sie «rechtmäßig» nicht zukommt und die sich mit diesem Akt der Aneignung von den Cherubim loslösen. Es sind dies die luziferischen Wesenheiten, die sich in diesem Moment auf ihre eigenen Füße stellen. Diese Loslösung ist ein Selbstständig-Werden, das zugleich auch bedeutet, dass im vorgesehenen Gang der Evolution eine Störung auftritt. Denn diese Wesen bleiben in der Entwicklung zurück, sind gewissermaßen unzeitgemäß und machen sich an der Weltentwicklung «schuldig». Die Schuld aber ist ein Preis der Freiheit. Jedes Kind macht seine erste Freiheitserfahrung im Ungehorsam gegenüber den Eltern. Und eben damit beginnt erst eigentlich die individuelle Entwicklung des Kindes. All dies geschieht auf der Grundlage des Verzichts, eines Rückzugs, der Raum gewährt.

Rudolf Steiner nennt diesen Verzicht auch den «schöpferischen» Verzicht. Durch ihn kommt etwas Neues in die Welt. Er lässt etwas zu, das der eigenen Intention zuwiderlaufen kann. Und dennoch erfüllt sich gerade in diesem Zuwiderlaufen der höhere, der heilige Sinn der Geschichte. Besonders deutlich wird dies an dem Verzicht Christi auf seine Selbsterrettung gegenüber dem Verrat durch Judas. Der größte

Verzicht begegnet uns, so Steiner, als Christus selber einen Gegner in seine Sphäre kommen lässt. Christus schafft erst die Bedingungen der Möglichkeit des Judas-Verrates. Das aber ist nicht der «Zweck» seines Verzichts. Der liegt vielmehr in seiner Erlösungstat, die jedoch durch Judas erst eigentlich möglich wird.

Ganz ähnlich hatten die Cherubim mit ihrem Verzicht nicht die Selbstständigkeit der luziferischen Wesenheiten beabsichtigt, die dann die Versuchung des Menschen zur Folge hat. Ihre Absicht war vielmehr, der entstandenen Zeit die Ewigkeit abzuringen. Das ist ihnen gelungen, aber eben zugleich mit dem Effekt der Selbstermächtigung der luziferischen Wesenheiten. Dass die luziferischen Wesenheiten dann aus dem normalen Entwicklungsgang herausgefallen und zurückgeblieben sind und schließlich den Menschen versuchen und damit seine Freiheit initialisieren, in deren Folge der Tod in die Welt kommt und damit die Zuspitzung der Zeitlichkeit – all das lag nicht in der Absicht der Cherubim. Aber sie scheinen eigenartigerweise mit ihrem Ziel des Erlangens der Ewigkeit geradezu auch auf die «Nebenwirkung» ihres Verzichts zu antworten. Ist die Sterblichkeit des Menschen die indirekte, die nicht beabsichtigte Folge des Opferverzichts der Cherubim, so sind Ewigkeit und

Unsterblichkeit das direkte Ziel, das die Überwindung des Todes wiederum erst ermöglicht. So führt der Verzicht der Cherubim in einen schöpferischen Strudel, der das tiefe Quellwasser von Entwicklung ist. Mit der erlangten Unsterblichkeit ist die Voraussetzung dafür geschaffen, dass das Böse wieder in das Gute verwandelt werden kann. Der Verzicht, der in die Ewigkeit führt, ist die Bedingung der Erlösung. Und Christus erlöst die Menschheit, indem er auf seine Errettung verzichtet und damit erst dem Tod die Auferstehung abringt. Es gilt also in einer in sich geschiedenen Einheit zu denken: zum einen die Geburt der Freiheit, das Auftreten des Bösen und die Sterblichkeit, und zum anderen die Erlösung aus der Zeitlichkeit, die Auferstehung und die damit verbundene Möglichkeit einer neuen, höheren Moralität.

Sündenfall und Unsterblichkeit, Verrat und Erlösung erscheinen jeweils wie die Wirkungen einer Tat, wobei das eine die Nebenwirkung und nur das andere die eigentlich beabsichtigte Wirkung ist. Merkwürdig nur, dass die Wirkung wie auf die Nebenwirkung antwortet. Die gewöhnliche Chronologie von Ursache und Wirkungen scheint hier zugunsten einer anderen Zeitlichkeit verlassen zu sein. Solche Verhältnisse des Verzichts ereignen sich auf vielen Ebenen und in verschiedensten Spielarten. Verzichten aber ist immer ein Gewähren-Lassen des Fremden, auch des Widersetzlichen, und ein Anteil-Nehmen am Überzeitlichen, denn man entzieht sich damit der in der Zeit ablaufenden Mechanik. Wer auf sein Recht verzichtet, auf Lohn, auf Ausgleich, auf Rache, der öffnet anderem den Raum, übersteigt die Ebene des Zeitlichen und vereinigt sich mit dem Göttlichen. Darin liegt eine neue Dimension von Freiheit, eine geistige Freiheit im Unterschied zur emanzipatorischen und zur Wahlfreiheit. In dieser Freiheit liegt die Möglichkeit zu einer Vereinigung mit dem «heiligen» Geist, der die Evolution zu einem immer wieder neuen schöpferischen Akt werden lässt.

Glaube ist Zusammenhang oder: Warum Rudolf Steiner glauben?

Es gehört zum Selbstverständnis der Anthroposophie, dass man von geistigen Wesen und Verhältnissen wissen kann wie von denen in der Natur, das heißt, man kann sie nicht bloß spekulativ erahnen, sondern empirisch beschreiben. Der Naturwissenschaft wird die Geisteswissenschaft zur Seite gestellt mit dem Anspruch darauf, dass es methodisch zwischen beiden Disziplinen keinen grundsätzlichen Unterschied gibt.[20] Auf dem Weg einer Schulung des Geistes durch Meditation und Konzentration sei es möglich, die Welt des Geistes erkennend zu erfassen und nicht «bloß» wie in den Religionen zu glauben. Diese Behauptung macht Sinn vor dem Hintergrund des Vorurteils, dass Anthroposophie etwas Nebelhaftes und Obskures sei.[21] Sie scheint mir nur nicht ganz nachvollziehbar, wenn man z.B. die in den Naturwissenschaften verlangte Wiederholbarkeit eines Experimentes bedenkt oder die ergebnisorientierte Zuverlässigkeit der angewendeten Techniken einfordert.

Die Schulung des Geistes ist keine Garantie dafür, irgendwann tatsächlich in die Welt des Geistes sehen zu können. Der Erfolg ist unverfügbar. Eine solche Methode würde in der Naturwissenschaft zweifellos wieder aufgegeben werden. In der Anthroposophie aber ist die Methode, der Schulungsweg um seiner selbst willen Teil der Geisteswissenschaft, die nicht zuletzt eine menschenbildende, eine pädagogische (griechisch *paideia* = Erziehung, Bildung) Aufgabe hat.

Dennoch: Es gibt die Einsicht in konkrete und wesenhafte Verhältnisse in der Welt des Geistes, und es gibt Menschen, die Einsichten haben. Und diese sind natürlich besonders interessant. Faktisch bleibt jedoch immer wieder ein gewisser Vorbehalt – ausgenommen gegenüber der Geistesforschung Rudolf Steiners. Das ist ein merkwürdiger Tatbestand, der es schwermachen kann, Anthroposophie nach außen zu vertreten, beruft man sich dabei doch fast ausschließlich auf die Mitteilungen eines einzigen Menschen. Warum besteht hier Vertrauen, und warum stellt es sich anderen Quellen gegenüber oft nicht ein?

In dieser etwas schizophrenen Situation möchte ich aus dem Wesen der Anthroposophie heraus und nur äußerlich ihr zum Trotz doch einen bestimmten Aspekt des Glaubens starkmachen. Wohl liegt er zunächst nicht auf der Hand, aber er scheint mir für die Anthroposophie wesentlich: Was nämlich die Ergebnisse von Steiners Geistesforschung von den meisten anderen unterscheidet, ist, dass sie einen großen und erlebbaren Zusammenhang darstellen, der sich freilich erst nach und nach erschließt, der aber vielleicht gerade deshalb – nämlich weil man mit ihm umgehen kann und muss – eine Erlebnisqualität hat.

Auch die Rede vom Zusammenhang ist abgegriffen, genau wie die, dass es in der Anthroposophie um Wissen und nicht um Glauben gehe. Was aber bedeutet dieses Wissen für den Nicht-Hellsichtigen? Der kann es nur glauben. Doch ist das nichts Schlechtes, wenn dieser Glaube letztlich etwas anderes als ein bloßes Für-wahr- oder Für-möglich-Halten dessen ist, was eine Autorität sagt. Ich möchte einmal versuchsweise die Rede vom Zusammenhang dadurch neu beleben, dass ich sie mit dem Glauben in eins setze: Glaube ist Zusammenhang.

Ehrlich gesagt ist es mir bei der Beschäftigung mit der Anthroposophie nicht unbedingt darum zu tun, auch irgendwann einmal «hellsichtig» zu werden. Nicht die Aussicht darauf, wie es Rudolf Steiner auch einmal etwas despektierlich formuliert, irgendwann einmal in der Lage zu sein, wenigstens «das Ende des

Schwänzchens eines Elementarwesens zu sehen»,[22] ist mir die treibende Kraft, mich mit den Inhalten des Geistes zu befassen, sondern die Suche nach dem großen Zusammenhang, in dem wir – hoffentlich – stehen. Die Kardinalfrage an die Anthroposophie war und ist dabei dieselbe, die man auch an eine Religion stellt, nämlich die nach dem Sinn, der uns immer wieder unter den Händen zu zerrinnen droht, wenn wir etwas nicht verstehen, wenn wir der Ungerechtigkeit, dem Leid, der Zerstückelung, den bloßen Assoziationen, dem «Ende der Geschichte» begegnen.

Es versteht sich, dass «Glaube» im gesuchten Sinne nicht als die bescheidenere Alternative zu einer gesicherten Erkenntnis zu denken ist. Der Begriff des Glaubens, der hier gemeint ist, ist tatsächlich der religiöse, dessen Gegensatz nicht das Wissen, sondern der Zweifel, ja vielleicht auch die Lebensunsicherheit und schließlich die Angst ist. Hier meint Glaube Vertrauen (griechisch: *pistis*). Dieser Glaube bezeichnet eine Seinsart des Menschen. Er betrifft die Art und Weise, wie der Mensch in der Welt steht. Und dennoch: Es gibt auch einen Übergang zwischen dem bloß mutmaßenden Glauben und der Daseinsqualität des Vertrauens, und eben dieser liegt in der Erschließung des Zusammenhangs.

Wenn Rudolf Steiner immer wieder dazu auffordert, die geisteswissenschaftlichen Inhalte zu prüfen und nicht bloß auf «Treu und Glauben» und damit auf Autorität hin (die Steiners, eines Lehrers, eines Wissenschaftlers) anzunehmen, so sind dabei das Denken, die Logik, die Urteilskraft gefordert. Diese Fähigkeiten sind es, die die entweder selbst beobachteten Tatsachen oder die geisteswissenschaftlich mitgeteilten zueinander in ein Verhältnis setzen. Die Methode hierfür nennt die akademische Geisteswissenschaft «Hermeneutik». Das ist ein Verstehen, Deuten oder Auslegen von Kunstwerken und geistigen Inhalten, ein sich Eindenken und -fühlen in das, was als Geistesprodukt vorliegt. Hermeneutik ist eine Welt- und Selbsterfahrung, die das Teil aus dem Ganzen heraus versteht und dabei selbst ein Teil des Ganzen ist. Ja, sie ist der Versuch, durch das Aufspüren der Zusammenhänge zu einem Evidenzerlebnis zu gelangen, das einen in der Welt verankert. Hermeneutik in diesem Sinne stiftet Vertrauen, ist die Eigenaktivität gegenüber dem, was Vertrauen beansprucht.

Das verstehende Ich setzt sich in einen Bezug – zu anderen Menschen, zu den Hierarchien, zu den Wesen und Tatsachen der Natur und schließlich auch zu sich selbst. Dieser Bezug ist ein Erleben des Geistes.

Und genau in diesem Zwischenreich des Bezugs spielt auch das, was «Glaube» im hier vorgeschlagenen Sinne meint. Der Verlust des Glaubens ist der Verlust des Zusammenhangs. Das merkt man häufig nicht gleich, weil wir ja heute wie nie zuvor miteinander «vernetzt» sind. Doch ist die technische Vernetzung nur die Karikatur eines Zusammenhangs, dessen Verlust sich schließlich in Depression, Angst und Demenz niederschlägt – alles Erscheinungsformen des Nicht-Verstehens in der Modalität der Krankheit.

Heilung geschieht in der Entdeckung des Zusammenhangs, denn der ist es, der Sinn erfahren lässt und aus der Isolation führt. Und der Glaube ist ein In-der-Welt-Sein, das sich im Zusammenhang weiß. Viele Heilungen, die Christus vornimmt, geschehen aufgrund des Glaubens. Ja der, der glaubt, ist schon geheilt, denn er steht im Bezug. «Dein Glaube hat dir geholfen» (Mt 9,22). Oder: «Euch geschehe nach eurem Glauben» (Mt 9,29). Wer glaubt, steht im Zusammenhang. Wer zweifelt, tritt aus ihm heraus in die Zweiheit, die Trennung.

Gleichwohl: Der Zweifel muss sein, muss sein können. Er ist es, der die Freiheit verbürgt. Und das Erstaunlichste ist vielleicht, dass die Geistesforschung Rudolf Steiners den Zweifel zulässt. Das heißt: Steiner zwingt nicht. Wer mit seinen Aussagen umgeht, bleibt frei in diesem Umgang. Sie haben nicht jenen Zugriff auf das Vorstellungsvermögen, wie sie die ganze Fotoserie von Schauungen eines solchen Hellsichtigen hat, dessen Mitteilungen nicht in einem atmenden Zusammenhang stehen. Und das ist immer dann der Fall, wenn allein irgendwelche ‹Fakten› aus der geistigen Welt mitgeteilt werden – Bilder ohne Hinblick auf die menschenbildende Kraft, Ergebnisse ohne das Ethos des Gesprächs. Hier glaube ich nichts, weil auch an mich nicht geglaubt wird.

Woher kommt der Glaube? Der Mensch ringt um den Glauben, der heilt. Dieses Ringen steht vor dem Hintergrund des Zweifels, der dazugehört. – Vermutlich ist das Besondere an dem Weg zum Zusammenhang, dass er von zwei Seiten gleichzeitig beschritten wird. Dann ist Heilung letztlich Koinzidenz eines Wirkens aus der geistigen und aus der sinnlichen Welt. Diese Koinzidenz ist vielleicht die höchste Art des Zusammenhangs. Hierin liegt die Ereignisqualität des Verstehens. Bei Rudolf Steiner ist das die höchste Erkenntnisart: die Intuition. In dieser fallen für mein Verständnis Glauben und Wissen zusammen. Ja, der Glaube adelt das Wissen zu jener Daseinsweise, in der es nicht einfach das Sammelsurium von Tatsachen ist, ganz gleich ob sinnlicher oder geistiger Art, sondern die Gewissheit, in jenem Zusammenhang zu stehen, der die Welt der Sinne und die Welt des Geistes verbindet. Eine Brücke zu dieser Glaubensgewissheit und damit auch zur Intuition ist der hermeneutische Umgang mit den von Steiner «gegebenen» Inhalten, die sich in ihrer Zusammenhangsträchtigkeit bis heute meist von anderer Geisteskundschaft unterscheiden.

«Wir wären nicht Menschen, ... wenn nicht das Weltenall fortwährend in uns erstürbe»

«Wenn die Kraft unvergänglich wäre, wenn der Stoff unvergänglich wäre, gäbe es keine moralische Weltordnung.» – Das sagt Rudolf Steiner in einem seiner Vorträge über *Die Brücke zwischen der Weltgeistigkeit und dem Physischen des Menschen.*[23] – Der zitierte Satz ist in zweifacher Hinsicht irritierend: Zum einen behauptet er, dass Stoff und Kraft vergänglich seien, was im Widerspruch zu den naturwissenschaftlichen Sätzen von der Energie- und der Masseerhaltung steht. Und zum anderen erklärt er, dass die Vergänglichkeit des Natürlichen eine Bedingung der Möglichkeit der moralischen Weltordnung sei. Was das Letztere angeht, so könnte man mutmaßen, dass wir es hier mit einem genealogischen Zusammenhang zu tun haben, bei dem aus dem vergehenden Natürlichen das Moralische hervorgeht. Das Vergehen der Natur wäre dann die Kehrseite der Entwicklung der Moral: Je mehr vergangene Natur, desto mehr gegenwärtige Moral. Aber so meint es Steiner nicht. Freilich, man denkt nicht selten und gerade in naturwissenschaftlichen Zusammenhängen so: Im Laufe der Evolution oder der individuellen Entwicklung geht das Höhere aus einem Niederen hervor: der Mensch aus dem Tier, das Geistige und Moralische aus einem verfeinerten Natürlichen oder auch eine kulturelle Errungenschaft aus einem unterdrückten Instinkt, aus einem nicht ausgelebten Trieb.

Anstelle dieser gewohnten Genealogie entfaltet Steiner einen völlig anderen, ja umgekehrten Zusammenhang, nämlich den einer Metamorphose des Moralischen ins Natürliche: Aus unseren freiheitlich verantworteten Taten werden die natürlichen Bedingungen unseres Lebens. Die Moralität ist nicht das sublime Ergebnis, sondern die Voraussetzung alles Natürlichen. Denn das Natürliche geht, so Steiner, aus den moralischen Idealen hervor. Sie sind der «Quell des Weltenschöpferischen». Doch ihre weltenschöpferische Kraft entfaltet sich erst im Durchgang durch den Schmelztiegel des Todes. Dann wird für den Kosmos fruchtbar, was als moralische Ideale in unserer Organisation gelebt und uns erwärmt hat. Ein moralisches Ideal gestaltet die natürliche Welt, sobald dieses Ideal durch den Tod gegangen ist und damit aus dem subjektiven Willen in die objektiven Tatsachen von Stoff und Kraft verwandelt wurde.

Dieser Zusammenhang ist für sich schon bedeutsam genug. Nun steht er aber außerdem noch in Verbindung mit der eingangs zitierten Aussage und den darin enthaltenen Schwierigkeiten: Warum soll Moralität nur möglich sein, wenn die Natur vergeht? Und was bedeutet es, dass Natur, dass Stoff und Kraft vergehen, was ja im Widerspruch zu den auf Antoine Lavoisier bzw. auf Julius Robert Mayer zurückgehenden Naturgesetzen steht. Darüber hinaus denkt Steiner ein Vergehen der Natur auch noch so radikal wie nur irgend möglich, nämlich geradezu als deren Vernichtung. Wo und wie aber soll denn diese «Vernichtung» geschehen?

Der Ort, an dem der Stoff vernichtet wird, ist der Mensch. Im Menschen wird Materie regelrecht aufgelöst, aber dieser Ort der Vernichtung ist zugleich der Ort, an dem Materie auch wieder entsteht – und zwar dann, wenn der Mensch von moralischen Idealen durchdrungen ist.[24]

Den zukunftsbezogenen und belebenden moralischen Idealen stellt Steiner die bloß theoretischen Ideen der modernen Naturwissenschaft gegenüber, die die Natur, so wie sie ist, zu beschreiben versuchen.

Diese Ideen wirken sich auf ihre Weise auf den Kosmos aus, nämlich so, dass das Weltall fortwährend in unserer Naturerkenntnis erstirbt. Wir stellen die Natur «fest» und töten sie damit. Wir formulieren ihre Gesetze und bringen sie um ihr Lebendiges. Wo sich Natur in unserem Bewusstsein darstellt, da ist sie schon tot. Jede erkenntnisrelevante Beschreibung der Natur hat die «Richtigkeit» des Leblosen wie der katalogisierte und dafür aufgepiekste Schmetterling.

Das könnte sich so anhören, als ginge es nun darum, diesen Naturzugang zu vermeiden: Wenn wir in unserem Erkennen die Natur, ja sogar das Weltall zu Tode bringen, müssen wir dann nicht damit aufhören? Nein, denn genau diese Naturerkenntnis ist erforderlich dafür, dass in uns das Selbstbewusstsein aufleuchtet: «Und wir wären ja nicht Menschen, wenn wir nicht theoretisch denken würden, wenn nicht das Weltenall fortwährend in uns erstürbe. Durch das Ersterben des Weltenalls sind wir eigentlich selbstbewusste Menschen, die zu Gedanken über das Weltenall kommen können. Aber indem das Weltenall sich in uns denkt, ist es schon Leiche. Der Gedanke über das Weltenall ist die Leiche des Weltenalls. Erst als Leiche wird uns das Weltenall bewusst und macht uns zum Menschen.»

Es ist also nicht allein erforderlich, dass die Natur vergeht, damit moralisches Handeln sein kann, sondern es ist auch erforderlich, dass das Weltall sich im Menschen denkt, dabei stirbt, zugleich aber im Menschen als Selbstbewusstsein aufersteht.

Wie hängt das mit dem anfangs zitierten Satz: «Wenn die Kraft unvergänglich wäre, wenn der Stoff unvergänglich wäre, gäbe es keine moralische Weltordnung» zusammen? Ist die Vergänglichkeit von Kraft und Stoff die Folge der Tatsache, dass der Mensch Kraft und Stoff in naturgesetzlicher Weise denkt? Oder noch mehr zugespitzt: Ist die theoretische Idee von der Unvergänglichkeit gerade die Ursache der Vergänglichkeit? Widerlegt der Erhaltungssatz sich selbst durch seine Handlungsdimension, nämlich durch die Tat, die als theoretisches Erkennen ein «Töten» ist?

Steiner sagt das so nicht, aber er stellt den Erhaltungssatz unmittelbar in den Kontext jener theoretischen Ideen, durch welche fortwährend das Weltall in uns stirbt. Wir töten die Natur, indem wir sie auf Gesetze bringen. So greifen hier auf eine schwer zu fassende, aber eben deshalb auch faszinierende Weise das, was kritisiert wird – der Informationsgehalt des Erhaltungssatzes –, und die Folgen seiner theoretischen Fixierung, also gewissermaßen das «Tun», die «Handlung» dieses Satzes ineinander: Das theoretische Gesetz von der Erhaltung von Stoff und Kraft tötet Stoff und Kraft, gerade indem es deren Unvergänglichkeit behauptet. Das Gesetz hat zwei «Tonarten», die einander widersprechen, eine äußere, in der es innerhalb seines Systems auch etwas Richtiges sagt, und eine innere, in der es die Wahrheit «tut», die seiner Aussage zuwiderläuft und das System sprengt. Es wird so zu einem produktiven Selbstwiderspruch und ist vielleicht gerade in dieser Ambivalenz wahr. Die Aufstellung dieses Gesetzes, wie auch die anderer vergleichbarer Gesetze, ist ein tödlicher Zugang zur Natur – und damit unwissentlich zugleich eine Voraussetzung der Moralität, die die Natur neu erschafft. Schlichtweg falsch ist der Erhaltungssatz also nicht, zumindest nicht für die äußere Natur. Nur rechnet er nicht mit dem Menschen und seinem Bewusstsein. Denn in ihm wird tatsächlich Materie vernichtet. Der Mensch ist der Brennofen für ein Eingehen ins Nichts und ein Hervorgehen aus dem Nichts. Er bringt, in der Nachfolge Gottes, das Neue in die Welt, während es nach dem Erhaltungssatz prinzipiell nichts Neues geben kann.

Nun handelt es sich dabei um viel mehr als um eine Variante des «Stirb und Werde». Denn es geht auch und vielleicht sogar in erster Linie um einen Weltzugang, in dem Natur und Moral sich nicht gegenseitig bestreiten müssen. Wo die Naturwissenschaft zur materialistischen Weltanschauung wird, da behauptet sie mit der Unvergänglichkeit der Stoffe indirekt zugleich, dass es nichts Neues unter der Sonne geben kann. Die Welt ginge dann tatsächlich ihrem Wärmetod, d.h. ihrer totalen Nivellierung entgegen.

Die Erhaltung von Stoff und Kraft erübrigt sich schließlich, wenn kein differenzbildender Impuls mehr wirksam werden kann, wenn keine Spannung mehr eintritt zu dem, was ist, und sich damit gar nichts mehr verändern kann. Die denkbar intensivste Spannung aber besteht zwischen Natur und Moral. Ohne eine Beziehung zwischen beiden erschöpft sich die Natur an sich selbst. Ihr fehlt dann das belebende, das schöpferische Prinzip. Eine unvergängliche Natur steht jenseits allen moralischen Handelns und damit auch jenseits des Geistes als des schöpferischen Prinzips.

Dass Natur auch für unsere Erfahrung zunächst jenseits aller Moral steht und Moral gegenüber der Natur als weniger real erscheint, ist in einer bestimmten Hinsicht auch richtig und sinnvoll. Denn in einer Welt, in der moralisches Handeln so real wäre wie in unserer Erfahrungswelt die Stoffe, gäbe es keine Freiheit. Wir sind nur deshalb frei, weil die moralische Welt nicht unmittelbar, sondern nur im Durchgang durch den Tod ihre Wirksamkeit in der Natur entfaltet. Wenn wir tatsächlich einen direkten, eingreifenden Zugang zur Natur hätten, so wäre unser Willensverhältnis zu ihr magisch. Dann könnten wir aus roten Kirschen blaue machen oder einem Sturm Einhalt gebieten oder Steine in Brot verwandeln. Unsere Gestaltungskraft in der Natur kann und darf sich nur kultivierend, aber nicht schöpferisch auf die gegenwärtige Natur beziehen. Unsere Schöpferkraft kann sich hier nur in dem durch die Vergänglichkeit von Stoff und Kraft ermöglichten Metamorphosezusammenhang zwischen Moral und Natur geltend machen, und der geht durch den Tod hindurch.

Im Raum gibt es keine Brücke zwischen Natur und Moral, es gibt sie aber in der Zeit. Diese Brücke liegt in der Vergänglichkeit. Sie ist die Grundlage der Metamorphose. Wo der Stoff sich auflöst, beginnt unsere Freiheit. Und unsere Freiheit ist es, die fortwährend neuen Stoff bildet. «Das Natürliche vergeht im Menschen; im Moralischen entsteht neues Natürliches.» Unser Bewusstsein tötet das Natürliche, und durch unseren Tod hindurch schafft unser Geist es neu. Es ist das Gesetz der Metamorphose, das dem Ineinandergreifen von Natur und Moral zugrunde liegt. «Eine vergangene Welt also», so Steiner, «erstirbt in uns bis zum Stoff, bis zur Kraft. Und nur weil gleich wiederum eine neue aufgeht, merken wir nicht, dass der Stoff vergeht und wieder entsteht.» Die unerschöpfliche Produktions- und Gestaltungskraft des Geistes gibt sich nur den Anschein einer unvergänglichen Natur, während in Wahrheit eine vergängliche Natur immer neu aus unserer Moralität hervorgeht.

Trauerzug und Vogelgrippe
Karma oder Zufall?

«Das Wort Zufall ist so recht eine Crux, ein Kreuz für jede Weltanschauung», sagt Rudolf Steiner in den *Offenbarungen des Karma*[25] und stellt schließlich fest, dass hinter dem Zufall als Erklärungsprinzip meist Ahriman steht. Er wirke da am stärksten, wo wir das Gefühl haben, mit dem Denken nicht mehr nachzukommen. Besonders tragisch scheint mir, dass dieses Gefühl insbesondere bei uns unerklärlichen Unglücksfällen auftritt. Aber nicht weniger problematisch ist es wohl, da Zusammenhänge zu unterstellen, wo gar keine bestehen. Psychologisch lässt sich von einer Paranoia sprechen, wenn jemand in einem unglücklichen Zufall das Wirken von Ursachen zu erkennen meint, die letztlich auf Vorurteile und Projektionen zurückgehen. Vielleicht kann man das im Unterschied zum ahrimanischen Erklärungsprinzip das «luziferische» nennen. Beide Erklärungsmodelle – also das des Zufalls und das eines mutmaßlichen, meist weltanschaulich bedingten Sinnzusammenhangs – können nur durch die Aufmerksamkeit einer trainierten Urteilskraft vor Täuschungen bewahrt werden. Dazu gehört zum Beispiel, versuchsweise einmal einen Sinnzusammenhang anzunehmen, wo nichts auf «Sinn» hinzudeuten scheint, und umgekehrt darauf zu verzichten, dort karmische Zusammenhänge zu konstruieren, wo bestimmte Koinzidenzen dies zu fordern scheinen. Auch das ist ein Aspekt der Unbefangenheitsübung, wie sie in dem Buch *Wie erlangt man Erkenntnisse der höheren Welten?* entwickelt wird.

In den Zeitungen war vor einigen Jahren einmal von zwei sehr traurigen Unglücksfällen die Rede, bei denen sich unmittelbar die Zufalls- und die Ursachen- bzw. Sinnfrage stellte. Diese würde der anthroposophische Leser vermutlich genau umgekehrt beantworten als der nichtanthroposophische Leser.

Drei Tote und bis zu vierzig Verletzte hatte es gegeben, als ein Paketauto, dessen Fahrer am Steuer einen Herzinfarkt erlitt und der deshalb die Kontrolle über sein Fahrzeug verlor, in einen Zug von 150 Trauergästen raste. Eine solche Meldung ist nicht zuletzt deshalb so erschütternd, weil hier der Tod irgendwie eine magische Anziehungskraft zu entfalten scheint und der zu Bestattende andere Menschen wie mit sich zieht. Das ist ein Gefühl, das man haben kann, und das durch vergleichbare Fälle bestärkt wird. Aber die wenigsten Menschen werden versucht sein, diesem Gefühl mehr Bedeutung beizumessen als einem Aberglauben. Das zeugt gewiss von einem gesunden Menschenverstand.

Dennoch macht es für unser Empfinden einen Unterschied, ob das Auto in einen Demonstrationszug rast oder eben in einen Trauerzug. Wir sind in letzterem Fall – ob Anthroposoph oder nicht – wohl eher geneigt, das Unglück als «etwas weniger» zufällig aufzufassen. Unterscheiden werden sich Anthroposophen und Nichtanthroposophen aber vermutlich in der Einschätzung der Gesamtsituation: Erstere werden hier karmische Zusammenhänge zumindest in Erwägung ziehen, denn gerade eine solche Gruppensituation legt karmische Gründe oder Ziele nahe. Hingegen wird sich der Nichtanthroposoph genau dagegen wehren und sich wohl auch gegen sein eigenes Gefühl der Unbehaglichkeit ob der merkwürdigen Todeskoinzidenz wenden und lieber von einem tragischen Zufall sprechen. Gerade damit bringt er seine ganze ohnmächtige Fassungslosigkeit und Trauer zum Ausdruck, die ihm durch eine karmische Sinnzuweisung womöglich geradezu beleidigt wird.

Die andere Unglücksnachricht, die ein Tag zuvor in der Presse zu lesen war, kann die Positionen in der genau entgegengesetzten Einstellung zeigen. Zwei Mädchen im Alter von 11 und 13 Jahren, die auf dieselbe Schule gingen und innerhalb von zwei Tagen gestorben waren, lösten Panik bei Eltern und Schülern dieser Schule aus. Fast alle der rund tausend Schüler kamen nach Verbreitung dieser Nachricht und eines Eintrags auf einer Internetseite, dass es noch «sehr begründete Hinweise auf einen weiteren Todesfall» an einem benachbarten Gymnasium gebe, nicht zur Schule. Das Gerücht einer Epidemie kursierte bis hin zur Angst vor ersten Fällen von Vogelgrippe beim Menschen. Dieses wurde dadurch noch geschürt, dass unmittelbar zuvor ein Fernsehfilm zu sehen war, der den fiktiven Fall der Infektion eines Jungen mit dem gefährlichen Virus durch einen Papagei darstellte. – Lauter Koinzidenzen, die einen Anthroposophen möglicherweise weniger stark berühren als einen Nichtanthroposophen oder zumindest weniger dazu veranlassen, sein Kind nicht zur Schule zu schicken. Vielleicht wird er den für ihr Alter so ungewöhnlichen Tod der beiden jungen Mädchen nicht zufällig nennen, weil er ihn in ihrem Karma liegen sieht, aber er wird viel weniger das Bedürfnis haben, äußere Gründe wie eine Epidemie für die

Gleichzeitigkeit dieser Tode zu finden, eben weil hier eher individuelle Schicksalsgründe vermutet werden.

Aber auch wenn der Anthroposoph hier der luziferischen Gefahr, dort Begründungszusammenhänge zu sehen, wo keine sind, entgeht, kann er ihr doch auf einer anderen Seite, der Kehrseite seiner Unbefangenheit in diesem Fall, wiederum erliegen. Denn wenn man grundsätzlich das Wirken des Karmas über alle äußeren Ursachen stellt, so geht man meist nicht davon aus, dass man sich irgendwo anstecken kann, wenn Infektion nicht im Karma liegt. Das scheint mir eine luziferische Fahrlässigkeit zu sein, zu der der Karmagedanke verführt und derentwegen es sinnvoll, ja vielleicht lebensnotwendig ist, die Perspektive zu wechseln, um allmählich zu einem Gespür dafür zu kommen, was tatsächlich karmisch ist. Auch wäre zu fragen, inwieweit eine im Karma liegende Infektion nicht doch auch verhindert werden kann. In jedem Fall kann man sich aber eine zusätzliche, nicht karmisch bedingte Infektion zuziehen, wenn man aufgrund des Karmagedankens die Vorbeugung versäumt.

Die Aussage Steiners, dass es letztlich keinen Zufall gibt, soll nicht bezweifelt werden. Dennoch wäre es vermessen, den Zufall in unserem Erleben zu leugnen, denn das könnten wir nur, wenn wir tatsächlich volle

Einsicht in die geistige Welt und eine Übersicht über gewaltige Zeiträume hätten. In der physischen Welt können tatsächlich äußere Dinge zusammentreffen, für die es zunächst keinen inneren Zusammenhang gibt. Das erläutert Steiner in einer Fragenbeantwortung von 1904: «In der physischen Welt von ‹Zufall› zu sprechen, ist gewiss nicht unberechtigt. Und so unbedingt der Satz gilt: ‹Es gibt keinen Zufall›, wenn man alle Welten in Betracht zieht, so unberechtigt wäre es, das Wort ‹Zufall› auszumerzen, wenn bloß von der Verkettung der Dinge in der physischen Welt die Rede ist. Der Zufall in der physischen Welt wird nämlich dadurch herbeigeführt, dass sich in dieser Welt die Dinge im sinnlichen Raume abspielen. Sie müssen, insofern sie sich in diesem Raume abspielen, auch den Gesetzen dieses Raumes gehorchen. In diesem Raume aber können äußerliche Dinge zusammentreffen, die zunächst innerlich nichts miteinander zu tun haben.»[26]

Was die Frage nach Zufall oder Ursache- bzw. Zweckzusammenhang angeht, so sieht man am anderen meist die Gefahr des Fehlurteils, dem man selbst am wenigsten ausgesetzt ist. Aber es kommt auch darauf an, die eigene Gefährdung zu sehen. Das bedeutet für die hier getroffene plakative Unterscheidung, dass, während der «Nichtanthroposoph» immer eher der ahrimanischen Gefahr erliegt, alles lieber dem Zufall zuzuschreiben als in einem Unglück auch einen Sinn zu suchen, der «Anthroposoph» die Hypothese Zufall geradezu braucht, um nicht der luziferischen Gefahr zu erliegen, falsche Sinnzusammenhänge zu behaupten, die ein Unglück relativieren oder Vorsicht versäumen lassen.

Die Schwelle erleben
Die wahre und die falsche Gestalt des Todes

Der Tod hat zweierlei Gestalt: Er ist Ende und Schwelle. Versteht man seine Schwellengestalt allzu selbstverständlich als Brücke zur geistigen Welt, so besteht die Gefahr seiner Verharmlosung. Zu dieser Brücke muss er erst werden. Das heißt, er muss seiner vernichtenden Gestalt, die uns mit dem Nichts bedroht, erst abgerungen werden. Dann wird er als Schwelle erlebbar und nicht übersprungen.

In den Kassler Vorträgen über das Johannes-Evangelium nennt Rudolf Steiner es «die Mission Christi auf Erden, dass er an die Stelle der falschen Gestalt des Todes durch seine Tat die wahre Gestalt des Todes hinstellte».[27] Dies geschehe in der Vereinigung mit dem Vater, denn der Tod sei «der immer lebendige Vater», er sei «in Wahrheit der Leben-Spender». Diese Erkenntnis aber ist das Ziel eines Weges. Wenn wir immer schon im Tod den Leben-Spender sehen, dann können wir keine wirkliche Erfahrung mit der Schwelle machen.

Die «wahre» Gestalt des Todes steht in einem Bezug, nämlich in dem zur «falschen». Erlebt werden kann die Schwelle nur in dem Verhältnis der beiden Gestalten zueinander. Was nun ist die «falsche» Gestalt des Todes? – Es ist die des Toten, das keinen Übergang kennt. Nicht selten ist unser unmittelbares und alltägliches Verhältnis zur Sinneswelt von diesem Eindruck bestimmt. Vor dem Hintergrund der wahren Gestalt des Todes ist die falsche mehr eine Interpretation der Sinneswelt, als dass sie ein besonderes Ereignis wäre. Erleben wir in der Sinneswelt vor allem ihre Stofflichkeit, so ist der Tod letztlich nichts anders als ein Seinsmodus, nämlich der der Materialität. Als bloße Materie aufgefasst ist die Sinneswelt tot. Darin zeigt sich seit dem Sündenfall die Wirkung Ahrimans: «Ahriman bewirkte, dass die äußere Welt dem Menschen nicht in ihrer wahren Gestalt erschien, sondern so, als ob sie nur eine materielle, eine stoffliche Welt wäre, als ob nicht hinter allem Stofflichen das Geistige wäre.» Es ist eine Konsequenz der Wirkung Ahrimans, in der Schöpfung schließlich nur das Gewordene und nicht das Werdende, und zwar das aus Geistigem Werdende, das Grenzüberschreitende, das Schöpferische zu sehen. Dies führt zu einer Auffassung vom Tod, in der dieser als das Tote gewissermaßen das Wesen alles Geschaffenen ist, das Letzt- und Endgültige: das Materielle, das keine Herkunft hat, sondern vielmehr selbst zum Ausgangspunkt gemacht wird, in dem es Herkunft ist. Das zeigt sich nicht zuletzt darin, dass der Weg der Evolution dann als vom Mineral zum Menschen führend angesehen wird und nicht umgekehrt. ‹Geistiges› erscheint schließlich als das Produkt materieller Verhältnisse und damit als eine mehr oder weniger komplizierte Kombination von Stoffen.

Wenn Steiner von der «wahren Gestalt des Todes» spricht, dann geht es darum, im Tod nicht das Tote, das Gewordene, sondern ein Werdendes zu erkennen: das eigentliche Vaterprinzip, das Schöpfungsprinzip. Wenn aber dem Geschaffenen seine geistige Herkunft bestritten wird, ja wenn sie schlicht vergessen wird und es nur noch die Faktizität des Materials gibt, dann haftet diesem das Perfekt des Toten an. Das ist die Illusion Ahrimans. In dieser Gestalt ist der Tod das «Zerrbild des Vaters» und vernichtend tödlich.

Doch hat auch die Illusion Ahrimans ihre Wahrheit. Eben sie gehört zum Erleben der Schwelle. Wir leben ja tatsächlich in der Unerbittlichkeit des Gewordenen und sehen nicht immer schon dahinter. Die Materie stellt ihre unwiderlegbaren Ansprüche an uns. Ja, sie macht uns ohnmächtig, indem sie uns mit ihrer Faktizität überwältigt, deren Sinn wir einfach nicht begreifen können, wenn die Sonne über Gerechte und Ungerechte gleichermaßen scheint und das Meer nach seiner Laune Schiffe versenkt. Mutmaßen wir gleich einen Sinn, so funktionalisieren wir und verlieren die Freiheit des Umgangs mit der Materie. Auch birgt jede Grenzüberschreitung in eine hinter ihr liegende geistige Welt die Gefahr der Illusion wie alles bloß Spekulative und in der Spekulation auch Interessenbehaftete. Die Wahrheit des Geistes enthüllt sich noch nicht dem bloßen Wunsch nach ihm.

Tatsächlich – und das ist die Dialektik freiheitlicher Entwicklung – ist es in einer gewissen Weise auch notwendig, dass sich der Mensch nicht immer in dieser Kontinuität seiner und der Welt geistigen Herkunft erfährt, dass er nicht immer schon hellsichtig ist und weiß, was das Schicksal mit ihm vorhat. Denn gerade das Erleben der Diskontinuität, der Grenze und Begrenzung, auch der Erkenntnisgrenze, gehört wesentlich zur Genese und Erfahrung seiner Selbstheit, des Ich.

Die unhintergehbaren Tatsachen, die Endlichkeit, die Isolation, die Bewusstwerdung am Widerlager der harten, toten Materie gehören zu den erschütterndsten Erlebnissen menschlichen Daseins. Der Tod in seiner Gestalt der Diskontinuität vereinzelt den Menschen. Diese Vereinzelung muss er durchleben und durch-leiden. Er macht in ihr die Erfahrung der Verlassenheit, die aber – und hier beginnt noch kaum merklich vielleicht das Erleben der Schwelle – ist kehrseitig die der Autonomie. Damit erst wird er zu einem verantwortlichen und freien Wesen, das sich selbst gestalten und bilden, ja das seinen Geist individuell betätigen kann und ihn so zu spüren beginnt. So haben wir es hier mit jener Dialektik zu tun, in der die geistige Entwicklung des Menschen sich gerade der verhüllten Schwelle, der Abschnürung von seiner geistigen Herkunft verdankt. Das ist die Wahrheit der «falschen Gestalt» des Todes.

Das Verhältnis von Materie und Geist, von Tod und Leben ist hoch dialektisch und nur so die Entwicklungsbedingung der individuellen Geistigkeit des Menschen. Seine Individualität ist an die Materie gebunden, seine Freiheit an die Erkenntnisgrenze, die ihm diese setzt – wäre er doch sonst nur der, der gar nicht anders kann, als den Orakelspruch seines Schicksals zu erfüllen. Und seine Geistigkeit erwächst aus dem Doppelsinn des Todes: dem der Abschnürung und Diskontinuität einerseits und des Schwellenphänomens der Kontinuität andererseits. Dass der Mensch Individualität wurde, so Steiner, «konnte ihm nicht unter anderen Verhältnissen gegeben werden als dadurch, dass ihm der Ausblick zur geistigen Welt zunächst durchschnitten wurde. Und was ihm diesen Ausblick durchschnitten hat, das eben war der Tod. Hätte der Mensch immer gewusst, dass der Tod der Same des Lebens ist, er wäre auch nicht zu einer selbstständigen Ichheit gekommen, denn er wäre geblieben im Zusammenhang mit der geistigen Welt. So aber trat der Tod ein, gab ihm die Illusion, dass er getrennt sei von der geistigen Welt, und erzog so den Menschen zur selbstständigen Ichheit». Das ist das Paradox, in das es verstehend einzutauchen gilt: Der Mensch verdankt sich in geistiger Beziehung seiner Trennung vom Geist.

Wie nun aber kommt er wieder zu einer Geisterfahrung? Wie erfährt er die Schwelle, ohne sie in einer simplen Zwei-Welten-Metaphysik schon übersprungen zu haben?

Christus hat auf Golgatha die Vereinigung mit der Todesschwelle geleistet, und zwar in einem in sich zwiespältigen Vorgang von Verlassenheit und Verbundenheit mit dem Vater. Die Schwelle ist Trennung und Brücke zugleich. Sie muss im Erleben vom einen in das andere verwandelt werden. Dass Golgatha, wie Steiner im letzten der Vorträge über *Die Evolution vom Gesichtspunkte des Wahrhaftigen*[28] sagt, kein Urbild in der geistigen Welt hat wie alle anderen geschichtlichen Ereignisse, macht es zu jener einzigartigen Brücke zwischen den Welten, die selbst ein Urbild ohne Metaphysik ist – das einzige Urbild, das seinen Ort in der Sinneswelt hat. Ihm wohnt die Faktizität des Todes als Abschnürung von der geistigen Welt inne, die aber in der Hingabe an den Vater, an den Tod gewendet wird. Diese Metamorphose des Todes – gewissermaßen von seiner ahrimanischen in seine väterliche Bedeutung – ist der Durchgang durch den Tiefstpunkt, der als Wendepunkt die Schwelle ist.

Das, was uns diese Ambivalenz wie in einer Art Todesvorwegnahme nachempfinden lassen kann, ist ein seelisches Phänomen, das wohl auch Christus auf dem Weg seiner Menschwerdung, die sich im Tod vollendete, kennengelernt hat: die *Angst*. Martin Heidegger nennt sie in seinem großen Werk *Sein und Zeit* eine «Grundbefindlichkeit» des Menschen. Im Anschluss an Kierkegaard werden Angst und Furcht unterschieden. Die Angst ist, anders als die Furcht, unbestimmt, sie kennt kein konkretes Wovor, das uns Gegenmaßnahmen und die Flucht ergreifen lässt. In Angst kann man nicht fliehen. Das heißt es gibt keinen Ausweg ins «Uneigentliche», um mit Heidegger zu sprechen, im Gegenteil: die Angst führt aus ihm heraus. Das Uneigentliche aber ist die Welt Luzifers und

Ahrimans: die Maja; bei Heidegger die eingeebnete Welt des «Man». Und insbesondere Ahriman hat wohl ein Interesse daran, dass wir zwar Furcht haben, aber nicht Angst. Die Furcht lässt uns Vorkehrungen treffen, die uns mit seiner Welt verstricken, vor allem in den Maßnahmen des Egoismus. Die Angst aber lässt sich nicht durch Maßnahmen gegen die Furcht vertreiben. Sie ist grundsätzlich und existenziell. Gerade so jedoch kann sie zu einem Offenbarungsgefühl werden, an dessen Tunnellende wir die Wahrheit sehen können. Mit der Angst durchleben wir die Schwelle. Ahriman will nicht, dass wir Angst haben, aber schließlich ist es gerade seine Welt, die uns Angst macht, weil die materiellen Beruhigungen das Geistige im Menschen nicht vor dem Gefühl ihrer letztendlichen Nichtigkeit bewahren können. Mit dem Angstgefühl fällt am Ende die ahrimanische Täuschung in sich zusammen. Die Verfallenheit an sie löst sich. Das Potenzial, das in der Angst liegt, beschreibt Heidegger als die Aufhebung unserer Verfallenheit an das «Man»: «Die Angst benimmt so dem Dasein die Möglichkeit, verfallend sich aus der ‹Welt› und der öffentlichen Ausgelegtheit zu verstehen. ... Die Angst offenbart im Dasein das Sein zum eigensten Seinkönnen, das heißt das *Freisein für* die Freiheit des Sich-selbst-wählens und -ergreifens.»[29]

Die Angst, deren etymologischer Zusammenhang mit der Enge für ihr Verständnis ergiebig ist, birgt die Potenz zur Befreiung in sich. Am Ende der Angst stülpt sich das Gefühl der Enge um in das der Weite. Dieser Weg lässt sich nachvollziehen, und zwar über eine bestimmte Qualität der Angst, die Heidegger bezeichnenderweise die «Unheimlichkeit» nennt. Diese meint ein «Nicht-zuhause-Sein», das bei Heidegger allerdings nicht die Frage nach einem Wo-denn-zuhause? aufwirft. «Die Angst dagegen holt das Dasein aus seinem verfallenden Aufgehen in der ‹Welt› zurück. Die alltägliche Vertrautheit bricht in sich zusammen.» Der so vereinzelte Mensch erlebt sich in dem «existenzialen ‹Modus› des *Un-zuhause*. Nichts anderes meint die Rede von der ‹Unheimlichkeit›.»[30] – «...dass wir nicht sehr verlässlich zu Haus sind in der gedeuteten Welt ...», sagt Rilke in den *Duineser Elegien* und überschreitet mit Orpheus die Grenze, was der Metaphysikkritiker Heidegger nicht tut. Gleichwohl birgt sein Denken den höchsten Respekt und eine hervorragende Kenntnis der Grenze, der Schwelle. Wie ein «Hüter der Schwelle» steht er vor ihrer unzulässigen Überschreitung und hat doch nichts anderes als ihre Ergründung und ihr Erleben im Sinn.

Hier soll nicht versucht werden, Steiner und Heidegger in eins zu setzen, aber für das Verständnis der Schwelle hilft es, den einen mit dem anderen zu erhellen. Heidegger hat als Kämpfer gegen die Seinsvergessenheit dieselbe Denkrichtung eingeschlagen wie Steiner gegen die Geistvergessenheit. Die Schwelle zu dem Vergessenen geht Heidegger mit seinem existenzphilosophischen Blick auf das menschliche Dasein von der subjektiven Seite an, der Angst, und Steiner aus seiner Perspektive auf die Welt der Sinne und die Welt des Geistes von der objektiven Seite her, dem Tod. Beides gehört zusammen. Dabei sind Angst und Tod Schwellen, die sich nicht einfach so überwinden lassen, ja sie werden überhaupt erst zu Schwellen, wenn sie durchlebt werden. Dieses Durchleben ist dann ein Verwandeln. Und sie können nur verwandelt werden, weil sie jenes Potenzial einer ‹Konversion› in ihr Gegenteil – Weite und Leben – in sich tragen. Sie bergen eine Ambivalenz in sich, aufgrund derer sie, wie Heidegger in Abgrenzung zur Rede vom «Überwinden» sagen würde, «verwunden» werden können – verwunden wie ein Schmerz, den man auch nicht einfach los wird, sondern durch-leiden muss, bis er transparent wird. Eben das ist das Erlebnis der Schwelle. Die Enge der Angst wird an ihrem

Krisenpunkt in die Weite der Offenheit (des Vertrauens?) verwunden: in die Weite eines neuen Zuhause, von dem Heidegger nicht spricht, aber man könnte es das Zuhause der Heimatlosigkeit des Eingeweihten (des Grenzverwinders?) nennen, von der Steiner spricht. Und der Tod begegnet uns in der tödlichen Gestalt seiner ahrimanischen Bedeutung, in der er, wie die Angst, eine Folge des Sündenfalls ist. Diesen Tod gilt es zu verwinden, d.h. in seine wahre Gestalt zu überführen, die es aber ohne seine falsche nie gegeben hätte. Denn diese ist die Folge des Sündenfalls, aufgrund dessen es überhaupt die Schwelle erst gibt.

Die Sünde des Intellekts

Ist man sich einer Schuld bewusst und bedauert, was geschehen ist, so wird man nicht groß auftreten, sondern eher leise Töne anschlagen, ja vielleicht sogar demütig sein und auch einen größeren Aufwand nicht scheuen, um das Geschehene wiedergutzumachen. Aber es gibt auch das Gegenteil: das Festschreiben einer Verfehlung, so als ließe sich an ihr nichts mehr ändern. Und schließlich findet man womöglich noch ein Gefallen daran. Bezogen auf die Erkenntnisresignation gegenüber der geistigen Welt diagnostiziert Rudolf Steiner dies in dem, was er den «intellektuellen Sündenfall» nennt.[31]

Von «Sünde» zu sprechen ist unangenehm, es macht aber Sinn, wenn man «Sünde» nicht als Grund einer Zerknirschung, sondern als Ausdruck unseres Verhältnisses zum Geist versteht. Ja, sie ist im Unterschied zur Schuld immer auf ein Geistiges bezogen. So «versündigt» man sich gegenüber dem Ich eines

Menschen, wenn man ihn in seinem Wesen missachtet und missbraucht. Oder man versündigt sich gegenüber der göttlich-geistigen Welt. Das heißt, man trennt sich von ihr, gibt die Beziehung auf, sagt sich los.

Ist vom «Sündenfall» die Rede, so wird alles noch etwas komplizierter, weil mit ihm, je nach theologisch-philosophischem Hintergrund, für die einen eine Art Urschuld des Menschen verbunden ist, während die anderen im Sündenfall die Emanzipation von einer göttlichen Führung und damit vor allem auch den Beginn der Freiheit sehen. Dann kann dieser «Fall» gar nicht schuldhaft sein, weil es erst in seiner Folge Freiheit und Schuldfähigkeit gibt. Unter beiden Gesichtspunkten aber bedeutet der Sündenfall eine Trennung vom Göttlich-Geistigen.

Wurde diese Trennung zunächst vor allem als ein Problem angesehen, dessen Konsequenzen der Schweiß der Arbeit, das Leid («unter Schmerzen gebären») und der Tod sind, so fühlte sich der Mensch, je mehr er mit seinem Intellekt tätig wurde, schließlich auch in seinen Erkenntnisfähigkeiten von den Konsequenzen des Sündenfalls betroffen, nämlich beeinträchtigt: Er kann die Welt des Geistes nicht mehr erkennen. Diese Unfähigkeit aber wurde auf ihrer Rückseite zu einer wachsenden Fähigkeit. Mit ihr schreitet der Emanzipationsakt des Sündenfalls voran. Denn die Trennung von der göttlich-geistigen Welt wird zunehmend weniger als ein Verlust erfahren, sondern als die Voraussetzung dafür, die Sinneswelt erkennend zu erobern. Der sich entfaltende Intellekt kann die Natur erkennen und nutzen. Gott kann er zwar noch konstruierend beweisen, aber eben nicht mehr erkennen, sondern nur noch glauben. Dieses Defizit macht sich der Intellekt nun jedoch selbst zu einem Fundament für alle gesicherte Erkenntnis in der Sinneswelt. Steiner betrachtet dies als den Ursprung der modernen naturwissenschaftlichen Rede von den Erkenntnisgrenzen, deren Selbstbeschränkung der «intellektuelle Sündenfall» ist.

In dieser Entwicklung sind erstaunliche Übergänge zu beobachten: Hielt sich der Mensch zunächst noch für zu schlecht, das Überirdische, das Geistige zu begreifen, so macht er diese Unfähigkeit schließlich zum Prinzip, um nicht mehr schlecht von sich denken zu müssen. Das Bedauern über den verlorenen Geistbezug weicht der Selbstgefälligkeit einer Erkenntnismacht, die sich in ihren Grenzen etabliert hat und hier Erstaunliches leistet. Mit Fernrohr und Mikroskop stößt man in immer größere Fernen und immer kleinere Details vor. Immer genauer wird die Sinneswelt erfasst, und schließlich lässt der Stolz auf diese selbst entwickelte Fähigkeit die Loslösung von der geistigen Welt als eine Errungenschaft und nicht als einen Verlust erscheinen: Das Übersinnliche lässt sich nicht erkennen, insofern tun wir gut daran, uns auf die Sinneswelt zu beschränken, um nicht dem Aberglauben zu verfallen. Auch das ist eine Errungenschaft.

Aus dem traurigen Bewusstsein vom verlorenen Zugang zum Geist wird das starke Selbstbewusstsein der erfolgreichen Konzentration auf die Materie. Die Begrenztheit unserer Erkenntnis ist schließlich weit davon entfernt, als eine auch selbstgemachte Trennung von der Welt des Geistes und damit als eine Art «Sünde wider den Geist» angesehen zu werden. Das hat auch etwas mit dem aufklärerischen Verständnis des Sündenfalls zu tun.

Wird der Sündenfall einzig im selbstbewussten Sinne als der Austritt aus der Unmündigkeit und als Eintritt in die Freiheit und Selbstständigkeit verstanden, die mit einer wachsenden Selbstmächtigkeit in der Erkenntnis der Sinneswelt einhergeht, so fehlt jene Erkenntnissehnsucht, mit der der Mensch sich erst eigentlich selbst gerecht werden kann. Insofern der Mensch das einzige geistige Wesen ist, das in der Sinneswelt lebt, muss ein Stück weit auch jene «romantische»

Sehnsucht zu ihm gehören, mit der er spürt, dass er mit dem Sündenfall etwas verloren hat, das es neu zu erlangen gilt. Das ist seine Schuldigkeit. Ohne die verliert er schließlich gar sein geistiges Wesen.

Rudolf Steiner spricht von einem «Missverständnis des Sündenfalls», wenn sich der Intellekt mit der Unerkennbarkeit des Geistes abfindet und sich in ihr selbstgefällig einrichtet. Das frühere Sündenbewusstsein ist eingeschlafen, die Erkenntnisgrenzen sind geblieben und verbinden sich nun mit einem emanzipatorischen Hochmut, der alles zum Aberglauben erklärt, was die Sinne nicht erkennen können.

Nun kann aber auch dieser emanzipatorische Hochmut noch in einer ganz anderen Hinsicht übertroffen werden, denn tatsächlich besteht eine bedeutende Gefahr gerade dort, wo ein neues Bewusstsein für die Möglichkeiten entsteht, die etablierten Erkenntnisgrenzen zu erweitern und zu überschreiten. Hier ist die Gefahr sogar die größte und nicht weniger eine «Sünde wider den Geist» als der intellektuelle Sündenfall, die Gefahr nämlich, die im Stolz auf jede höhere Erkenntnis liegt. Wenn der Stolz im Hinblick auf die Naturerkenntnis noch ein Recht hat, so hat er es in der Geisterkenntnis nicht. Die Aufhebung der Erkenntnisgrenze macht nur unter der Bedingung der Demut Sinn. Ja, nur dann kann überhaupt Geisterkenntnis sein.

Steiner stellt dem «intellektuellen Sündenfall», der die Erkenntnisgrenzen festschreibt, das gegenüber, was er die «spirituelle Sündenerhebung» nennt, d.h. den Aufschwung zu einer neuen Geisterkenntnis. Die aber muss mit jener Demut gepaart sein, die das alte Sündenbewusstsein begleitet hat: «Und so muss eben mit der Notwendigkeit der Sündenerhebung zugleich eingesehen werden, dass der Mensch die Erziehung in Demut, die er durchgemacht hat, nun mit vollem Bewusstsein auch in sich aufnehmen muss. Und er kann das ja. Denn wenn aus der Erkenntnis Hochmut kommt, dann ist das immer ein Zeichen davon, dass es eigentlich mit der Erkenntnis gewaltig hapert.»[32]

Erkenntnisdemut hat nichts mit Kleinmütigkeit oder mit moralischer Zerknirschung zu tun. Dennoch hat sie tatsächlich etwas mit einer Schuld zu tun, aber im Sinne der Zukunftsdimension von Schuld: Ich schulde etwas. Ich schulde der Welt des Geistes alle Anstrengung einer neuen Vereinigung mit ihr. Diese Wiedervereinigung vollzieht sich in der gewandelten geschichtlichen Situation nicht dadurch, dass man sich vom Baum der Erkenntnis fernhält, sondern umgekehrt in dem Versuch, durch ein demütig mutiges

Essen vom Baum der Erkenntnis die Sonderung aufzuheben. Das ist die «spirituelle Sündenerhebung». – Was heißt das? Diese Sündenerhebung heißt «nichts anderes», so Steiner, «als den Christus wirklich verstehen», die Sprache des Himmels zu lernen, «um einen Sinn zu verbinden mit dem, was der Christus auf Erden wollte».[33] Auch ist ja Christus als die lösende Antwort auf den Sündenfall gekommen.

Das Jüngern des Ätherleibes

Es gibt so etwas wie einen «horror contradictionis», unter dem viele denkende Menschen leiden, eine Angst vor dem Widerspruch. Aber vielleicht ist dieser «horror» gar nicht nötig, im Gegenteil: vielleicht ist er sogar hinderlich. Widersprüche können ja auch etwas Faszinierendes haben. Rudolf Steiner jedenfalls spart nicht mit ihnen. Oft führen sie zu ganz neuen Gedanken und katapultieren uns über unser gewöhnliches Denken hinaus.

Noch kein Widerspruch, sondern einfach kontraintuitiv ist es, wenn Steiner ausgerechnet über den Ätherleib, also den Lebensleib sagt, dass dieser im Gegensatz zum physischen Leib im Laufe des Lebens immer jünger werde. Im Alt-Werden «jüngert» der Ätherleib, wie es bei Steiner heißt. Ätherleib und physischer Leib verhalten sich also gegenläufig zueinander: Während unsere Haut Falten bekommt und wir kahlköpfig werden, wird unser Ätherleib pausbackig und blühend.[34]

So steht der Ätherleib in einem erstaunlichen Gegensatz zum physischen Leib. Darüber hinaus aber steht er offenbar in einem Widerspruch zu sich selbst. Das jedenfalls ergibt sich aus anderen Ausführungen Steiners zum Ätherleib: Wenn er nämlich in der Zeit des Ersten Weltkriegs der jungen Toten gedenkt, dann erfahren wir, dass bei jenen früh Gefallenen noch unverbrauchte Ätherkräfte vorhanden waren – Ätherkräfte, die an sich noch ein ganzes Menschenleben bis ins Alter von sechzig, achtzig oder mehr Jahren ausgereicht hätten und nun gewissermaßen übrig bleiben.[35]

Bei einem normalen Lebensverlauf werden die Ätherkräfte immer weniger. Das leuchtet ein. Aber vor dem Hintergrund der erstgenannten Aussage heißt das nun: Der Ätherleib jüngert im physischen Alterungsprozess, und er verbraucht dabei seine Kräfte. Das klingt doch widersprüchlich. Aber es hält die Perspektive für neue Einsichten offen: für Einsichten in die Welt des Geistes.

Steiners Blick beim Gedenken an die jungen Toten geht nun nicht auf den Widerspruch in der Entwicklung des Ätherleibes, sondern ist auf eine Spiritualisierung des Erdenlebens durch die zur Verfügung stehenden Ätherkräfte gerichtet. Denn durch den frühen Tod eines Menschen werden Ätherkräfte frei, die nun der geistigen Weiterentwicklung der ganzen Menschheit zugute kommen können. Von den Ätherleibern der Frühverstorbenen spricht Steiner als von den «großen Mitarbeitern in der Spiritualisierung der menschlichen Kultur.»[36]

Als bedeutsames Beispiel für die Wirksamkeit des Ätherleibes eines Frühverstorbenen erwähnt Steiner wiederholt die Geschichte des kleinen Theodor Faiß. Dieser Junge wurde im Alter von sieben Jahren in Dornach durch einen umstürzenden Möbelwagen getötet. Die Umstände dabei waren so außerordentlich, dass viel dafür spricht, hier nicht an einen Zufall zu denken. Ja, hier darf man vielleicht von karmischer Fügung und einem Opfer, das gebracht wurde, sprechen. Der Ätherleib des Jungen, so erklärt Steiner, stand nach dessen Tod als helfende Kraft dem Dornacher Bau zur Verfügung. Seine «Vermittlerkräfte» inspirierten damit auf entscheidende Weise das geistige Leben auf der Erde.[37]

Es geht hier nicht um die ökonomische Rechtfertigung eines Unglücks und auch nicht um die des damals wütenden Ersten Weltkriegs, sondern um ein geisteswissenschaftliches Verständnis von äußerst schmerzhaften Ereignissen und jene Weisheit, die die Perle des

Schmerzes ist. Dabei spielen geistige Welt und physische Welt auf wunderbare Weise zusammen. So gäbe es nach Steiner keinen Homer, keinen Shakespeare, keinen Goethe, Michelangelo, Raffael und viele andere nicht, «auf denen die Fortentwicklung der Menschheit beruht, insofern die Fortentwicklung der Menschheit Genialität braucht, [...] wenn nicht der Boden dazu bereitet würde dadurch, dass auch Menschen jung sterben müssen».[38] Und ergänzen darf man, dass die genannten Persönlichkeiten mehr als andere offen für jene Kräfte aus der geistigen Sphäre waren und sie unter schöpferischen Schmerzen für die Welt fruchtbar gemacht haben. Hier findet ein Austausch von füreinander bestimmten Kräften statt, in dem der Schmerz nicht weniger zu den Taten des Genies als zu dem Opfer der Frühverstorbenen gehört.

Wie aber verhält es sich nun mit dem genannten Widerspruch? Wenn das Leben seinen normalen Gang geht, der Mensch alt wird, dann jüngert sein Ätherleib. Dann muss bei einem Menschen, der jung stirbt, der Ätherleib quasi ‹alt› sein, aber unverbraucht, weshalb er seine Kräfte der Menschheit zur Verfügung stellen kann. – Das Verhältnis von alt und unverbraucht einerseits und jung und verbraucht andererseits wirkt ungereimt. Ja, wir empfinden das als Widerspruch, weil wir in unserer Beurteilung stets die Standards des physischen Leibes zugrunde legen, der nur entweder jung und unverbraucht oder eben alt und verbraucht ist. Beim Ätherleib verhält sich nun aber alles anders.

Bei der Geburt oder der Empfängnis wird uns der Ätherleib wie ein großes Kapital übergeben. Da ist er, wie Steiner sagt, «ausgeprägt und ausziseliert, da hat er viele, viele innere Formungen».[39] Da hat er Falten, könnte man sagen, aber eben diese Falten sind sein Reichtum, der im Laufe des physischen Lebens verbraucht wird. Es treten dann die Formungen zurück, und die «Haut» des Ätherleibes wird wieder glatt wie die physische Haut eines Kindes. Aber sollte man deshalb sagen können, dieser Ätherleib sei nun undifferenziert, ihm seien seine Eigenarten im Laufe der Jahre eingeebnet worden und damit verschwunden? Glatt und ohne Charakteristika am Ende eines Lebens? – Das wird man so auch nicht sagen können, denn ist nicht der Ätherleib dasjenige Wesensglied, in dem sich die im Leben erworbenen Fähigkeiten niederschlagen? In ihn prägt sich, je älter der Mensch wird, Weisheit ein, wohl aber nicht so, dass dies in jedem Moment auch für die Umgebung sichtbar würde, denn es kann ein Mensch im Alter dement sein, und doch haben Jahrzehnte wachen Lebens an seinem Ätherleib gearbeitet.[40]

So hätten wir also dreierlei gleichzeitig zu denken: Der Ätherleib eines physisch alt gewordenen Menschen ist erstens jung, zweitens verbraucht und drittens angereichert mit der Weisheit des durchlebten Lebens. Das fordert uns in ein Denken, das wir nicht gewohnt sind, und zwar deshalb nicht, weil wir gewöhnlich weniger in Verhältnisbestimmungen und Beziehungen, also weniger aus einem Zwischenbereich der Relationen denken als vielmehr in isolierten Zustandsbeschreibungen. Die drei Charakteristika des Ätherleibes eines alten Menschen sind aber eher als Metaphern für Verhältnisse zu verstehen. Sie sind relational und im Fluss. Sie zeugen von einer zunehmenden Lösung des Ätherleibes vom physischen Leib und vom Verhältnis des Vergangenen zum Künftigen. Während bei einem jungen Menschen eine starke Verbindung zwischen physischem Leib und Ätherleib besteht, löst sich diese im Alter. Nur deshalb kann der Ätherleib jünger werden und dabei gleichzeitig den physischen Leib altern lassen, ihm also immer weniger belebende Kräfte zukommen lassen. Und nur deshalb kann sich der Ätherleib im Jüngerwerden verbrauchen, weil das Kapital, das er sich in einem früheren Leben erworben hat und das sich im Nachtodlichen beziehungsweise Vorgeburtlichen mit kosmischen Kräften vereinigt hat, im Laufe seines physischen Lebens zugleich zur Neige geht. Dafür wird er aber von einem Weisheitscharakter durchströmt, der die Ebenmäßigkeit individueller Schönheit entfaltet. Der Reichtum aus einem früheren Leben verbraucht sich, während die Weisheit wächst. Und hier eröffnet sich sein Verhältnis zum Kommenden, denn schließlich wächst mit der Weisheit ein Potenzial an zukünftigen Fähigkeiten, das erst in der endgültigen Loslösung vom physischen Leib zu einem neuen, größeren Kapital für eine nächste Verkörperung wird.

Aus dem Leib wird der Kopf

Der Kopf des Menschen zeigt sich bei seiner Geburt sogleich in einer gewissen Vollkommenheit. Er muss nicht noch in demselben Maße wachsen und sich wandeln wie der übrige Organismus. Der Kopf, so Rudolf Steiner, weist auf eine Entwicklung hin, die der Mensch schon hinter sich hat, während der übrige Organismus erst am Anfang einer Entwicklung steht.[41] Das hat seinen Grund darin, dass sich der Leib einer früheren Inkarnation im Durchgang durch das Leben zwischen Tod und neuer Geburt in den Kopf der neuen Inkarnation verwandelt hat. Der Kopf hat also eine Vorgeschichte, die zur Reinkarnation des Individuums gehört, während sich der Leib in seinen Anlagen von den Vorfahren herschreibt.[42] Das Haupt zeige, so Steiner, «dass es ein umgewandelter übriger Organismus ist; der übrige Organismus, dass er ein noch nicht gewordenes Haupt ist. Gewissermaßen so wie das grüne Blatt ein noch nicht gewordenes Blumenblatt ist, und das gefärbte Blumenblatt ein umgewandeltes Laubblatt. Und dasjenige, was der Mensch durch seinen übrigen Organismus ausbildet, das verleibt sich der Seele ein. Und wenn der Mensch durch die Pforte des Todes geht, tritt das in eine geistige Welt ein, macht eine Entwickelung zwischen dem Tod und einer neuen Geburt durch und wird in einem späteren Leben zu den Kräften, die dann im Haupte sich ausbilden, so wie das Haupt der Gegenwart sich aus dem Organismus eines früheren Erdenlebens herausgebildet hat»[43]

Dieses Umwandlungsverhältnis wirft ein Licht auf den besonderen Reinkarnationsgedanken Rudolf Steiners. Reinkarnation betrifft nämlich damit auch das Physische des Menschen. Sein seelisch-geistiger Kern tritt nicht einfach nur in einer neuen Hülle auf, sondern im gegenwärtigen Kopf hält sich das vergangene Leben auch in physischer Hinsicht präsent. Mein Kopf ist die Umstülpung der Gliedmaßen meiner früheren Inkarnation. Und während der Kopf damit an das Ende einer Entwicklung kommt, gewährleisten die Gliedmaßen – natürlich nicht dem Stoff, sondern der individualisierten Form nach – die leibliche Kontinuität mit einem künftigen Leben.

Im Vortrag vom 7. August 1916 aus der Reihe *Das Rätsel des Menschen. Die geistigen Hintergründe der menschlichen Geschichte,*[44] in dem Steiner meines Wissens zum ersten Mal von diesem Metamorphosezusammenhang spricht, stellt er auch sogleich die Frage, durch welche Kräfte denn diese Umwandlung geschieht. Seine Antwort auf diese Frage ist nicht weniger denkwürdig als die Verwandlung selbst. Denn die Kräfte, die diese Verwandlung leisten und zu ihr bestimmt sind, verwenden wir heute gewöhnlich zu einem ganz anderen Zweck, nämlich zu dem der Erkenntnis der Welt. So könnte man in einer gewissen Hinsicht sagen, dass ein und dieselben Kräfte zunächst die leibliche Grundlage unseres Denkens, also den Kopf, schaffen und dass sie sich dann eben des Kopfes bedienen. Aber es ist doch etwas anders. Denn letztlich ist es eine Alternative, ob wir diese Kräfte für die Vorbereitung jener im Nachtodlichen sich vollziehenden Umwandlung der Gliedmaßen in den künftigen Kopf verwenden oder ob wir sie jetzt unmittelbar zum Erkennen gebrauchen – oder genauer gesprochen: zum Erkennen verbrauchen.

Zur Erläuterung bedient sich Steiner des Bildes vom Weizenkorn, das wir entweder zum Brotbacken oder zur Aussaat für neuen Weizen verwenden können. Was die Natur angeht, so ist die innere Bestimmung des Weizenkorns nicht die Ernährung des Menschen, sondern eine neue Weizenpflanze. In einer gewissen Hinsicht verhält es sich mit den Kräften, die wir heute mit der größten Selbstverständlichkeit zum Erkennen verwenden ähnlich, denn eigentlich sind sie gar nicht zum Erkennen bestimmt, sondern eben zu jener Metamorphose der Gliedmaßen in den Kopf. Und ein Teil der Kräfte folgt ja auch weiterhin unbewusst dieser Bestimmung, denn der Mensch tritt immer noch mit einem Menschenkopf auf. Aber was der Mensch für die Erkenntnis der Welt aufwendet, geht in gewisser Weise für seine eigene Weiterentwicklung verloren wie das Weizenkorn, aus dem keine neue Pflanze wird, weil man damit Brot gebacken hat.

Nun hat es diese Alternative von bestimmungsgemäßem oder -fremdem Gebrauch der Kräfte nicht immer so gegeben. In die «Gefahr», dass sich der Mensch immer mehr der äußeren Welt zuwendet und sie mit seiner Erkenntnis zu erfassen strebt, ist er erst nach und nach und im Besonderen erst im Übergang von der Antike zur Neuzeit gekommen. Denn solange das Wissen noch mehr ein inneres und gewissermaßen unbewusstes und zweckfreies, ja mehr eine Seinsweise war, wie etwa bei den alten Ägyptern oder Chaldäern, war der Anteil äußerer Erkenntnis nur gering. Das hat auch damit zu tun, dass die äußere Welt noch schlichtweg einen wesentlich kleineren Radius hatte. Schon rein geografisch wusste man eben noch nichts von vielen Teilen der Erde. Diese hat sich der Mensch erst nach und nach erobert, bis dahin, dass uns heute die Erde klein geworden ist und sich der Forscherdrang bis auf die konkreten Verhältnisse auf anderen Planeten ausdehnt.

Sollte man nun auf die Radius- und Erkenntnisausweitung verzichten? Ist es falsch, die Welt zu erforschen und die Dinge bis in ihre Bestandteile zu untersuchen? Sind Weltraumfahrt und Genforschung Gründe dafür, dass sich der Mensch innerlich nicht weiterentwickeln kann, so dass er schließlich für eine nächste Inkarnation so wenig Bildekräfte angesammelt hätte, dass er Gefahr läuft, mit einem Kopf zur Welt zu kommen, der aussieht wie der eines Tieres? Ist denn äußere Erkenntnis «schädlich»?

Steiner stellt diese Fragen so nicht, aber indirekt gibt er eine Antwort auf sie, und diese hat eine fundamentale Bedeutung für die Menschheitsentwicklung in unserer Gegenwart. Es geht ihm nicht um ein «Zurück zur Natur», sondern eher um eine Verwandlung von Zivilisation in Kultur. Es geht nicht darum, auf das Erkennen zu verzichten, sondern es in einer ganz anderen Haltung zu vollziehen – einer Haltung, die

Erkenntnis in einen höheren Dienst stellt als den der unmittelbar materiellen Nützlichkeit.

Wie das Weizenkorn schließlich auch dadurch geadelt wird, dass es nicht nur neuen Weizen hervorbringt, sondern den Menschen ernährt, so muss entsprechend die äußere Erkenntnis des Menschen geadelt werden, die nicht unmittelbar seine eigene Fortentwicklung betrifft. Erkenntnis muss «Götterdienst» werden: «Erwirbst du Erkenntnisse, die du dem fortlaufenden Strom entziehst, so sei dir klar, dass Erkenntnis-Erwerben ein Götterdienst sein muss. Was an Erkenntnis erworben wird, ohne dass wir uns bewusst sind, dass das ein heiliger Dienst in der Entwickelung der Menschheit ist, ohne dass wir das, was wir uns aneignen von der Außenwelt, den höheren Geistern übergeben, die sich davon nähren, die das in sich aufnehmen – was wir an solcher Erkenntnis erwerben, die wir nicht mit dieser Empfindung begleiten, die wir einfach gedankenlos erwerben, das ist wie Weizenkörner, die in die Erde fallen und verfaulen, das heißt die keine Ziele erreichen, nicht die ihren und nicht die anderen, die zur menschlichen Nahrung dienen.»[45]

Das äußere Wissen des Menschen muss also Nahrung für die göttliche Welt werden, und als solche ist es auch für die geistdurchwirkte Entwicklung der Menschheit geheiligt. Hingegen verfehlt jedes rein profane Wissen den Sinn der Evolution. Denn was nur im Dienst technischer «Verbesserungen» steht, was nur der Nützlichkeit dient, wie die gentechnisch optimierte Tomate, geht dem göttlichen Dienst verloren und ist wie ein verfaulendes Weizenkorn. Wird Wissen aber Götterdienst, dann steht der Mensch gerade auch in der Zuwendung zur äußeren Welt im Austausch mit der geistigen Welt. Er ernährt dann die geistige Welt, die auch ihn ernährt und davor bewahrt, irgendwann mit dem Kopf eines Tieres anzutreten.

Wodurch aber wird dieser Götterdienst möglich? Im Grunde dadurch, dass Christus sich mit der Erde verbunden hat, dass er zum Brot der Menschen geworden ist. Das ist die Voraussetzung dafür, dass das Wissen des Menschen zum Brot der Götter werden kann.

Zu der schönen Symmetrie der Weltentwicklung, die uns Steiner vor Augen führt, gehört es, dass mit der Ausweitung des äußeren Wissenshorizontes, die die Gefahr einer Entwicklungshemmung, einer Vertierung der Kopfgestalt mit sich bringt, zugleich jenes Ereignis eintritt, das dem drohenden Absterben des Menschen die entscheidende Wende gibt. Wurde der Horizont mit der griechisch-lateinischen Kulturepoche zunehmend weiter, so trat zur selben Zeit die Möglichkeit ein, das mit den Sinnen erworbene Wissen von der äußeren Welt zu einem Götterdienst zu machen. Christi Zuwendung zur Erde schuf die Voraussetzung dafür, dass Welterkenntnis auch Religion sein kann.

Umgestülpt oder: Anders denken lernen, als man denkt

Wenn man die dem sozialen Leben zugrunde liegende Ordnung mit der des menschlichen Organismus vergleicht – welches der inneren Systeme des Menschen entspricht dann dem Wirtschaftsleben? Das Nerven-Sinnessystem, das rhythmische System oder das Stoffwechselsystem? – Unbefangen würde man hier wahrscheinlich auf das Stoffwechselsystem tippen: Das Wirtschaftsleben gilt der Herstellung, der Verteilung und dem Verbrauch von Gütern des menschlichen Bedarfs. Es schafft die stofflich-materiellen Grundlagen für das Rechts- und das Geistesleben. Für das Geistesleben liegt es nahe, es dem Nerven-Sinnessystem zuzuordnen, das den denkenden ‹Kopf› des Ganzen bildet. Das Rechtsleben steht in der Mitte zwischen Wirtschafts- und Geistesleben und entspricht deshalb den alles in Einklang bringenden rhythmischen Tätigkeiten von Herz und Atmung. Zu diesem Ergebnis kommt man, wenn man in Analogien denkt und die Phänomene in ihrer unmittelbaren Aussage miteinander vergleicht. Das ist dann ein Vergleich, der sich auf die Außenseite der Dinge bezieht. Die Innenseite, die Wesenswahrheit kann sich demgegenüber ganz anders, ja geradezu gegensätzlich verhalten.

Friedrich Nietzsche schreibt einmal in *Jenseits von Gut und Böse* im Hinblick auf die Wahrheiten der tiefsten Dinge: «Alles, was tief ist, liebt die Maske; die allertiefsten Dinge haben sogar einen Hass auf Bild und Gleichnis. Sollte nicht erst der Gegensatz die rechte Verkleidung sein, in der die Scham eines Gottes einherginge? ... Jeder tiefe Geist braucht eine Maske: mehr noch, um jeden tiefen Geist wächst fortwährend eine Maske, dank der beständig falschen, nämlich flachen Auslegung jedes Wortes, jedes Schrittes, jedes Lebens-Zeichens, das er gibt» (Zweites Hauptstück, 40). – Das ist kein grundsätzliches Plädoyer Nietzsches für Maskierungen, sondern die Aufforderung zu einem größeren Bewusstsein und einer tieferen Erkenntnistätigkeit.

Rudolf Steiner hat eine besondere Methode tieferer Erkenntnis entwickelt, eine andere Art des Denkens. Es folgt dem Prinzip der Umstülpung, die auf dem Weg zur geistigen Wahrheit einer Sache durchlaufen werden muss. So gehört es für Steiner, entgegen dem äußeren

Eindruck, zur Wirklichkeit in einem tieferen Sinn, dass eben nicht das Geistesleben, sondern das Wirtschaftsleben den Kopf des sozialen Organismus ausmacht, während das Geistesleben im Sozialen dem Stoffwechselsystem im Menschen entspricht.[46] Denn nicht das Wirtschaftsleben kann das Geistesleben ernähren, sondern umgekehrt: Das Geistige muss die Grundlage der Produktionsverhältnisse sein. Es ist der Magen, die Leber, die Milz, ohne deren Tätigkeit das Wirtschaftsleben zugrunde gehen müsste. Ja, eine Ursache für dieses Zugrundegehen besteht gerade in dem falsch gedachten, ungeistigen Verhältnis zwischen Geistes- und Wirtschaftsleben. Denn hält man das Geistesleben gewissermaßen nur für das ‹Hobby›, das sich ein vermeintlich erfolgreiches Wirtschaftsleben leisten kann, so muss dieses Wirtschaftsleben an geistiger Unterernährung zugrunde gehen. Das geschieht um so sicherer, je mehr man nur das Wachstum des Wirtschaftslebens zur Grundlage seiner Existenz macht und eben nicht das Geistesleben und die darin zu verwirklichende Freiheit, die auch eine Freiheit von wirtschaftlichen Interessen ist. Im Wirtschaftsleben waltet sogar ‹naturgemäß› ein Tödliches, so wie beim menschlichen Organismus die Bewusstseinsprozesse Sterbeprozesse sind. «Das Wirtschaftsleben ist dasjenige, welches den geschichtlichen

Fortgang der Menschheit fortwährend zum Absterben bringt, das nicht etwa das Übrige aus sich hervortreibt, sondern nur den Tod von allem hervorbringt. Und dieser Tod muss fortwährend wieder ausgeglichen werden durch dasjenige, was im geistigen Organismus hervorgebracht wird.»[47]

Steiners Art des Denkens ist hier von einer Konkretheit, die alle Abstraktion, die stets die Grundlage eines nur äußerlichen Vergleichs ist, hinter sich lässt. So ist es z.B. abstrakt, wenn man zwischen einer Kirsche und einem Steak mit den Begriffen «rot», «weich», «saftig» die Beziehung «Fleisch» herstellt. Freilich gibt es wohl zwischen diesen beiden ‹Lebensmitteln› auch kaum noch eine tiefere Beziehung. Da aber, wo es eine geistige Beziehung gibt, muss ein Denken unternommen werden, das uns unseren Gewohnheiten entgegen erkennen lässt, dass z.B. die Erde im Sommer gerade nicht wach ist, sondern schläft, während sie im Winter wacht. Das ist die geistige Dimension der Erde, die ihr wesenhaft zugrunde liegt. Dass im Winter alles unter einer weißen Decke zu ruhen scheint, ist die Maske, unter der sich das Gegenteil verbirgt. Natürlich hat die Maske, die Maja, die die Analogie herstellt, auch recht, aber nur da, wo sie sich transparent macht für das Übersinnliche: an der Schwelle. So ist der Tod als Tod eine Lebenswandlung. Ein Sterben im Irdischen ist ein Geboren-Werden im Geistigen und umgekehrt. Ein solches Verbergen des Geistigen unter seinem gegensätzlichen Ausdruck kann ein natürliches, also von selbst geschehendes oder ein absichtliches sein. Letzteres hat Nietzsche in *Jenseits von Gut und Böse* gemeint. Es ist das Prinzip seiner Moral, die eine ganz eigene Tiefe hat, die Tiefe der Scham: «Es sind nicht die schlimmsten Dinge, deren man sich am schlimmsten schämt: Es ist nicht nur Arglist hinter einer Maske, – es gibt so viel Güte in der List. Ich könnte mir denken, dass ein Mensch, der etwas Kostbares und Verletzliches zu bergen hätte, grob und rund wie ein grünes altes schwer beschlagenes Weinfass durchs Leben rollte: die Feinheit seiner Scham will es so» (a.a.O.). Das ist gewissermaßen eine ‹esoterische Moral›, deren Größe bei Nietzsche nicht selten verkannt wird, aber vielleicht wollte das seine Scham so.

Anders zwar, aber doch vergleichbar steht zu dieser esoterischen Moral die esoterische Erkenntnis, die im Nachvollzug der Umstülpungsverhältnisse liegt, wie sie auch in den Verwandlungen des menschlichen Leibes vom einen Leben ins andere geschieht. So wie sich das Gute, um als solches bewahrt zu werden, nicht selbst demonstrieren darf, weil es dann seine Wahrhaftigkeit verliert, so sind auch Analogie schlüsse im Erkennen überall da nicht ausreichend und oft auch nicht sinnvoll, wo es um die geistige Tiefe einer Sache geht. Bezogen auf das Beispiel vom sozialen und vom leiblichen Organismus bedeutet das: Der soziale Organismus verhält sich, wenn wir ihn tief verstehen wollen, zum Leibesorganismus des Menschen wie die Reinkarnation einer Individualität zu einer vorangegangenen Inkarnation. Dass sich der Leib von der einen Inkarnation zur anderen in den Kopf verwandelt, die Füße dabei zu Augen werden und die Arme zu Ohren, ist nur einem Erkennen zugänglich, das sich von der Abstraktion der Analogie gelöst hat und selbst aktiv in die Sphäre des Geistes eintaucht. Sich in ein solches Denken einzuüben ist naturgemäß schwer. Vielleicht muss sich das Evidenzerleben hier zunächst auf den Nachvollzug beschränken, also auf das Nach-Denken der von Steiner angeführten Umstülpungsverhältnisse. In jedem Fall aber wird hier das Erkennen in einer Weise aktiv, wie wir sie nur dem Willenselement zuschreiben können.

Wenn wir die Prädikate «theoretisch» und «praktisch» zu vergeben haben, dann beschreiben wir mit «theoretisch» gewöhnlich das Denken und mit «praktisch» das Handeln. Und so sehr wir davon überzeugt sind, dass wir zum Handeln den Leib brauchen und im Denken uns von demselben weitestgehend frei halten, ebenso fern liegt uns zunächst die Erfahrung, dass wir beim Denken gerade dann abstrakt verfahren, wenn wir es auf den Leib abstützen, wohingegen wir uns eigentlich erst dann vom Leib frei zu machen vermögen, wenn wir im Steinerschen Sinne ‹konkret› zu denken lernen. Im Grunde ist nämlich nur das leibgebundene Denken theoretisch und abstrakt – ausgerechnet dieses, wo wir doch gemäß der Analogie dachten, alles, was mit dem Leib zu tun hat, sei praktisch und das, was von ihm losgelöst ist, eher theoretisch. In der Loslösung aber liegt eine wesentliche Tat des Denkens. Es ist die Loslösung von der Analogie, in der der Wille gewissermaßen noch schläft, während er in den Relationen der Umstülpung für das Erkennen erwacht. Dieses Erkennen ist unterwegs zur Geistesschau.

«Haarsträubender Idealismus»? oder: Geliebte Pflichten, gelassene Rechte und das soziale Hauptgesetz

Wenn von Pflichten und Rechten die Rede ist, beschleicht einen leicht ein ungutes Gefühl: Jetzt wird es auf eine unangenehme Weise moralisch. Dem ‹altmodischen›, konservativen Klischee der Pflichterfüllung steht dabei das ‹neumodisch› revolutionäre der eingeforderten Rechte kaum nach. Geltend gemachte Rechte können etwas von einer selbstsüchtigen Penetranz haben, wie auf der anderen Seite die Forderung nach Pflichterfüllung etwas zurechtweisend Autoritäres hat. Umgibt den Begriff der Pflicht die Aura einer geforderten Unterwerfung, so hat der des Rechts die Aura des Aufbegehrens. Der eine Pol gebiert den anderen: Unterwerfung wehrt sich durch Aufbegehren, und die Revolte des Aufbegehrens wird durch Maßregeln wieder zur Raison gebracht. Es ist ein Pingpong-Spiel zwischen Ahriman (Pflicht) und Luzifer (Recht). Und dieses bleibt so lange rein reaktiv, also in wechselseitiger Abhängigkeit, als es nicht gelingt, Luzifer und

Ahriman zu ‹erlösen›, indem man den einen auf den anderen einwirken lässt. Die Rechte bedürfen der Abkühlung durch Ahriman, die Pflichten der Erwärmung durch Luzifer. Beide erfüllen nämlich in der Anwendung auf ihr Gegenüber ihre höchste Aufgabe.[48]

So einfach das klingt, so schwer ist es, denn die Sache geht schließlich mit einem den Gewohnheiten zuwiderlaufenden Perspektivenwechsel einher: Die Pflicht wird erwärmt, dadurch dass die Außenwelt zur eigenen Sache wird, zu meinem Anliegen. Und die Rechtsansprüche kühlen ab, wenn mit Gelassenheit das von außen Kommende – etwa im Sinne einer karmischen Betrachtung – auch als das Eigene angesehen werden kann. Die gewöhnliche Subjekt-Objekt-Beziehung – hier Ich, da Welt – wird in dieser neuen Tingierung der Pflichten und Rechte ein Stück weit aufgehoben. Genau darin liegt eine Mittefindung.

Es geht bei dieser Mitte nicht um ein Mittleres zwischen Pflicht und Recht. Das gibt es nicht. Doch erringt das Ich auf diesem Weg seine eigene bewegliche Mitte, die eine besondere Qualität hat. Sie bildet sich nämlich nicht zwischen zwei Extremen, wie etwa die Mitte zwischen Tollkühnheit und Feigheit, die in Mut und Vorsicht liegt. Nein, diese Mitte ist mehr eine Beziehung, ein Verhältnis, eine Nähe: die Mitte zwischen Zentrum und Umkreis oder Innen und Außen.

In diese Richtung denkt auch die französische Philosophin Simone Weil. Freilich: Sie beschreibt den Perspektivenwechsel bei den Pflichten und Rechten in einer Weise, die auf den ersten Blick das Schwergewicht ganz auf die Pflicht zu legen scheint und deshalb rigide und gewissermaßen ahrimanisch anmutet. In ihrem Buch *Die Einwurzelung,* das den Untertitel «Einführung in die Pflichten dem menschlichen Wesen gegenüber» trägt, schreibt sie gleich zu Beginn: «Der Begriff der Verpflichtung hat den Vorrang vor dem des Rechtes, der ihm untergeordnet und von ihm abhängig ist. Ein Recht ist nicht wirksam durch sich selbst, sondern einzig durch die Verpflichtung, der es entspricht; die tatsächliche Erfüllung eines Rechtes geschieht nicht durch den, der es besitzt, sondern durch die anderen, die ihm gegenüber eine Pflichtleistung ihrerseits anerkennen. ... Ein Mensch für sich betrachtet hat nur Pflichten, unter denen sich gewisse Pflichten gegen sich selbst befinden. Die anderen haben, von ihm aus gesehen, nur Rechte. Er wiederum hat Rechte, wenn man ihn vom Standpunkt der anderen aus betrachtet, die ihm gegenüber Verpflichtungen ihrerseits anerkennen.»[49]

Das diesen Gedanken zugrunde liegende Prinzip ist der Standortwechsel, der auch eine Qualität der Mitte ist: Ich betrachte, was zu tun ist, aus der Sicht der anderen und diese aus meiner. Das ist, solange der Wechsel nicht vollzogen ist, äußerst schwer, denn das Luziferische in uns wehrt sich naturgemäß gegen die Ansprüche Ahrimans. Ist es aber geleistet, so macht gerade Luzifer die Sache leicht, und Ahriman verhindert, dass die eigene Kontur verschwimmt.

Nun betrifft aber das Verhältnis von Pflichten und Rechten gewissermaßen nur die ‹passive› Seite unserer Lebensverhältnisse. Der Standortwechsel erfährt noch einmal eine Steigerung, wenn wir vom Rechtsleben ins Wirtschaftsleben wechseln. Die Pflicht, die sich aus dem Recht des anderen ergibt, ist noch keine selbst gesetzte produktive Aufgabe, sondern gilt allein der Wahrung von Rechtsverhältnissen. Geht es aber nicht mehr allein um ein Handeln im juristischen Sinne, sondern um Produktionsverhältnisse, in denen Erträge erwirtschaftet werden, dann kommen wir von der Relation von Pflicht und Recht zu der von Aufwand und Ertrag, Arbeit und Lohn. Wenn wir auch hier einen Standortwechsel vollziehen und eine neue Mitte suchen, dann bedeutet das, dass sich Aufwand und Ertrag nicht mehr auf dieselbe Person konzentrieren, und das heißt letztlich: Der Ertrag meiner Leistung kommt anderen zugute. Nicht ich bin der Nutznießer meiner Arbeit, sondern die anderen. Die aber arbeiten für mich. Das ist die Idee des «sozialen Hauptgesetzes», wie es Rudolf Steiner in seinem Aufsatz *Geisteswissenschaft und soziale Frage* formuliert hat. Im Grunde ist dieses «soziale» Gesetz ein Gesetz mit religiöser Dimension, weshalb es Steiner auch – für unsere Ohren ungewohnt – als ein Gesetz des «Okkultismus» versteht, in dem das erste Wort bezeichnenderweise nicht das «Wohl», sondern das «Heil» ist: «Das Heil einer Gesamtheit von zusammenarbeitenden Menschen ist umso größer, je weniger der Einzelne die Erträgnisse seiner Leistungen für sich beansprucht, das heißt, je mehr er von diesen Erträgnissen an seine Mitarbeiter abgibt, und je mehr seine eigenen Bedürfnisse nicht aus seinen Leistungen, sondern aus den Leistungen der anderen befriedigt werden.»[50]

Was dieses Gesetz enthält, ist nichts weniger als ein Schwellenübertritt. Steiner trägt dem auch Rechnung, wenn er aus der Sicht diesseits der Schwelle die «soziale Frage» zunächst so formuliert, wie wir sie gewohnt sind: «Welche gesellschaftlichen Einrichtungen müssen getroffen werden, damit ein jeder für sich das Erträgnis seiner Arbeit haben kann?» Man rechne dabei damit, so Steiner, «dass das Ganze einer menschlichen Gemeinschaft am besten gedeihen könne, wenn der Einzelne den ‹vollen› oder den größtmöglichen Ertrag seiner Arbeit auch einheimsen kann.»[51] – Das ist mit einem Wort wie «einheimsen» tendenziell formuliert und verschenkt damit etwas von dem revolutionären Gestus des «sozialen Hauptgesetzes», so als verstünde sich dieses von selbst. Das «soziale Hauptgesetz» aber rückt ja an die Stelle dessen, was diesseits der Schwelle im Wirtschaftsleben als «gerecht» empfunden wird, nämlich die Werkgerechtigkeit von Lohn für Arbeit in einer Person, eine andere Gerechtigkeit und an die Stelle des Wohl-Standes das Heil. Dieses liegt in einer Umstülpung des Herkömmlichen, des Diesseitigen: «Genau das Gegenteil davon lehrt nun der Okkultismus, der auf eine tiefere Erkenntnis des Menschen und der Welt begründet ist.»

Diese tiefere Erkenntnis trägt im Grunde jeder Mensch in sich. Gleichwohl ist das «soziale Hauptgesetz» erschütternd – erschütternd in seiner Befremdlichkeit einerseits und zugleich seiner höheren Selbstverständlichkeit andererseits, denn im Grunde hat es den Charakter eines «Naturgesetzes»: «Alle Einrichtungen innerhalb einer Gesamtheit von Menschen, welche diesem Gesetz widersprechen, müssen bei längerer Dauer irgendwo Elend und Not erzeugen. – Dieses Hauptgesetz gilt für das soziale Leben mit einer solchen Ausschließlichkeit und Notwendigkeit, wie nur irgendein Naturgesetz in Bezug auf irgendein gewisses Gebiet von Naturwirkungen gilt.»[52] – Wir wissen, dass das wahr ist. Wir kennen dieses Naturgesetz. Das «soziale Hauptgesetz» ist keine moralische Forderung, sondern nur die Beschreibung dessen, was ist. Wir wissen um es, auch wenn es zu jener «tieferen Erkenntnis des Menschen und der Welt» gehört, die eben nicht an der Oberfläche liegt. Ja, wir staunen über es gerade deshalb, weil wir es im Verborgenen, im «Okkulten» kennen. Es wiederzuerkennen, es ins Bewusstsein zu bringen ist eine Sache der anthroposophischen Geisteswissenschaft, die hier die Grenze von Natur und Moral überwunden hat. Wenn man das «haarsträubenden Idealismus» nennt, wie Steiner es von denjenigen vermutet, die sich einbilden, «praktische Menschen» zu sein,[53] so geschieht das wahrscheinlich aus Angst. Das ist verständlich, und es wäre anmaßend, sich über diese Angst hinwegzusetzen. Was kann das Mittel gegen sie sein, gegen das fehlende Vertrauen? – Das lässt sich wohl nur ganz blass sagen. Es liegt im Finden des je eigenen Naturgesetzes, das man sich zur Aufgabe macht: «Was aber jeder tun kann, das ist, im Sinne obigen Gesetzes in seinem Bereiche zu wirken.»[54] Das niedere Selbst hat die Aufgabe, sein höheres zu finden, das ihm beim Suchen schließlich zur Sehnsucht wird. «Es wird ihm [dem Menschen] das Gefühl davon aufgehen, dass er einen höheren Sinn erfüllt, wenn er im Sinne seines Platzes in der Welt und im Sinne seiner Fähigkeiten arbeitet. Kein schattenhafter Idealismus wird aus dieser Einsicht folgen, sondern ein mächtiger Impuls aller seiner Kräfte, und er wird dieses Handeln in solcher Richtung als etwas so Selbstverständliches ansehen, wie in einer anderen Beziehung Essen und Trinken.»[55] – An dieser Stelle treffen Recht und Pflicht zusammen. Wir haben das Recht und die Pflicht zu essen und zu trinken, wie unseren Ort im Ganzen auszufüllen. Darin sind Natur und Moral eins.

In der Mitte der Zeit: das Ich

Unsere Erde durchläuft eine Entwicklungsgeschichte, die aus dem Geistigen kommt, im Zustand der Wärme einen ersten Anhauch von Sinnlichkeit erfährt, dann über das Gasförmige und Flüssige bis hin zur äußersten materiellen Verdichtung geht. Diese hat in unserem Zeitalter ihren Höhepunkt. Dann wendet sich die Bewegung, um bis zum Ende der Erdenzeit in eine neue Vergeistigung zu führen. Auch in der Biografie jedes Menschen, also in der Bewegung seines Lebens von der Geburt bis zum Tod, spiegelt sich dieser Verlauf zwischen den beiden Geistpolen. In der Mitte dazwischen liegt der Wendepunkt, der zugleich ein Tiefstpunkt und ein Höhepunkt ist. Er ist markiert durch die Geburt des Ich. Dieses ist das Zentrum des Steinerschen Geschichts- und Menschenbildes. Auch liegt keiner anderen bekannten Geschichtsidee so deutlich jene Figur einer Kurve, einer Parabel zugrunde. Mit ihr wird der Akzent ganz auf die Mitte gelegt, denn sie ist das Entwicklungsziel, mit dem erst die Voraussetzung geschaffen ist, einer neuen Vergeistigung entgegengehen zu können. Dieses zweite Ziel, das Ende, wird hier ebenso wie der Anfang ganz von der Mitte der Ich-Geburt her gedacht.

Im jüdisch-christlichen Verständnis verläuft Geschichte linear zwischen Anfang und Ende, zwischen Schöpfung und himmlischem Jerusalem. Auch hier gibt es eine Mitte der Zeit, diese aber ist nicht die Bedingung dafür, dass jenes himmlische Jerusalem überhaupt sein kann, sondern ist inhaltlich immer schon ganz von der Erwartung der letzten Dinge erfüllt: der Wiederkunft Christi, der Auferstehung der Toten, des allgemeinen Gerichts, des Endes der Welt. Was am Ende steht, hat die eigentliche Bedeutung. Die Grundgeste der Gegenwart ist dabei die der Hoffnung auf das Verheißene.

Im Osten hingegen, im Buddhismus und Hinduismus gibt es ein solches Ziel nicht oder wenn, dann als Austritt aus der Kreisbewegung. Alles kehrt ewig wieder, weshalb sich die Sehnsucht auf ein Aufhören, ein Erlöschen (Nirwana) richtet, das nicht am Ende einer wirklichen Entwicklung steht, sondern die Befreiung von der ewigen Wiederkehr bedeutet, in der es naturgemäß keine Mitte gibt.

Das spiralige Geschichtsverständnis schließlich, das das Moment des Zyklischen und des Linearen in sich vereint, wie das der Theosophie, kennt ebenfalls keine Mitte, sondern eine Zielbewegung in immer neuen Runden, die aus einer immanenten Schubkraft hervorgeht.

Ein Geschichtsbild, das demgegenüber so sehr aus der Mitte heraus denkt wie die Anthroposophie, revolutioniert mit diesem Akzent das Selbstverständnis und die Verantwortung des Menschen. Zu seiner Grundgeste wird dabei das Gegenwärtigsein zwischen Vergangenheit und Zukunft. Das heißt, es kommt in einem emphatischen Sinne jetzt auf mich an. Denn in der Mitte aller Entwicklung steht das Ich, das Zentralorgan des Menschen, dessen er in seiner größten Entfernung vom geistigen Ursprung mächtig wird und das zugleich – denkt man im Kontext der Viergliederung in physischen Leib, Ätherleib, Astralleib und Ich – das Geistigste auf Erden an ihm ist.

Die Geistigkeit des Ich ist nicht die Geistigkeit eines Jenseits, denn sie wirkt in der Verwandlung der Leiblichkeit, und die ist es, die unser irdisches Leben reich macht. Das Ich erfüllt auch hier eine Mitte, nämlich als Mittler zwischen Geist und Materie, ohne den es nur die Langeweile des Geistes gäbe: keinen Eros, keine Kunst, keine Religion. Denn das sind zentrale Gebiete, auf denen der metaphysische Dualismus von Geist und Materie überwunden werden kann, dadurch dass sie zueinander in ein sich durchdringendes Verhältnis gesetzt werden: sei es in dem Spannungsverhältnis von Verzicht und Erfüllung (Astralleib), in der ästhetischen Umgestaltung der ‹Natur›, des Charakters oder Temperaments (Ätherleib) oder schließlich etwa in der zu erringenden Einflussnahme auf die Zeichen von Scham und Angst, wie sie im unwillkürlichen Erröten und Erblassen zwar ein Missverhältnis, aber dennoch einen Bezug zum Göttlichen anzeigen (physischer Leib).

Das Ich ist Mittler und als dieser hat es seinen Ort «in der Mitte der Zeit», in der auch der Messias erwartet wurde. Wann aber ist das? – In der Atlantis, die ja das geschichtliche Zentrum aller Epochen ausmacht? Nein. Christus ist nicht in dieser exakten Zeitenmitte gekommen, sondern danach.

Die Mitte der Zeit ist eine «Zwischenzeit», nämlich die Zeit zwischen dem Herantreten Luzifers an den Menschen in der Lemuris und der Inkarnation Christi in der nachatlantischen Zeit. Diese Mitte hat sowohl einen geschichtlichen Ort auf dem Weg, den die Parabel der Welt- und Menschheitsgeschichte vom Geist in die Materie wieder zum Geist vorzeichnet, als auch eine Mittleraufgabe, die in der Verwandlungsbeziehung zwischen Astralleib und Geistselbst, Ätherleib und Lebensgeist, physischem Leib und Geistesmensch besteht.

Die Verwandlungskraft aber liegt im Ich, das sich zwischen Luzifer und Christus, zwischen Sündenfall und Erlösung entwickelt.

Das macht die Größe von Steiners Geschichts- und Menschenbild aus, dass er stets aus dem Bewusstsein dieser Zwischensphäre denkt. Damit ist die Mitte nicht, wie geometrisch schematisch veranlagt, ein exakter und notwendiger Punkt auf einer Kurvenlinie, sondern ein freier Zwischenbereich zwischen den exzentrisch bewegenden Momenten der Geschichte: zwischen dem Einfluss Luzifers auf den Menschen und der Tat Christi für ihn. Beide nun verhalten sich zur Mitte der Zeit anachronistisch. Luzifer wirkt hier in der Verfrühung, Christus in der Verzögerung.

Die geschichtlich-mathematische Mitte der Zeit liegt in der Epoche der Atlantis auf der Erde. In ihrer Mitte hätte der Mensch seiner natürlichen Entwicklung nach seine volle leibliche Ausgestaltung erreicht und damit zugleich den ihm geometrisch bestimmten Moment seiner Ich-Geburt erlangt. Durch den Einfluss Luzifers in der lemurischen Zeit aber wird das menschliche Ich anachronistisch, d.h. unzeitgemäß, was hier heißt: es kommt zu früh. Mit diesem Austritt aus der Geometrie der Geschichte tritt das Moment der Freiheit in die Notwendigkeit ein, und zugleich verbindet sich der Mensch nun mit der Materie in einer Weise, die die Wiederloslösung zu einer moralischen, also nicht mehr nur natürlichen Aufgabe macht, zu deren Bewältigung er schließlich die Hilfe des Christus braucht. Der aber nun kommt jetzt erst später, als es die geometrische Mitte anzeigt, nämlich in der vierten nachatlantischen Kulturepoche, in der unsere Zeitrechnung mit Jesu Geburt auf Erden beginnt.

Die Entwicklung des Menschen wird durch jene luziferisch bedingte Verfrühung des Ich, diesen Geniestreich des Unzeitgemäßen, zu einer bewussten und auf Autonomie gegründeten Entwicklung. Diese Freiheit erhält ihr Gegengewicht in einer allzu engen Verbindung mit der Materie, die von jetzt an Verfall, Krankheit und Tod bedeutet. Es sind diese Erscheinungen des Eintritts in die materielle Welt, die nun zu einer Herausforderung des Ich werden, wie es sie ohne Luzifer nicht hätte kennen und erleiden lernen können. Sie sind die Voraussetzung für eine reifende Höherentwicklung, in der schließlich die luziferische Freiheit durch eine Freiheit in Christus abgelöst werden kann. Ein Engel hingegen ist weder frei, noch kann er es werden wie ein Mensch, weil er nicht sterblich ist und die Ich-Stufe seiner Entwicklung nicht im Einzugsgebiet der Materie durchlaufen hat.

Nun wäre – und das ist wohl wiederum eine Besonderheit in Steiners Geschichtsbild, die man sich bewusst machen muss – Christus auch ohne die Wirkung Luzifers auf den Menschen gekommen. Und ohne die Verfrühung Luzifers wäre er tatsächlich in der geometrischen Mitte der Zeit gekommen: «Wäre der Mensch ohne Freiheit, daher auch ohne sein Verdienst, bloß wie durch einen geistigen, höheren Instinkt in der Mitte der atlantischen Zeit angekommen, er hätte die Reife gehabt, dass schon damals jenes Prinzip auf die Erde heruntergestiegen wäre, das wir das Christusprinzip nennen: Dann wäre der Christus schon damals erschienen. So aber war die Freiheit des Menschen gegeben, der Mensch dadurch unter seine instinktive, normale Entwicklungsstufe heruntergedrängt worden, und die Folge war, dass er jetzt erst durch sich selber heranreifen musste, sodass er also das Christusprinzip um dieselbe Zeit später empfangen konnte, als vorher die luziferischen Wesen eingegriffen hatten. Wir müssen uns klar sein darüber, dass das Herabsteigen und Wirken des Christus durch das Eingreifen der luziferischen Wesenheiten verzögert worden ist. Dadurch aber waren die Menschen in einer reiferen Form, als der Christus niederstieg.»[56]

Eine Verfrühung, die Tat einer Unreife wird also zur Bedingung eines Reifeprozesses, der erst die wirkliche Aufnahme Christi ermöglicht. Mit Luzifer beginnt die Zeit der Inkubation mit dem Ich, die sich mit der Erfüllung durch Christus vollendet. Die Bedingung für diese Erfüllung ist am Ende der Zwischenzeit in einer Hinsicht mit der Inkarnation Jesu gegeben. Das ist Weihnachten. Sachlich aber lebt das Ich als Organ der Mitte fortwährend in der Mitte der Zeit, die um die Erfüllung mit dem Christusprinzip ringt. Und das nun drückt sich in jener anderen Perspektive auf die Weihnachtszeit aus, die ja auch eine Zwischenzeit in der Mitte der Zeit ist, die keine rechnerische Qualität, wohl aber jedes Jahr eine besonders spürbare geistige Beschaffenheit hat. Es sind jene zwölf heiligen Nächte, in denen aus der Finsternis das Geisteslicht leuchtet: die Zeit zwischen dem 24. Dezember und dem 6. Januar, die nicht selten bei aller ersehnten Ruhe und Besinnlichkeit auch eine Krisenzeit ist. Sie fordert unser Ich zu einer Metamorphose auf, die es schließlich in einem immer höheren Grad geistempfänglich macht. Der 24. Dezember als der Adam-und-Eva-Tag ist der luziferische Auftakt zu jener Zwischenzeit, die am 6. Januar, dem Tag der Jordantaufe, mit dem Einzug des Geistes Christi in Jesus ihre Vollendung findet. Diese Zeit ist vielleicht im Besonderen unsere alljährliche Reifezeit.

Die Religion der Götter

Der Mensch ist auf der Erde das am weitesten entwickelte und entwicklungsfähigste Wesen. Alle übrigen Wesen verändern sich zwar, folgen aber auf den Wegen ihrer Verwandlung keinem Ideal. Ziele einer Selbstgestaltung, Vorbilder, Ideale kennt nur der Mensch. Und nur er hat so etwas wie Religion. Zwischen beidem, dem Ideal und der Religion, der Entwicklung des Menschen und seiner Verbindung zur geistigen Welt, besteht eine Beziehung: «Alles, was über den Menschen hinausgeht, hat man hier auf der Erde als Religion.» Das sagt Rudolf Steiner in einem seiner Vorträge über *Inneres Wesen des Menschen und Leben zwischen Tod und neuer Geburt.*[57] Diesem Gedanken gesellt er einen anderen hinzu, mit dem deutlich wird, dass Religion nicht nur in einer Richtung die Verbindung zwischen irdischer und geistiger Welt ist. Denn auch in der geistigen Welt gibt es eine Religion, nämlich die, die sich auf den im Irdischen sich entwickelnden Menschen bezieht. Steiner nennt sie die «Götterreligion». Inhalt dieser Religion ist der Mensch, und zwar mit der Perspektive auf die Verwirklichung des Menschenideals. Das nämlich schwebt den Göttern, d.h. den Wesen aus der vielfältigen Welt der Hierarchien, als Ziel ihrer Schöpfung vor. Die Vervollkommnung des Menschen, seine Vergöttlichung ist die Religion der geistigen Welt. Mit dieser Vergöttlichung ist gewiss keine uniforme Größe gemeint, sondern das volle Ausschöpfen der grundsätzlich individuell angelegten Möglichkeiten jedes Einzelnen.

Kann nun der Mensch im irdischen Leben auch Atheist sein, weil er etwa an der Realisierbarkeit von Idealen zweifelt und eine geistige Welt nicht gelten lassen will, so kann er dies in der geistigen Welt nicht, denn hier zwingt ihn die unmittelbare Begegnung mit den geistigen Realitäten zu deren Anerkenntnis. Auf der Erde können wir das bezweifeln, hier ist Religion unsere freie Tat. Hier kann der Mensch den Geist auch ignorieren, ja er kann ihn, wie Steiner sagt, auch «übersehen», denn der Zugang zur Welt des Geistes ist hier auch eine Frage der Erkenntnis. Das gilt nicht für die Situation, in der er sich in der geistigen Welt befindet. Im Leben zwischen dem Tod und einer neuen Geburt stehen die Götter und mit ihnen ihr

Menschheitsideal unübersehbar vor uns. Hier gibt es kein Erkenntnisringen um die Frage nach der Wirklichkeit des Geistes und der Möglichkeit höherer Entwicklung. Es gibt keinen Atheismus in der geistigen Welt, denn im Zusammenleben mit den Göttern wäre dies ein Widerspruch in sich. Und doch gibt es auch in der Sphäre des Geistes eine Form des Areligiösen. Wie das?

Das Areligiöse des Menschen in der geistigen Welt liegt – so würde ich Steiner hier interpretieren – im verweigerten Bezug des Menschen zur irdischen Welt. Es gibt nämlich auch in der geistigen Welt den Augenblick einer Krisis, einer Entscheidungssituation, ja einer Versuchung: «Jedes Mal, bevor wir zu einer Erdeninkarnation gehen, tritt an uns die Versuchung heran, in der geistigen Welt zu bleiben, in den Geist einzutreten und sich vorwärts zu entwickeln mit demjenigen, was man schon ist, was jetzt ganz durchgöttlicht ist, und zu verzichten auf das, was man als Mensch noch immer mehr werden könnte auf der Bahn nach dem fernen religiösen Ideal der göttlich-geistigen Welt hin. Es tritt die Versuchung heran, irreligiös für das Geisterland zu werden.»[58]

Die Versuchung besteht darin, den Weg der Vervollkommnung vorzeitig abzubrechen. Der Versucher ist auch hier Luzifer, der «Anachronist». So wie er, der selbst Verspätete und «Zurückgebliebene» uns einst durch seine Versuchung vorzeitig in die physische Welt brachte, so will er uns jetzt vorzeitig in der geistigen Welt halten, indem er uns eine Vergeistigung anbietet, bei der all das, was wir in unserer Entwicklung schon erreicht haben, in Vollkommenheit überführt wird, aber eben nur das und nicht die Anlagen, die wir noch auszubilden haben. Man kann sich das vielleicht so vorstellen wie bei der Entwicklung der Tierarten, die ja auch jeweils in ihren spezifischen Fähigkeiten weitaus vollkommener sind als der Mensch, die aber nicht in der Lage sind, weitere Anlagen auszubilden, weil sie nämlich aus der Entwicklung herausgefallen sind. So will uns Luzifer aus unserer Entwicklung herausreißen, indem er uns zur Vollkommenheit des schon Erreichten durch die göttliche Vergeistigung versucht, uns aber den Weg zum Menschen- und Menschheitsideal, also zu unserer wirklichen Vergöttlichung abschneidet. Das ist der Atheismus Luzifers. Er verweigert die Göttlichkeit des Menschen.

Um der luziferischen Versuchung in der geistigen Welt zu widerstehen, bedarf der Mensch der Hilfe der Götter. Sie kämpfen um den Menschen und sein zu erreichendes Ideal. Dieser Kampf ist Teil ihrer Religion. Religion aber bedeutet jetzt die Rückbindung an die physische Welt, denn ohne sie ist die Vervollkommnung des Menschen nicht möglich, weil nur hier die Freiheit zu ihr besteht, ohne die unsere Entwicklung auch für die Götter wertlos wäre. Sie zu ermöglichen, kämpfen die Götter um uns, indem sie schließlich das Projekt des Menschen für seine nächste Inkarnation «hinauswerfen» in die Raumeswelt, damit der Mensch der Versuchung zu einer vorzeitigen Vergeistigung und damit unvollkommenen Entwicklung entzogen ist. Steiner beschreibt nun, wie der Mensch als Projekt der Götter (lateinisch *proiectum* = «das nach vorn Geworfene») im Gravitationsbereich der neuen Inkarnation wie magnetisch angezogen wird von der irdischen Welt, und zwar ganz konkret von einem bestimmten Elternpaar. So wird ihm die Versuchung durch die Umhüllung mit einer neuen Leiblichkeit verhüllt. Der Mensch tritt in ein neues Erdenleben ein, um hier seine Anlagen eigenständig und voll verantwortlich weiter auszubilden, auf dass in der geistigen Welt immer mehr von ihm vergöttlicht werden kann. Denn das, was die Götter in der geistigen Welt aus uns machen können, ist abhängig von unserem irdischen Leben. Dieses unser irdisches Leben ist unabdingbar für die Götterreligion.

Interessant an diesen Gedanken Steiners ist nicht

zuletzt, dass zur Entwicklung des Menschen Religion gehört, ja dass der Entwicklungsgedanke selbst nicht anders als religiös sein kann, und das in zwei Richtungen: In der einen Richtung setzt das Menschenideal, das über den Menschen hinausgeht, ein religiöses Verhältnis zur Welt des Geistes voraus. In der anderen Richtung erfüllt sich Religion als Götterreligion aber nur dann, wenn der Mensch wieder in das irdische Leben eintritt, um dort in einer neuen Inkarnation in schöpferischer Freiheit neue Fähigkeiten zu entwickeln, die dann in der geistigen Welt vervollkommnet werden. Auf das Leben in der Welt des Geistes zwischen Tod und Geburt muss ein neues Leben zwischen Geburt und Tod auf der Erde folgen. Die geistige und irdische Welt sind über die Reinkarnation des Menschen durchlässig miteinander verbunden. Religion als die durchlaufene Verbindung beider Welten schlägt sich nieder in der Vervollkommnung des Menschen. Was Rudolf Steiners Gedanken dabei auszeichnet, ist eine Leidenschaft gegenüber der Schwelle, denn in ihr liegt die Quellkraft von Entwicklung. Darin unterscheidet er sich sowohl vom konfessionellen Christentum als auch vom östlichen Reinkarnationsgedanken, deren Perspektive jeweils auf einen endgültigen Erlösungszustand geht. Und während im

Osten eine Entwicklung des Menschen dazu da ist, aus dem endlosen Kreislauf von Geburt und Wiedergeburt herauszutreten, so ist bei Steiner gerade jede neue Geburt ein Schritt auf dem Entwicklungsweg, der die Religion der Götter erfüllt.

Glaube, Liebe, Hoffnung
Fähigkeiten der Wesensglieder

Die Anthropologie Rudolf Steiners, wie er sie zum Beispiel im Kapitel über das «Wesen der Menschheit» in seiner *Geheimwissenschaft* darstellt, erscheint ebenso schlicht wie einzigartig, wenn man sich vor Augen führt, welche fundamentalen Seinsqualitäten durch das Hinzutreten eines jeden weiteren Wesensgliedes verständlich werden: Welch ungeheurer, ja namenloser Unterschied besteht zwischen Leben und Tod? Und welch entscheidende Bedeutung kommt dementsprechend dem Lebensleib bzw. Ätherleib zu, durch den erst das Stoffliche lebendig wird? Und wie radikal unterscheidet sich wiederum das ‹bloße› Leben von der Möglichkeit eines Wechsels zwischen Wachen und Schlafen? Diese nächste Seinsstufe erklärt sich bekanntlich durch das Hinzutreten des Astralleibes, jenes dritten Wesensgliedes, über das die Pflanzen noch nicht, aber die Tiere schon verfügen, und mit dem es überhaupt erst möglich ist, wach zu sein und über Lust und Leid, über Sympathie und Antipathie, Triebe und Begierden eine Beziehung zur Umwelt aufzunehmen. Und schließlich der Schritt zum Menschentum: Mit ihm kommt das Mysterium des Ichs in die Welt. Das Ich erst kann Vorstellungen im Bewusstsein erzeugen und halten, ohne dabei auf die objektive Gegenwart der Inhalte angewiesen zu sein. Das Erinnern, das Erleben eines Bleibenden im Wechsel der Eindrücke, das ist eine entscheidende Fähigkeit des Ich. Ohne diese bliebe die ganze Weltgeschichte stumpf. Ja, es gäbe gar keine Geschichte, kein Denken, keine Kultur, keine Moralität ohne das Erinnern.

Mit jedem hinzutretenden Wesensglied wird also eine weitere Stufe in der Evolution verständlich, deren Bedeutung ein rein physikalisch-chemischer, also substanzbezogener Erklärungsversuch nicht erfassen kann, weil ihm die qualitativen Unterschiede zwischen Tod, Schlaf und Vergessen einerseits und Leben, Wachen und Erinnern andererseits nicht zugänglich sind. Es zeichnet die Menschenkunde der Anthroposophie aus, dass sie ein organisches System freigelegt hat, dessen Glieder eine Vorstellung von den besonderen Fähigkeiten oder Begabungen der einzelnen Naturreiche und im Besonderen des Menschen geben. Es werden Steigerungsstufen deutlich, deren jede sowohl einen Übergang als auch einen gewaltigen Sprung bedeutet.

In Anbetracht des vollständigen Systems der Wesensglieder müsste nun eigentlich die Frage gestellt werden: Wie geht es weiter? Das heißt, welche Qualitätsmerkmale oder Fähigkeiten treten noch hinzu, die den zwar veranlagten, aber noch nicht ausgebildeten geistigen Wesensgliedern von Geistselbst, Lebensgeist und Geistesmensch entsprechen?

Wir sind bislang zur Ausbildung des spezifisch Seelischen gekommen, für dessen Fähigkeit das Verhältnis von Erinnern und Vergessen steht und das ein nach Empfindungsseele (vorstellendes Erinnern), Verstandesseele (Begriffsbildung) und Bewusstseinsseele (meditatives Verinnerlichen) differenziertes Vorstellungsleben ermöglicht. Diese Seelenqualitäten sind im Ich zusammengefasst. Was aber wird noch hinzutreten, wenn die Stufen der geistigen Wesensglieder zu erklimmen sind? Oder ist die Frage falsch gestellt? Können die Geistesglieder überhaupt solche Aufgaben haben, wie sie der Ätherleib hat, der alles erst zum Leben erweckt, oder der Astralleib, der das Leben aus seinem Schlaf reißt?

So klar und deutlich die Aufgaben auf der Ebene der Leiblichkeit sind, innerhalb derer mit jedem Schritt

Umwälzendes geschieht, so wenig sind uns die ‹Gewinne› durch die Stufen der geistigen Entwicklung deutlich. Das könnte auch damit zusammenhängen, dass die Steigerungsstufen in der Seinsqualität in einer gewissen Hinsicht immer kleiner werden. So besteht doch zwischen der Pflanze und dem Mineral und damit zwischen Leben und Tod ein größerer Unterschied als zwischen den Wechselzuständen von Wachen und Schlafen, die das Tier der Pflanze voraus hat, oder gar zwischen Erinnern und Vergessen, jenem vergleichsweise kontrastarmen Wechsel, um den der Mensch noch das Tier übertrifft, das sich keine Vorstellungen eines früher Erlebten in ein Bewusstsein rufen kann, weil es eben kein Vorstellungsbewusstsein hat. Und ist nicht überhaupt *der* Unterschied der größte, der mit der alten philosophischen Frage: «Warum ist überhaupt etwas und nicht vielmehr nichts?» angesprochen ist? Diese betrifft ja den Unterschied zwischen Sein und Nichtsein, wie er mit dem Auftreten des allerersten Wesensgliedes, des physischen Leibes, zur Welt kam. Verblassen also die Fähigkeiten, die mit den drei Geistesgliedern noch hinzukommen können, aufgrund der geringeren Intensität, also der weniger werdenden Seinsdichte des noch zu Erreichenden? – Das wäre wohl eine sehr ungeistige und damit in Bezug auf die höheren Wesensglieder unsachgemäße Unterstellung. Hingegen steht eher zu vermuten, dass es erneut um einen ganz radikalen Unterschied zu dem bisher Erlangten geht, wobei zugleich auch eine Kontinuität zu wahren ist, wie sie ja tatsächlich auch zwischen Sein, Leben, Wachen und Erinnern besteht.

Eine Spur, die über das von Steiner Ausgesagte zu den besonderen Aufgaben der drei geistigen Entwicklungsstufen führen kann, ist die Tatsache, dass sich in den Geistesgliedern die durch das Ich umgewandelten Aspekte der Leibesglieder verwirklichen. Welche seelisch-geistigen Eigenschaften oder Fähigkeiten können nun als Umwandlungsformen von Sein, Lebendigsein und Wachsein zutage treten?

In den Vorträgen vom 2. und 3.12.1911[59] nennt Steiner im Zusammenhang mit den Leibesgliedern drei Grundkräfte menschlichen oder eigentlich menschheitlichen Lebens von höchster Spiritualität, nämlich die, die mit den alten evangelischen Weisheitsworten von Glaube, Liebe und Hoffnung angesprochen sind. Der Glaube sei eine Kraft des Astralleibes, die Liebe eine des Ätherleibes und die Hoffnung eine des physischen Leibes. Das wird vielleicht erst dann verständlich, wenn man die Entwicklungsdimension der Leiblichkeit im Hinblick auf ihr Geistiges mitdenkt.

Dann nämlich kommt man zu einer bewussten Ausbildung dieser Kräfte im Zugehen auf die Wesensglieder Geistselbst, Lebensgeist und Geistesmensch, von denen Steiner in den beiden Vorträgen mit dem Titel *Glaube, Liebe, Hoffnung – drei Stufen des menschheitlichen Lebens*[60] allerdings nicht spricht. Er macht aber deutlich, dass mit diesen Weisheitsworten auch die Menschheitszukunft angedacht ist. Dabei scheine allerdings schon jetzt die Glaubenskraft des Astralleibes in die Seele herein, was unserer Gegenwart das Charakteristikum gebe.[61]

Wir leben in der fünften Kulturepoche des nachatlantischen Zeitalters. Es ist die Epoche der Bewusstseinsseele. Diese nun deutet zugleich vor auf das bewusst zu entwickelnde Wesensglied des Geistselbstes. Im Sinne einer Vordeutung gibt uns der Glaubenscharakter des Astralleibes, sobald wir ihn in der Bewusstseinsseele ergreifen, eine Ahnung von dem, was mit dem Geistselbst zu entwickeln sein wird. Die Seelenglieder, die im Ich zum Zentrum des Menschen gehören, sind die Spiegelachse zwischen den Leibes- und den Geistesgliedern. Rückbezug und Vordeutung haben hier ihren Knotenpunkt. «So dass wir in unserem Zeitraum die Eigentümlichkeit haben, dass in der Seele der Menschen etwas vorhanden ist, wie wenn sich in der Seele spiegelte der Glaubenscharakter des astralischen Leibes. Im sechsten nachatlantischen Zeitraum wird sich spiegeln im Inneren des Menschen der Liebescharakter des Ätherleibes und im siebenten, vor der großen Katastrophe, der Hoffnungscharakter des physischen Leibes.»[62]

Glaube, Liebe und Hoffnung sind uns gewöhnlich mehr als seelische denn als leibliche Qualitäten vertraut. Doch haben sie alle etwas von jenem unbewussten Charakter des Leiblichen. Das heißt, sie stehen unserem denkenden, fühlenden und wollenden Wesen nicht einfach so zur Verfügung. Während der Leib sie gewissermaßen auf natürliche Weise hat, gilt für die Seele, dass sie sich diese Fähigkeiten erst erwerben muss. Erwirbt man sie sich aber, so ist der Glaube die Vordeutung auf das Geistselbst, die Liebe die Vordeutung auf den Lebensgeist und die Hoffnung die auf den Geistesmenschen.

Welcher Glaube ist hier gemeint? Doch nicht der, der überall da als Lückenbüßer eintritt, wo wir etwas nicht wissen. Vielmehr geht es um den Glauben, der gerade als eine wissende Lebenshaltung auftritt, die über alle Angst und Depression unserer Gegenwart hinaus ist, weil sie den Sinn nicht aufgeben muss, wo unser bloßes Faktenwissen unser Leben banalisiert. Die

Bewusstseinsseele hat die Geste der Öffnung, der Empfänglichkeit, wie sie der Zuversicht des Glaubens eignet, ohne blind zu sein. Die Entwicklung des Lebensgeistes beträfe dann die durch die Verstandesseele hindurchgegangene Liebeskraft des ätherischen Leibes. Sie meint, wie es Steiner in dem ersten der beiden Vorträge entfaltet, noch etwas anderes als das, «was die Menschen durch entsprechende Bande zusammenhält, sondern etwas, was auch der einzelne Mensch braucht. Der Mensch, der keine Liebeskraft entwickeln kann, verödet und verdorrt auch in seinem Wesen.» [63] Insofern ist die Liebeskraft eine aus dem bloß Vegetativen heraus metamorphosierte und ins Höchste vergeistigte Lebenskraft. Und auf der letzten Stufe schließlich begegnen wir der für den physischen Leib ebenso kontraintuitiven wie deshalb notwendigen Dimension der Hoffnung, die mit dem Geistesmenschen in einer uns heute noch unbekannten Qualität zu entfalten ist. Der physische Leib ist ja gerade der am meisten ausgestaltete und verfestigte Leib, der im Sinne der Wahrscheinlichkeit zu wenig Hoffnung Anlass gibt, wie das z.B. bei einer tödlichen Krankheit deutlich wird. Aber Hoffnung ist eben etwas anderes als die Wahrscheinlichkeit des Überlebens oder Sterbens. In ihr ist schon im Leib die Geistdimension des erst am Ende der nachatlantischen Zeit auszubildenden

Geistesmenschen angelegt. Und was für das Ende der nachatlantischen Zeit im Kleinen gilt, gilt für das Ende der Erdenzeit im Großen. Hoffnung ist die spiritualisierte Kraft des Physischen, mit der der Geistesmensch über die «große Katastrophe» hinauskommt.

Denn was ist die große Katastrophe? Das Aufhören von allem, das Ende, die Vernichtung, das Nicht-Sein. So wie der physische Leib alles aus dem Nichts gezogen hat, so droht am Ende der Zeiten sich wieder alles in nichts aufzulösen. Die geistige Verfassung, die dem entspricht, ist die Verzweiflung, ihr Gegenstück die Hoffnung, die Kraft, die die größte Seinsmacht hat, denn solange es Hoffnung gibt, ist nicht nichts. Diese Kraft bedarf der Ermächtigung durch das Ich. Und das gilt für alle drei: für Glaube, Liebe, Hoffnung, in denen die noch zu entfaltenden Wesensglieder schon gegenwärtig sind. Doch sind es nur Vordeutungen. Die erfragten besonderen Fähigkeiten der Geistesglieder sind für unser gegenwärtiges Bewusstsein noch nicht wirklich fassbar. Unterwegs zu ihnen aber ist das spirituelle Leben. «Und dass Sie dieses spirituelle Leben», so Steiner, «nicht umsonst aufgenommen haben, dafür wird Ihnen bürgen, was als starke Kräfte der Hoffnung in Ihnen leben wird, dass nach einer großen Katastrophe ein neues Menschenalter kommen wird, in dem heraufkommen wird auch im äußeren Leben in einer neuen Menschheitsbildung dasjenige, was innerlich spirituell in den Seelen vorbereitet worden ist.»[64]

Anmerkungen

1 Tatsächlich gab es lange Zeit eine Zuckersteuer. Mit dem Aufblühen des Überseehandels mit Rohrzucker im 16. Jahrhundert entdeckte man eine neue Steuerquelle, den Zuckerzoll. 1841 wurde dann in Deutschland eine echte Zuckersteuer eingeführt, die nach dem Gewicht der angelieferten Zuckerrüben bemessen wurde. – Zum 01.01.1993 wurde die Zuckersteuer im Hinblick auf den EG-Binnenmarkt zur Vermeidung von Wettbewerbsverzerrung und zur Anpassung des Umsatzsteuergesetzes abgeschafft.

2 Rudolf Steiner, *Mitteleuropa zwischen Ost und West,* GA 174a, Dornach ²1982, Vortrag vom 2.5.1918.

3 Rudolf Steiner, *Ursprungsimpulse der Geisteswissenschaft,* GA 96, Dornach ²1989, Vortrag vom 22.10.1906.

4 Rudolf Steiner, *Die pädagogische Praxis vom Gesichtspunkte geisteswissenschaftlicher Menschenerkenntnis,* GA 306, Dornach ⁴1989, Vortrag vom 22.4.1923.

5 Rudolf Steiner, *Welche Bedeutung hat die okkulte Ent-*

wicklung des Menschen für seine Hüllen und sein Selbst?, GA 145, Dornach [6]2005, Vortrag vom 21.3.1913.

6 Rudolf Steiner, *Erfahrungen des Übersinnlichen*, GA 143, Dornach [4]1994, Vortrag vom 25.2.1912.

7 In dem von Wolfgang G. Vögele herausgegebenen Buch *Der andere Rudolf Steiner* (Dornach 2005) ist erstmals eine kurze Begegnung zwischen Schnitzler und Steiner aus dem Jahr 1890 dokumentiert, die aber für Ersteren wohl keine nachhaltige Bedeutung hatte. 1919 versuchten Walter Johannes Stein und Ludwig Graf Poltzer-Hoditz Schnitzler für den Aufruf «An das deutsche Volk und die Kulturwelt» zu gewinnen, jedoch ohne Erfolg. Schnitzler notiert diesbezüglich im Tagebuch: «Mein unzerstörbares Misstrauen gegen Wundermänner.» (20.2.1919). Zwei Tage später heißt es lapidar: «Begann ein Rud. Steinersches Buch über Geheimwissenschaften zu lesen.» Mehr scheint über Schnitzlers Beschäftigung mit Steiner nicht überliefert zu sein.

8 Vortrag vom 9.2.1912, in: *Das esoterische Christentum und die geistige Führung der Menschheit*, GA 130, Dornach [4]1995. Und Vortrag vom 20.2.1912, in: *Wiederverkörperung und Karma und ihre Bedeutung für die Kultur der Gegenwart*, GA 135, Dornach [4]1989.

9 Rudolf Steiner, *Esoterische Betrachtungen karmischer Zusammenhänge*, 2. Band, GA 236, Dornach [6]1988, Vortrag vom 27.6.1924.

10 Rudolf Steiner, *Geisteswissenschaftliche Menschenkunde*, GA 107, Dornach [5]1988, Vortrag vom 1.1.1909.

11 Vgl. *Ursprungsimpulse der Geisteswissenschaft*, GA 96, Dornach [2]1988, Vortrag vom 16.4.1906. Die im Folgenden zitierten Stellen sind aus diesem Vortrag Rudolf Steiners.

12 Rudolf Steiner, *Die Brücke zwischen der Weltgeistigkeit und dem Physischen des Menschen*, GA 202, Dornach [4]1993, Vortrag vom 23.12.1920. Aus diesem Vortrag stammen auch alle folgenden Zitate.

13 Andere Quellen sprechen vom Weihnachtsbaum seit dem 15. Jahrhundert. Vgl. den Artikel «Weihnachten» bei Wikipedia.

14 «Wir wissen auch aus andern Vorträgen, dass Jahve oder Jehova sich für den, der tiefer in das Wesen des Christentums eindringt, eigentlich wesenhaft gar nicht unterscheidet von dem Christus selber. Wir müssen uns vielmehr klarmachen, dass ein inniger Zusammenhang der Jahve-Idee und der Christus-Idee besteht. ... Wir brauchen nur an ein Bild zu erinnern, auf das auch schon öfter aufmerksam gemacht worden ist, das Bild des Sonnenlichtes, wie es uns entweder direkt von der Sonne erscheint oder, in mondhellen Nächten besonders, vom Vollmonde zurückgestrahlt wird. Es ist ja Sonnenlicht, was uns vom Vollmond als Licht entgegenstrahlt, aber es ist reflektiertes Sonnenlicht, das doch wieder etwas anderes

ist als das direkt empfangene Sonnenlicht. Würden wir uns, um einen Vergleich zu haben, den Christus symbolisieren durch das direkte Sonnenlicht, so müssten wir dann Jahve oder Jehova als Sonnenlicht symbolisieren, das vom Monde zurückgeworfen wird, und wir würden damit genau den Sinn, der gemeint ist in der Menschheitsentwickelung, treffen.» (*Exkurse in das Gebiet des Markus-Evangeliums*, GA 124, 13.3.1911)

15 Rudolf Steiner, *Das Johannes-Evangelium*, GA 103, Dornach [11]1995, Vortrag vom 30.5.1908.

16 Siehe den Vortrag vom 10.6.1923 in: *Die Geschichte und die Bedingungen der anthroposophischen Bewegung im Verhältnis zur Anthroposophischen Gesellschaft*, GA 258, Dornach [3]1981.

17 Emil Bock, *Moses und sein Zeitalter*, Stuttgart 1983, S. 92.

18 Rudolf Steiner, *Das Johannes-Evangelium*, GA 103, Vortrag vom 30.5.1908.

19 *Die Evolution vom Gesichtspunkte des Wahrhaftigen*, GA 132, Dornach [7]1999, Vortrag vom 14.11.1911.

20 Dabei wird der ältere akademische Begriff von Geisteswissenschaft übergangen, was bei der Erstbegegnung mit der anthroposophischen Geisteswissenschaft zu Missverständnissen führen kann. Zu den akademischen Geisteswissenschaften zählen die Philosophie, Theologie, Rechtswissenschaft, die Philologie oder

Literaturwissenschaft, Geschichte, Kunstgeschichte. Aus anthroposophischer Sicht nennt man diese gerne «Kulturwissenschaften», um sie von einer Wissenschaft der geistigen Welten zu unterscheiden. Wilhelm Dilthey, der die Bezeichnung «Geisteswissenschaft» präzisierte und popularisierte (*Einleitung in die Geisteswissenschaften,* 1883), sah ihren Auftrag darin, den Zusammenhang zwischen «Leben, Ausdruck und Verstehen» zu untersuchen, und verstand unter «geistiger Welt» die erlebbare Welt der künstlerischen und schriftstellerischen Werke der Menschen.

21 z.B. Rudolf Steiners Vortrag «Was wollte das Goetheanum und was soll die Anthroposophie?» vom 9.4.1923 in dem gleichnamigen Band GA 84, Dornach ^{2}1986.

22 Vgl. den Vortrag vom 13.11.1909, in: *Die tieferen Geheimnisse des Menschheitswerdens im Lichte der Evangelien,* GA 117, Dornach ^{2}1986.

23 Vortrag vom 18.12.1920 in GA 202 (s. Anm. 12). Auch die nachfolgenden Zitate stammen, soweit nicht anders angegeben, aus diesem Vortrag Steiners.

24 Vgl. z.B. den Vortrag vom 27.9.1921 in: *Vorträge und Kurse über christlich-religiöses Wirken,* II, GA 343, Dornach 1993.

25 *Die Offenbarungen des Karma,* GA 120, Dornach ^{8}1992, Vortrag vom 20.5.1910.

26 «Gibt es einen Zufall?» in: *Luzifer-Gnosis, Grundlegende Aufsätze zur Anthroposophie und Berichte aus den Zeitschriften «Luzifer» und «Luzifer-Gnosis» 1903-1908*, GA 34, Dornach 1960.

27 Rudolf Steiner, *Das Johannes-Evangelium im Verhältnis zu den drei anderen Evangelien*, GA 112, Dornach ^{7}2007, Vortrag vom 6.7.1909. Soweit nicht anders angegeben stammen alle obigen Zitate aus diesem Vortrag.

28 Vortrag vom 5.12.1911 in: *Die Evolution vom Gesichtspunkte des Wahrhaftigen*, GA 132.

29 Martin Heidegger, *Sein und Zeit*, § 40.

30 Ebd.

31 Rudolf Steiner, *Lebendiges Naturerkennen. Intellektueller Sündenfall und spirituelle Sündenerhebung*, GA 220, Dornach ^{2}1982, Vorträge vom 21. und 26.1.1923.

32 A.a.O., Vortrag vom 21.1.1923.

33 Ebd.

34 Rudolf Steiner, *Erdensterben und Weltenleben*, GA 181, Dornach ^{3}1991, Vortrag vom 29.1.1918.

35 Vgl. *Wege der geistigen Erkenntnis und der Erneuerung künstlerischer Weltanschauung*, GA 161, Dornach ^{2}1999, Vortrag vom 6.2.1915, und *Menschenschicksale und Völkerschicksale*, GA 157, Dornach ^{3}1981, Vortrag vom 9.3.1915.

36 *Menschenschicksale und Völkerschicksale*, GA 157, a.a.O.

37 *Das Geheimnis des Todes*, GA 159, Dornach [3]2005, Vortrag vom 13.6.1915.

38 *Zufall, Notwendigkeit und Vorsehung. Imaginative Erkenntnis und Vorgänge nach dem Tode*, GA 163, Dornach [2]1986, Vortrag vom 5.9.1915.

39 *Menschenschicksale und Völkerschicksale*, GA 157, Vortrag vom 7.12.1915.

40 Vortrag vom 5.9.1915, siehe Anm. 38.

41 *Geist und Stoff, Leben und Tod*, GA 66, Dornach [2]1988, Vortrag vom 31.3.1917.

42 Leibliches wird vererbt, und das natürlich auch nach Maßgabe des karmischen Verhältnisses zu den Eltern. In anderen (späteren) Vorträgen legt Rudolf Steiner dar, wie sich der Leib vom Kopf aus schon während der Embryonalzeit und dann während der ersten Lebensjahre neu bildet. In diesem ganzen Prozess durchdringen sich die Anteile des Erbstroms mit denen des Reinkarnationsweges. Vor allem das erste Jahrsiebt ist eine Auseinandersetzung zwischen diesen beiden Kräften.

43 GA 66, a.a.O.

44 Rudolf Steiner, *Das Rätsel des Menschen. Die geistigen Hintergründe der menschlichen Geschichte*, GA 170, Dornach [3]1992, Vortrag vom 7.8.1916.

45 Ebd.

46 Vgl. *Gegensätze in der Menschheitsentwicklung. West*

und Ost – Materialismus und Mystik – Wissen und Glauben, GA 197, Dornach [3]1996, Vortrag vom 24.6.1920.

47 Ebd.

48 Rudolf Steiner, *Der Zusammenhang des Menschen mit der elementarischen Welt*, GA 158, Dornach [4]1993, Vortrag vom 22.11.1914.

49 Simone Weil, *Die Einwurzelung*, München 1956, S. 11.

50 Rudolf Steiner, *Luzifer-Gnosis, Grundlegende Aufsätze zur Anthroposophie und Berichte aus den Zeitschriften «Luzifer» und «Luzifer-Gnosis» 1903-1908*, GA 34, Dornach 1960, S. 213.

51 Ebd., S. 211.

52 Ebd., S. 213.

53 Ebd.

54 Ebd., S. 218.

55 Ebd., S. 219.

56 *Welt, Erde und Mensch*, GA 105, Dornach [5]1983, Vortrag vom 10.8.1908. – Zur «Datierung» des Mysteriums von Golgatha aus geisteswissenschaftlicher Sicht gehört auch noch das Folgende: 333 n. Chr. ist die exakte Mitte der Verstandesseelenepoche, die selbst die Mitte der nachatlantischen Zeit ausmacht. Für 333 Jahre nach dieser Mitte, also für das Jahr 666 n. Chr., hatte Sorat die verfrühte Begabung des Menschen mit der Bewusstseinsseele angebahnt, was zur Folge gehabt hätte, dass der

Mensch das Geistselbst nicht hätte entwickeln können. Deshalb musste das Mysterium von Golgatha als entscheidendes Gegengewicht ebenso viele Jahre (333) vor der Mitte der Verstandesseelenepoche stattfinden wie der Sorateinfluss danach. Vgl. GA 184, 11.10.1918.

57 *Inneres Wesen des Menschen und Leben zwischen Tod und neuer Geburt,* GA 153, Dornach [6]1997, Vortrag vom 10.4.1914.

58 Ebd.

59 Die beiden Vorträge tragen den Titel «Glaube, Liebe, Hoffnung – drei Stufen des menschheitlichen Lebens». Sie sind enthalten in: *Das esoterische Christentum und die geistige Führung der Menschheit,* GA 130.

60 A.a.O.

61 Ebd., 3.12.1911.

62 Ebd.

63 Ebd., 2.12.1911.

64 Ebd., 3.12.1911.

Ruth Ewertowski

Revolution im Ich

Einweihung als Wiedergeburt
in Anthroposophie und Literatur

255 Seiten, gebunden mit Schutzumschlag

«Zwei Vorzüge sind es, die die Literatur mitbringt und mit denen sie uns das Thema unmittelbar nahebringt ... dass sie Einblick gibt in das, was sich dabei seelisch im Verborgenen abspielt und nur schwer zu fassen ist, und zum anderen, dass sie unmittelbar Zugang zu höheren Wirklichkeitsformen schaffen kann als denen, die uns umgeben.»

Ruth Ewertowski

Einweihung hat viele Formen. Vor allem im Sinne von Lebenswandlung und Wiedergeburt betrifft sie die ganze Existenz eines Menschen. Eine neue Daseinsqualität wird errungen – eine Unerschütterlichkeit, die nur das Ergebnis eines durchlaufenen Untergangs sein kann. Der Mensch bringt sich selbst neu hervor, durchläuft eine Revolution in seinem Ich.

Verlag Freies Geistesleben

Rudolf Steiner

Die Kunst des Wartens

Impulse 5

Werde ein Mensch mit Initiative: *Ressourcen*.

Herausgegeben von Jean-Claude Lin

mit einer Einleitung von Ruth Ewertowski

Zum wirklichkeitsgemäßen Umgang mit Ideen und Initiativen gehört, den richtigen Zeitpunkt ihrer Verwirklichung abwarten zu können. In innerer, geistiger Betätigung können unsere Ideen und Initiativen sogar «von den Göttern getauft» werden.

Verlag Freies Geistesleben

Jörg Ewertowski

Die Entdeckung der Bewusstseinsseele

Wegmarken des Geistes

Rudolf Steiner – Augustinus – Petrarca – Heinrich von Kleist

236 Seiten, gebunden mit Schutzumschlag

«Die Bewusstseinsseele ist die Gestalt unserer geschichtlichen Epoche und die Signatur der biografischen Lebensmitte. Sie ist Emanzipationsprinzip. Aber auch Prinzip zur Geburt des höheren Menschen.»

Jörg Ewertowski

«Ewertowskis genaue Ausführungen zur Bewusstseinsseele mit ihrer Gestaltung und ihren Möglichkeiten vermitteln dem Leser höchste Achtung für die entscheidenden geistigen Leistungen der Vergangenheit; er erlebt sie mit, sie werden zur Erfahrung.»

Maja Rehbein, Anthroposophie

Verlag Freies Geistesleben

Adalbert Stifter – Dichtung als Weg zur Einweihung
Herausgegeben von Günter Röschert
Mit Beiträgen von Ariane Eichenberg, Jörg Ewertowski, Ruth Ewertowski und Günter Röschert

169 Seiten, gebunden mit Schutzumschlag

«Stifters Erzählungen und Romane sind kunstvolle und durch seine eigene ‹Lebenseinweihung› mit Erfahrung gesättigte beispielhafte Wege, auf denen wir uns selber die Organe heranbilden können, um das Leben ringsum, aber auch unseren eigenen Lebenslauf als ‹Schwellengang› zu erleben. Den Leser dazu anzuregen und zu ermutigen, wieder zu Stifters Werken zu greifen, sie mit Genuss zu lesen und gleichzeitig im Sinne solcher übenden Betrachtung fruchtbar zu machen, ist das große Verdienst dieses Buches.»

Joachim von Königslöw